Code of Peace

CODE OF PEACE

Ethics and Security in the World of the Warlord States

Dorothy V. Jones

THE UNIVERSITY OF CHICAGO PRESS

Chicago and London

Dorothy V. Jones is a research associate of the Newberry Library, Chicago. She is the author of *License for Empire: Colonialism by Treaty in Early America* (1982), published by the University of Chicago Press, and *Splendid Encounters: The Thought and Conduct of Diplomacy* (1984), published by the University of Chicago Library and distributed by the University of Chicago Press.

The University of Chicago Press, Chicago 60637
The University of Chicago Press, Ltd., London
© 1989, 1991 by The University of Chicago
All rights reserved. Published 1991
Printed in the United States of America

00 99 98 97 96 95 94 93 92 91   5 4 3 2 1

ISBN (cloth): 0-226-40646-6

Library of Congress Cataloging-in-Publication Data

Jones, Dorothy V.
    Code of peace : ethics and security in the world of the warlord states / Dorothy V. Jones.
        p.   cm.
    Includes bibliographical references and index.
        1. International relations—Moral and ethical aspects.
    2. Security, International.   I. Title.
    JX1255.J66   1991
    172'.4—dc20   91-13010
                                                            CIP

⊗ The paper used in this publication meets the minimum requirements of the American National Standard for Information Sciences—Permanence of Paper for Printed Library Materials, ANSI Z39.48-1984.

In memory of

Robert Rosenthal

whose faith in an earlier project
helped make this one possible

Great Bodies of Men have seldom judged what they ought to do by any other Rule than what they could do. What Nation is there that has not oppressed any other, when the same could be done with Advantage and Security?

Cato's Letters 61
John Trenchard and Gordon Thomas
13 January 1721

Contents

Introduction

War and trade are the most obvious constants in the relationships between states in the international system. The constant that is much less obvious—in fact, almost hidden—is the search by those same states for international standards of behavior. This book is about that search.

The commonest reaction to the phrase *standards of behavior*, when taken in connection with international affairs, is skepticism, followed by a barrage of questions that add up to various polite forms of, "Are you kidding?" This study addresses three of the questions that are most often asked:

—Are there ethical standards that apply to relations between states in the international system?

—If there are such standards, are they or can they be universal, given the diversity of cultural traditions represented in the international system today?

—If such standards exist and they are universal, what difference does it make, since the most obvious rule of behavior followed by the states is that of self-interest?

It is the argument of this book that the answer to the first two questions is yes. The answer to the third question is that the standards matter in ways that will be evident as the analysis proceeds. The method of argument is historical. To say that is not to announce that later events come after earlier events—something that everybody already knows, although the fact is sometimes forgotten in assertions of causation. Rather, it is to say that context and change are crucial variables in the development of this code of international ethics by the states and that understanding requires a knowledge of both.

The code that the states have developed is not a rigid set of rules derived from static principles. It is a set of guidelines pointing toward the goal of peace and security but not specifying the path to be taken. In that respect, it is flexible, and it is, and has been, responsive to changing conditions and concepts. There are nine basic principles on which the code relies. They give it its distinctive shape and a consistency that allows its characterization as a code. The nine principles are:

1. Sovereign equality of states
2. Territorial integrity and political independence of states
3. Equal rights and self-determination of peoples
4. Nonintervention in the internal affairs of states
5. Peaceful settlement of disputes between states
6. Abstention from the threat or use of force
7. Fulfillment in good faith of international obligations
8. Cooperation with other states
9. Respect for human rights and fundamental freedoms

In addition to these nine basic principles are two principles that have come to the fore in the period since World War II. There is broad agreement on these two, but agreement is not universal, as it is with the basic nine. They are listed here as auxiliary principles that may one day achieve wide enough acceptance to be included in the basic set:

Creation of an equitable international economic order

Protection of the environment

How has this set of standards been derived? The states of the international system have derived it from their own experiences of trading with each other and fighting with each other through the centuries. They have also drawn on a rich heritage of law and philosophy, and religious and social concerns. The results of their reflections have been embodied in numerous treaties, conventions, protocols, declarations, and other international instruments. It is on these instruments that this study is based.

A compilation was made of the major, state-level agreements and declarations that either dealt specifically with the principles underlying relations between states, or stipulated actions based on a specific principle (see appendix 1). Since most of this explicit philosophizing by the states on the matter of their own relations has taken place since World War I, it was appropriate to set the beginning date for the compilation at 1919. The end date, though set at 1989, could, in theory, be reset indefinitely as more international declarations are issued or international instruments ratified by the states. The point can be made, however, with the seventy-nine major instruments and declarations considered here.

No nongovernmental documents or reflections are included, not because they lack importance but because the point of the study is to see what the states themselves have done and said. The influence of private organizations and individuals will become apparent during the course of the argument. Resolutions by the states are excluded on the grounds that they require less commitment than either a formal agreement, such as a treaty or a convention, or a formal declaration, and thus are not as good an indicator of state opinion. With one exception, proposals that never became agreements at the state level are excluded on the same grounds. The exception is the Dumbarton Oaks proposal of 1944 that, the following year, provided the basis for the Charter of the United Nations.

With two exceptions, all the agreements and declarations are multi-lateral and thus represent the opinion of a number of states. The exceptions to this again have to do with influence. The 1941 Atlantic Charter—a wartime declaration issued by the United Kingdom and the United States—embodied much state reflection from the past and, during the war years and immediately after, became a vehicle for the expression of multilateral ideals; it is therefore included. Similarly, the Sino-Indian trade agreement of 1954 had an influence unrelated to its trade arrangements because of the five Buddhist principles of coexis-tence included in its preamble. This, too, became a vehicle for multilateral expression, and so is one of the seventy-nine state agree-ments and declarations.

Of these seventy-nine components of the code, forty deal entirely with human rights either through a listing of those rights, as in the 1948 Universal Declaration, or else through the articulation of one par-ticular right, as in the 1926 convention on the abolition of slavery. This leaves thirty-nine agreements and declarations that deal in a more comprehensive manner with the fundamental principles that under-lie—or that the states think *ought* to underlie—relations between states. Respect for human rights and fundamental freedoms is included as a principle in twenty of those thirty-nine remaining instruments. Counting the forty instruments devoted entirely to human rights, it is thus the most often asserted and elaborately detailed of the nine basic principles articulated by the states, a development that has taken place almost entirely since World War II.

Twenty of the thirty-nine comprehensive instruments include the sovereign equality of states among their lists of fundamental prin-ciples. Twenty-two include the territorial integrity and political independence of states. Equal rights and self-determination of peoples is included in eighteen of the instruments, again, almost all in the peri-od since World War II. The peaceful settlement of disputes and the related principle of restraint from the threat or use of force are each included in twenty-eight of the thirty-nine instruments. Twenty-five of the thirty-nine include the principle of nonintervention, twenty-eight the principle of cooperation, and fifteen the principle of the good-faith fulfillment of obligations.

These simple aggregates say nothing about the principles themselves. What the numbers do tell us is that these particular principles have been repeatedly affirmed by many states over a seventy-year period that has seen tremendous changes in the international system. That fact alone should suggest a degree of consensus and universality that begins to address the questions listed above. If that fact, even in its bare, numerical form, were more widely known, it could inform much current debate on international affairs. As experienced an observer as George Kennan has argued that there are no standards that apply to international affairs and that a prudent pursuit of national interest is the best that can be hoped for there.[1] If the argument of this book is correct, Kennan's is a position with which the states themselves do not agree.

At the beginning of this introduction it was stated that the states' search for international standards of behavior was so obscure as to be almost hidden. It is a statement that needs clarification. Why *almost hidden?* Part of the reason lies in the simple fact of dramatic impact. The movement of the earth by an earthquake makes news; the movement of the earth by an earthworm does not, although in the long term it may be more important because of its effect on the productivity of soil. This search by the states is intellectually exciting both for what it reveals about the states and because of its long-term potential. It does not, however, have the immediate impact of an earthquake.

Beyond the lack of short-term drama are other reasons for the obscurity of the search, one of which is mislabeling. The states have applied the term *law* to what is, in fact, a philosophical endeavor. They have consistently said that what they are doing is formulating the principles of international law. Sometimes this effort is part of a movement for codification of that law. Sometimes it is part of what is called the law's "progressive development." Sometimes the two are linked, as in article 13 of the United Nations Charter, which calls on the General Assembly to take initiatives looking toward "the progressive development of international law and its codification."[2]

The term *development,* left undefined, seems to throw the whole effort into the camp of speculative moral philosophy, a fact that the term *law* seems to deny. The confusion between *becoming* and *being,* between *ought* and *is,* characterizes the whole enterprise. What has been done for the purposes of this study is to say that the clearly normative portions of international law can be studied on their own, separate from the usual topics in a textbook on the subject; that these normative portions deal with what the states think *ought* to be, not with what actually *is;* and that, therefore, what we are dealing with is not law in the usual sense of the word but, rather, with ethical standards.

The work of Felix Cohen, Lon Fuller, Edmund Cahn, and H. L. A. Hart provides a kind of precedent for this emphasis on the normative underpinning of the law, but since their focus was on domestic rather than international law, the parallel is not exact. The degree to which international law meets the requirements of a legal system is a subject of study in itself, one that will not be pursued here. What is germane to this study is the fact that that law, as it stands, is shot through with philosophical assumptions and speculations that, taken together, set out a detailed picture of a world of peace, justice, and international cooperation. International lawyers have been saying for at least a hundred years that theirs is an exact science. What they have not said, what, perhaps, they stand too close even to perceive, is that international law is also a venture into moral imagination. In the period covered by this study, it is a venture that has been carried forward by the states of the international system.

In this analysis, the states are treated as unitary actors. The purpose is to see what the states have actually said and done, not to trace the processes by which they decided what to say and do. State decision-making at the international level is a complex procedure involving many considerations, numbers of people, and, usually, several competing centers of power. It is a challenging subject of study, but it is not what is being studied here. Where the focus is on decisions already made, one can fairly speak of "the state" and "states" as the actor or actors that made the decisions.

There remains one point to be clarified, and that is why those states are characterized as warlords in the title of this book. Some readers have suggested that this pejorative term tells more about the author's moral presuppositions than it does about the states, which are, after all, the legitimate national authorities of the world's various peoples.

Warlords is indeed a pejorative term, but its force is directed not against the states, as such. It is directed against the states in their warmaking mode. It denigrates exactly what the states have repeatedly condemned: the illegitimate use of force in the international system. What is remarkable about this endeavor by the states is their recognition of their own warlordish tendencies, and their persistent attempts to devise an ethical code and an international system in which the rewards that go to force—and they are frequently handsome—will be so overbalanced by other considerations that force will no longer mean war in the traditional sense. Its only use will be in collective action, should that become necessary to maintain peace.

This may be hypocritical pretense on the part of the states, but, if so, it is one of the most elaborate and extended bits of hypocrisy on record. Even as hypocrisy, it is worthy of study. One might ask, why do they bother? What is the audience for this elaborate charade?—if indeed it is a charade. Is the audience other states? If other states believe the hypocrisy theory, why should they be impressed? Perhaps the audience is world public opinion. But that amorphous, ever-changing body of the attentive few is far more likely to draw its own conclusions than to take the states' words for anything, nor are any of the news media likely to be impressed. That leaves the leaders and representatives of the states—that passing parade of those who sit in public office, participate in international conferences and organizations, negotiate treaties, and, in general, tend to the international business of their particular state. Is it their own consciences that are salved by this tribute to some standard other than that of naked self-interest? But, again, if the tribute is indeed hypocritical, why bother?

A different way of looking at this search by the states for international standards of behavior is to see it as a serious attempt on their part. That attempt is hampered by the same conflicting desires and impulses that make it difficult for individual human beings to behave according to standards they themselves have set. The problem is compounded by the fact that the states are collectivities with institutional impediments to clear-cut policy formulation. Further, they are collectivities that are always girded for self-defense, so that they react with entrenched caution even when they are sure what it is they want to do.

As for the way the title of this book reveals the author's moral commitments, those commitments include fidelity to the complexity and variety of the historical record, as well as a preference for peace over war. The preference may have led to the choice of subject, but the argument that is made in this book is as faithful to the historical record as the author's skill and training could make it.

Work on this book was made possible by the support of the John D. and Catherine T. MacArthur Foundation. A Social Science Research Council/MacArthur Foundation Fellowship in International Peace and Security provided not only the means and the time for research but the stimulus to try to expand the conceptual base of security studies. During the period of the fellowship, the history department of the University of Chicago furnished an academic base, while the Newberry Library in Chicago continued to provide the institutional and intellectual setting that has benefited so many scholars, including this one.

My research assistant, Barbara Welke, while doing indispensable digging in the sources, also challenged some of my initial assumptions and thereby helped clarify the conceptual base of this particular study.

Hers were the first of many challenges from many different people. I am grateful to students in the University of Chicago's International History Workshop directed by Akira Iriye; students in the graduate colloquium, "Peace Movements in Modern History," directed by John W. Chambers of Rutgers; and participants in the Newberry Library's Fellows' Seminar. Responding to their challenging questions has made this a better book.

For guidance through the unfamiliar terrain of moral and political philosophy and applied ethics, I am indebted to James Gustafson, Russell Hardin, and Mark Siegler, M.D., all of the University of Chicago. Members of the Working Group on International Ethics continued my education in these fields, and helped me appreciate how difficult and necessary it is to communicate across the boundaries of separate disciplines. Terry Nardin of the University of Wisconsin—Milwaukee and Frank Ninkovich of St. John's University gave sympathetic and critical readings to portions of this book, readings that bettered the argument and tightened the prose. Both the argument and the prose also benefited from the attention of Bob Jones and Priscilla Murphy. As a sample of what the reader has been spared: a ninety-seven word sentence has now, at one editor's suggestion, been broken into three sentences.

If this list of acknowledgments gives the reader the idea that scholarship is a cooperative enterprise, the list will have served its purpose. The visible structure that bears the author's name rests on a foundation laid by many hands. To acknowledge that is a pleasure which, in the case of this final acknowledgment, is mixed with sadness. Robert Rosenthal, to whom this book is dedicated, did not live to see this indirect outcome of a project undertaken for him in 1983. As curator of special collections at the University of Chicago's Joseph Regenstein library, Bob Rosenthal enthusiastically pushed scholars to use the resources of special collections in innovative ways. One project in which he believed and for which he pushed was my proposal for an exhibition to explore the concepts and practice of diplomacy. That exhibition set me on the road that has led to this book. One of Bob Rosenthal's favorite admonitions was to "look at the big picture." In this book I have tried to do just that.

Prologue

Once there was a convention of cats. There were cats of all different sizes and colors, but they had one thing in common. They were afraid. Mice were scarce and smart that year and, in desperation, the cats had begun attacking and eating each other.

"This has got to stop," said a large green-eyed tabby, who was not exactly the chief cat since the other cats would not allow that. He was, however, bigger and tougher than everyone else, so he always spoke first at conventions.

A murmur of agreement ran round the room. "It's madness," said one cat.

"It's suicide," said another.

"Furthermore, it's against the law of the cats," said a very small calico cat, whose size made it certain that, if things continued as they were, she would soon be killed and eaten.

"What's that?" asked the tabby sharply.

The calico cat licked one paw nervously and tried to blend into the crowd. Instead, the crowd pulled back from her and she found herself alone in a circle of gleaming eyes and twitching tails.

She swallowed hard. "It's—it's the law, you know," she said, stammering and hiccoughing until she could hardly be understood. "We're not to kill—each other, I mean. It's been that way right from the beginning. Only we've forgotten. And now see what's happened. We don't—we can't—there's not even any—we don't trust each other anymore."

This last came out in a rush, and the calico cat closed her eyes to shut out the sight of all those gleaming eyes and twitching tails.

"The law," said the tabby slowly as if he were remembering something from a time long past.

"The law," said the other cats. It certainly had a nice solid sound—a compelling sort of sound. And if they wanted to survive, they needed to do something. But what? "What do you suggest?" they asked the calico cat.

She opened one cautious eye. "We could write it all down so that we would never forget again."

1

So they did. They wrote down everything they could remember about not killing each other and not stealing each other's mice, about telling the truth, about sharing their mice with nursing mothers and those who were too old to hunt. And when they were finished they were very proud of the list they had made and they called it the Code of the Cats.

"Now what?" they asked the calico cat, who had remembered more than anybody else about the code.

"We proclaim it," she said without hesitation.

So they proclaimed the code with speeches and songs and patriotic poetry, with abundant references to their glorious history and still more glorious destiny, and they said that all cats everywhere had to obey the code on pain of . . .

"On pain of what?" asked the calico cat, who was trembling with eagerness because of the progress they were making.

But that brought the cats up short. Suppose they were able to come up with a suitable punishment. Who could they trust to administer the code and mete out the punishment justly? And without that, who could they trust not to cheat?—to hoard mice, for example, or, on the other hand, to lie and say that they hadn't caught any mice and let others do all the work. For that matter, who could they trust not to kill on the sly?

The cats began to growl a little in their throats. They looked suspiciously all around and moved away from each other.

"Well?" said the calico cat, still eager and expectant.

"I tell you what we *could* do," said the cat who had first spoken, and he looked from one tabby cat to another. "We tabbies could all stick together."

"And all of us grays," said the gray cats to each other.

And so it went around the room, black cats to black cats, yellow cats to yellow cats, white-footed cats to white-footed cats, until most of the cats were divided up into tight little groups. "Too strong for anyone to attack," they said. And "just for defense, you know."

"I don't understand," said the calico cat. "What about the code?"

"What about it?" they answered, and their eyes began to gleam and their tails began to twitch.

"You've got to learn to face *facts*," said the first tabby. "You've got to see things the way they *are*."

"But—" said the calico cat.

"But, nothing," they said, and poised themselves to jump, some with their eyes on the calico cat, some with their eyes on each other.

And here the fable stops because it is not yet finished. The most likely ending is easily imagined, but the most likely ending is not the necessary ending. Whether or not the cats will jump depends on whether or not they remember the code, and on *that* depends the drawing of the moral with which all good fables should end.

1 The World the Warlords Made

We cannot in the least admit that Russia had from the first any serious or genuine desire for peace. She has rejected the proposals of Our Government; the safety of Korea is in danger; the vital interests of Our Empire are menaced. The guarantees for the future which We have failed to secure by peaceful negotiations, We can now only seek by an appeal to arms.

Japanese declaration of war
10 February 1904

Early in February 1904, Japanese leaders demonstrated their clear understanding of the world they lived in by ordering a surprise attack against the ships of the Russian Pacific fleet anchored in the roadstead just outside the harbor at Port Arthur. This heavily fortified port at the tip of the Liao-tung peninsula on the south coast of Manchuria was a key to naval supremacy in the waters around eastern Russia, northeast China, the Korean peninsula, and the islands of Japan. Moving swiftly, the first Japanese torpedo boats headed toward the line of anchored Russian ships, swung to port, and, one after another as they sped along a course parallel with the ships, fired their torpedoes. Swinging about again, they raced, untouched, out of range of return fire. A second Japanese group followed almost immediately. These boats too fired their torpedoes and got away before Russian gun crews could inflict any damage. Nearly an hour later the last of the Japanese torpedo boats, which had become separated from the others, launched their attack and also escaped unscathed. The Russo-Japanese War of 1904–1905 had begun.

From a military point of view, the Japanese attack was a great success. The Russian battleships *Tzesarevich* and *Retzivan* and the cruiser *Pallada* had all been taken out of action at no cost to the attacking force. Equally important was the effect on Japanese morale. The entire nation had been organized for this war, but it was still a tremendous gamble. Imperial Russia was without question one of the great powers of the international system. And Japan? Japan had fought against China in 1894–1895 and had won that war, but the China of the late

5

Ch'ing (Xing) dynasty was scarcely able to keep internal order, much less to defend itself.

This war was wholly different and not just in the relative power that could be brought to bear. For the Japanese, the victory at Port Arthur was as much a vindication of their claims to great power status as it was a military triumph. And when this triumph was matched by another, they were sure of the validity of their claims. At about the time of the attack on Port Arthur, the Fourth Division of the Japanese fleet under Rear Admiral Sotokichi Uriu trapped two Russian warships in the Harbor of Chemulpo (Inchon) on the west coast of Korea. After a brief and disastrous sortie against the Japanese, the Russian commanders ordered their vessels back into the harbor. There they scuttled the ships rather than allow them to be captured. The sinking of the *Varyag* and the *Koreetz* put the world on notice that the victory at Port Arthur was not simply a fluke. From that point on, Japan had to be figured into the endless power calculations of the early twentieth century.

It was a tight little club that Japan sought to enter. For years the club's focus had been on Europe, and its membership had been exclusively European. The admittance of Turkey in 1856 following the Crimean War did nothing to broaden the base of membership or shift attention from Europe. The Turks were only there on sufferance, and the more they lost their grip on the Ottoman Empire, the more contemptuous the sufferance became. In the "old boy" world of nineteenth-century diplomacy, Turkey was a kind of permanent indigent presence, allowed inside the club but not allowed to vote.

Japanese leaders had carefully studied the operation of the international system as it was manipulated by a few European powers. On the Continent the powers that mattered were Prussia and Austria (and their later manifestations as the German Empire and Austria-Hungary), and Russia and France. Across the Channel, it was Great Britain that mattered. Increasingly, the United States was mattering, too, especially since the Spanish-American War had left it with possessions in the western Pacific, but it still was a hesitant player in the global game of power. Japanese leaders did not think it likely that their aspirations would disturb the United States since the Japanese goals were well defined and close to home. Moreover, they intended to pursue those goals by the rules of the game as they understood them after close observation of the actions of the European founders.

And what counted in the eyes of the powers that mattered? Force counted. Through force Russia had acquired Turkestan and the Caucasus. Through force Prussia and Austria had gained the duchies of Schleswig and Holstein. Savoy and Nice had been given to France (after a show of a plebiscite) as a reward for French aid in the Italian wars of unification. Alsace and Lorraine were annexed by Germany after victory in the Franco-Prussian War. And this was just on the Continent. Wherever Europeans went in Asia, Africa, the Middle East, their armies were at their right hand and their navies at their left, and few indigenous powers could long hold out against them.

Japanese leaders drew the obvious conclusion that force was not only an acceptable means to great power standing, but an effective one. They instituted a system of nationwide conscription and training, opened military schools, hired French and (after the French defeat in 1871) German military advisers, and set about creating a national army that would combine the best in modern weapons and tactics with the best of the traditional Japanese values of loyalty, frugality, and self-sacrifice. At the same time, they hired British experts to help them create what they were determined was going to be the finest navy in the world. Since Japan was, like Great Britain, an island nation, it was clear to Japanese leaders that effective use of the military might they were developing would depend on control of the seas around their homeland.

It was clear also that guile and secrecy were part of the arsenal of the Europeans, and, further, that Europeans admired the clever move that led to success, whether or not the move had been made according to the publicly proclaimed rules. Deception was practiced and expected even while it was condemned. Napoleon III met Cavour in Plombières and plotted against Austria. France maneuvered secretly against Belgium and Luxembourg. Bismarck was a master of disinformation and of the calculated, carefully timed leak to the press. Spying was routine.

As part of their long-range plan to achieve international recognition as a great power, the Japanese began secretly to gather information on potential enemies and friends. Army and navy officers sent abroad for language training were expected to engage in intelligence operations, as were career diplomats. "Intelligence rides" similar to those undertaken by European cavalry officers on frontier duty were engaged in by Japanese officers to gather information and map areas of special interest in the northeast provinces of China, in Manchuria, and in Korea. Close watch was kept on the progress of the Trans-Siberian Railway across Russia and the Chinese Eastern Railway linking the Siberian railroad to the fort at Port Arthur.

Japanese diplomats and military attaches in St. Petersburg carried out their public duties with every show of friendship while gathering information on army strength and morale and establishing a network of contacts with dissident Russians. Spies in Korea prepared the ground for a friendly reception of Japanese troops when they should arrive and sent back to Tokyo detailed information on road conditions, available food, and the width and depth of rivers to be forded or bridged as the army moved north through the peninsula.

None of this is to suggest that the Japanese emerged into the modern world from some primal state of innocence in which violence, secrecy, and lying were unknown. It is simply to state that when the Japanese began their push for entry into the great power club in the 1890s and on into the 1900s, this was the kind of world they found. They learned quickly what seemed to work and what did not work in such a world, and they made their plans accordingly.

Their victory over China in the war of 1894–1895 had taught them another lesson about the world in which they wanted to play a leading part. Even victory was not enough if the European powers refused to recognize the victor's demands. A group of European powers had forced Japan to give up Port Arthur, one prize of the war that Japan had wanted badly to keep. The city with its fort and magnificent harbor had been returned to China, which was too weak to hold it. It was now in Russian hands, but Japanese leaders were determined that it not stay there. They watched how Bismarck maneuvered the European alliance system to the advantage of Prussia and later of the German empire, and they moved to protect their own flank by similar means. A defensive alliance with Great Britain, concluded in 1902, freed them from the fear of European intervention.

While they negotiated with Russia, they continued their preparations for war. When they were ready, they recalled their minister from St. Petersburg, attacked the Russians at Port Arthur, and sent troops of the First Army to land on the west coast of Korea. From there the troops were to move north through that weak and formally neutral country toward the Yalu River, the border between Korea and Manchuria. Just across the river was the "Eastern Force" of the Russian army, ready to contest any movement toward Port Arthur from the landward side.

The Japanese took the world as they found it when they emerged from centuries of isolation, and the tactics they adopted to achieve their goals are a telling commentary on the kind of place it was. It was a world of warlord states. Their very existence rested on force, and their relations with each other were shaped by well-deserved suspicion. In London, Paris, Rome, Vienna, Washington, St. Petersburg, and Tokyo, there was a perpetual casting up of the accounts of power and a compulsion to act if these were seen to be out of balance.

It was a world of states that asserted their sovereignty against all comers. They held themselves answerable to no authority except perhaps a vaguely defined public opinion that in most countries was poorly organized and had few means of bringing pressure to bear. The states acted as they saw fit, which, in practice, often meant whatever they thought they could get away with. They set themselves up as judges of their own actions and bowed, when they had to, not to the judgment of others but to the force, or the fear of force, that others might bring against them.

The last lingering sense of a community of nations seemed to have disappeared from day-to-day international politics in the early twentieth century. Gladstone, that champion of community, was dead. Wilson's time to speak of such matters was yet to come. With no one of influence to articulate a wider view of international relationships, the states fell back upon narrow self-interest as a guide. They elevated this narrowness to a formal policy they called "pursuing the national interest," and they clung to the policy as to a lifeline.

Narrow as that policy was, it might have served them better if they had been more skillful. But without anyone of the stature of Bismarck—dead the same year as Gladstone—to manipulate this narrow, power-oriented view of state relationships, diplomacy turned easily into a game of grab. From self-interest it was a very short step to self-aggrandizement. When the states took that step, they called it "securing their legitimate sphere of influence."

No one saw more clearly than Theodore Roosevelt the kind of world being created in the early 1900s. For Roosevelt, China was the terrible example of the cost of weakness in such a world. Distracted by turmoil within and demands from without, the feeble Chi'ing dynasty had been forced to grant economic concessions, spheres of influence, and control of its customs to stronger powers. "China is not making aggressions on anybody," Roosevelt pointed out to a Harvard audience in 1911. "China is not endeavoring to attack anybody; and it is only saved from destruction—and it is not saved from spoliation and hectoring and attempted division—by the fact that there are many outside powers jealous of one another."[1]

From this and the spoliation of other weak powers in Asia, Africa, and the Middle East, Roosevelt drew a lesson that he never failed to urge upon his countrymen, even though the United States was separated by two oceans from the main theaters of conflict. "Good will, and the friendship of foreign powers, are utterly insufficient substitutes for ability to protect ourselves," he told his audience of young men in 1911—soon to be sucked into a war for which they and the country were unprepared. "No foreign nation, not the most friendly, will respect us or give us its slightest aid, save on condition that we make it evident that in case of need we can fight for our own land."[2] In the world created by the warlord states, strength and a readiness to fight were essential for survival.

But they were essential for something else as well. It was here that Roosevelt and his friend Captain Alfred Thayer Mahan, a military strategist, saw clearly to the root of a problem the states had created for themselves. When a wrong or an injustice occurred in relations between the states, there were few satisfactory means for redress short of force. Binding arbitration of disputes was not an all-sufficient answer, as Mahan pointed out to his fellow delegates at the first Hague Peace Conference in 1899. What about those states that would not be bound by the rules? Who then would stand for justice? "Until it is demonstrable that no evil exists, or threatens the world, which cannot be obviated without recourse to force, the obligation to readiness must remain; and, where evil is mighty and defiant, the obligation to use force—that is, war—arises."[3]

Mahan's style of speech was stilted even for the formal speech of the late nineteenth century, but his perception of the world of the warlord states was acute. What was a peace-loving state to do?—and there *were* some even in such a world. To lay down its arms was to invite aggression, if not against itself then against a weaker, dependent state. To remain armed was to risk war when peace was the desired goal.

But not just any peace; and that was part of the problem that Mahan and Roosevelt perceived. Peace was an ambiguous term. It had many faces, not all of them pleasant. As Roosevelt pointed out in his 1904 presidential message to Congress, "The peace of tyrannous terror, the peace of craven weakness, the peace of injustice, all these should be shunned as we shun unrighteous war."[4] It was the duty of the powerful states to help the world along toward a peace based on justice. It was equally their duty to remain strong "to repel any wrong, and in exceptional cases to take action which in a more advanced state of international relations would come under the head of the exercise of international peace."[5]

Whatever route was chosen through the world created by the warlord states, war seemed to lie at the end of the road. Whether policy was shaped by national interest, or spheres of influence, or the pursuit of peace, somewhere along the line the states would be faced with the necessity for war.

But this boxing-in of choice was not quite the constraint in the early twentieth century that it is today. Attitudes were different then partly because the wars were different. Not nearly so many people were involved, and the weapons were not nearly so destructive. Those were limited, manageable, winnable wars; and they had—or could have— enormous intellectual and emotional appeal. For these reasons war had become, by the early twentieth century, an acceptable instrument of national policy, and it remained so until the bloody stalemate of World War I.

And there was yet another reason for war's acceptance. If the state was a moral community, a community with shared values, a common heritage, and hopes for the future—and many people thought it was— then national policy became an expression of the collective ideals of the people of the state. It followed that war as an instrument of national policy was war with a high moral purpose. This helps to explain the confident and righteous tone of the Japanese declaration of war, a war they had been planning for at least a decade. And it helps to explain the fervor with which they pursued their goal of victory over the Russians.

The Almost Manageable War

The advance of the Japanese First Army through Korea to the Yalu River on the northern border was a model of organization and perseverance in the face of weather conditions seemingly far more hostile than were the Russians. For the most part, the Russians stayed on the far side of the Yalu, and their scouting parties were no more than an occasional annoyance. Bad weather, on the other hand, was a frequent visitor, and it disrupted Japanese schedules and communication, mired troops and transport, and made the carrying of supplies by sea a hazardous undertaking. Japanese leaders had chosen February for their strike against the Russians precisely because of the weather. Now they and their troops were paying the price.

It was a price they were willing to pay since in other respects the bad weather was serving them well. For one thing, it had helped to make their initial attack at Port Arthur a complete surprise. Although everyone knew that relations between Japan and Russia were strained, the Russians were still unprepared for hostilities. From a reasonable point of view, if war were contemplated, it made sense to wait until roads were passable and harbors free of ice. The Russians were a reasonable people; they would be ready to fight when fighting was practical. Meanwhile, many of the guns in their shore batteries at Port Arthur were coated with grease to protect them against the Manchurian winter. It took time to get the guns ready for action when the Japanese attacked the Russian ships outside the harbor, a fact that helps to explain how the Japanese torpedo boats got away untouched.

So as Japanese troops struggled northward through Korea, they could take comfort in the knowledge that the bad weather hampering them could also be expected to hamper the Russians in far more serious ways. The Russians had about eighty thousand troops stationed in the east. The Trans-Siberian Railway could deliver about a thousand men a day to the railhead at Mukden under ideal conditions; but this was February, far from ideal, and conditions would not be much better in March.

Furthermore, the railway was not yet complete around Lake Baikal, a large inland lake in the south of Russia near the border with Mongolia. All troops, weapons, and supplies had to be hauled across forty miles of ridged and treacherous ice that was in winter often swept by gale force winds, or else they had to be transported many miles out of the way around the southern end of the lake. The Japanese, with a well-trained and tightly disciplined army of some seven hundred thousand, could afford to cope with weather that was helping to preserve their numerical advantage.

Yet speed was also an essential part of the Japanese plan. It had to be. Time would give the Russians the opportunity to call on their immense reserves of men and materiel. At full wartime strength, their army numbered more than 4.5 million men. The Japanese would not be able to muster more than a million men if they brought every reservist into the field.

Russia also had one of the finest navies in the world, and only part of it was at Port Arthur. Even as the Japanese blocked the entrance to the harbor at Port Arthur to prevent harassment of their troop transports, they were aware that the strength of the Russian navy relative to theirs put them in a precarious position. It was a position that demanded both boldness and caution, careful planning and at the same time all possible speed. The tasks of blockading, mine laying and sweeping, and transporting troops, were stretching the Japanese navy to the utmost. There were no ships in reserve, and their own shipyards were not yet capable of replacing any losses. Part of the Russian Pacific fleet was at Vladivostok, where it was an immediate threat to naval operations and a possible threat to the home islands. There was also the Baltic fleet. If the Russians brought that fleet into the Pacific, the naval odds would shift heavily in their favor.

With these thoughts in mind, the Japanese drove themselves hard to take full advantage of foul weather and their temporary command of the sea. They maintained a ceaseless patrol off Port Arthur and sent a squadron of cruisers to search out the Russian ships based at Vladivostok and keep them occupied. As melting ice gradually freed harbors on the Korean coast, they moved their points of debarkation farther northward. This reduced the distance that the troops of the First Army had to travel on the few Korean roads that led to the town of Wiju, their destination on the Yalu River. The roads were barely adequate at best. As the season advanced and the thaw became general, they turned into troughs of mud that sometimes held the forward movement of men and animals to five miles a day. It became impossible to supply the troops by land. Supply depots were set up on the nearby coast, and supplies were run in at great risk in small boats commanded by army officers, since the navy could not spare any men for the job.

Mile by mile, the army moved north toward the Yalu. Scouts moved ahead and to either side of the advance but encountered only a few Cossack patrols whose orders were clearly to avoid any serious engagement. The engineers also were well in front of the main body of men, which because of the weather and the condition of the route was strung out to a depth of six days march. This army traveled on the skill and ingenuity of its engineers as much as on its stomach. The engineers saw to the felling of trees and their placement when roads turned into sink holes. They saw that movable obstacles were removed and found ways around those that could not be moved. They searched out passable fords in the streams and drove in posts with lines and handholds to help the men across. Where there was no ford, the engineers built bridges, often working through the night in the rushing, icy water in order to keep the army moving forward with as little delay as possible. The work was dangerous, for the streams and rivers were swollen with runoff from melting snow in the mountains, and the weather was still unpredictable.

All in all, it took almost six weeks to move the First Army 130 miles, but when at last the scattered troops converged upon Wiju, the men were ready for battle. They had confidence in their commander, General Tamesada Kuroki, and they were determined to be worthy of the confidence placed in them by the Japanese government and by the nation as a whole.

This determination was what had sustained them in the march north through Korea. If their war—their unprecedented war—against a European power were to succeed at all, a victory was needed right at the outset. It was the job of the First Army to provide one. They knew that the Second Army was only waiting word of the favorable outcome of events on the Yalu before attempting a landing on the Liao-tung peninsula north of Port Arthur. The two armies would then coordinate an advance toward the main body of the Russian forces concentrated at Liao-Yang, some two hundred miles above Port Arthur. Other Japanese troops would move south against Port Arthur itself. But first the Russians entrenched on the far side of the Yalu River, across from the First Army, had to be taken care of. It would not be enough simply to drive them back. What was demanded of the Japanese at Wiju, by their leaders and by themselves, was a victory.

So preparations began for the Battle of the Yalu. Now that the main body of infantry had arrived at its initial goal, the problems for General Kuroki and his staff were tactical ones. Emplacements had to be chosen and prepared for the big guns, still several days behind with the artillery detachments. Russian positions and strength had to be reconnoitered and reckoned. Decisions had to be made about sites for crossing the Yalu and, just beyond it at this point, the Aiho River, flowing in a parallel course and connected to the Yalu by numerous channels.

The islands between the channels were a matter for special thought, as was the high and rocky hill on the river bank opposite Wiju. Tiger's Hill, it was called, and it rose five hundred feet straight up from the Yalu riverbed on one side and the Aiho on the other. At this point the Aiho flowed in from the northwest, turned, and ran a brief parallel course before joining the Yalu below the town. There were other hills, too, where Russian batteries might be placed and that would be difficult for infantry to storm.

General Kuroki and his staff spent much time studying the terrain, their maps, and intelligence reports. Meanwhile, Japanese engineers began erecting screens of young trees and millet stalks along the roads wherever they were open enough to be visible to Russian observers. When the guns had come up and men and guns were brought forward into position for the assault, their movements would be hidden from view. The longer the Russians could be kept in the dark about the numbers and placement of the Japanese forces, the longer it would be possible to fool them about the sites where crossing would actually be made. To help keep the Russians guessing, Japanese gunboats came up the Yalu and began shelling the Russian right flank, as if in preparation for an infantry attack on the Russian right.

These kinds of maneuvers and calculations were an integral part of war in the early twentieth century, and they gave to those wars a strong intellectual and emotional appeal completely separate from the stated goals of the war. Besides having ultimate and serious purposes in abundance, war was also a kind of game. It was the ultimate game in which the stakes were high and victory could be won by bold, imaginative, skillful use of the forces available. In a game context, war could be seen as a set of supremely challenging problems calling for the best efforts of the military strategists of both sides as they maneuvered for the tactical advantages that would lead eventually to the prize of victory.

The mood is difficult to recover now, but it is clearly there in the writings of the time, both factual and imaginative. An element of play was involved, and a level of competition that demanded the best of the players. Since the wars were also reported in detail by the numerous war correspondents who accompanied the contending armies, it was a game that allowed a high level of vicarious participation. Every newspaper reader could be a military expert and, over the breakfast or dinner table, work out the problems of a campaign at a safe remove from the battlefield yet with a pleasurable sense of involvement:

The objective? A quick-firing field gun on the brow of a hill overlooking your fortified position. The gun must be put out of action—captured, if possible, and turned against the enemy. The gentle rear slope of the hill is sure to be heavily guarded, but the steep face below the overhanging brow is another matter. Ascent would be risky but it offers the possibility of surprise. The big gun can't be depressed enough to sweep the face, so the assault troops would only have to contend with small arms fire. With a diversionary force to the rear . . .

And so the problem is set. It is a concrete problem with factors of terrain, morale, weather, supplies, and overall strategy to be figured in. Then all possible skill and intelligence is brought to bear to reduce chance to a minimum and apply the lessons learned from hard experience. Captain Mahan knew the thrill of this kind of contest and tried to convey it to his fellow citizens along with the assurance that there were ways to secure a favorable outcome. War was not just blind, indiscriminate slaughter. There were principles to rely on. There was exact, aquirable knowledge to be applied: "Strategy is a game of wits, with many unknown quantities; as Napoleon and Nelson have said—and not they alone—the unforeseen and chance must always be allowed for. But, if there are in it no absolute certainties, there are practical certainties, raised by experience to maxims, reasonable observance of which gives long odds. Prominent among these certainties are the value of the defensive, the advantage of a central position, and of interior lines."[6]

The maxims are set out with striking confidence, but Mahan was not alone in such confidence. For students of military affairs, it was a confident time. The case-study method was used to demonstrate various problems, to warn against the mistakes made by the untalented or unlucky, and to explain the solutions that had been worked out by leaders of genius. Throughout much of the nineteenth century, Napoleon was the reigning genius, and his campaigns were studied in minute detail. After the German success in the Franco-Prussian War, Helmuth von Moltke became the leader to follow, if only vicariously. A study of his campaigns, and those of other talented leaders, would, it was felt, yield sure principles of successful warfare.

It was this belief that gave such confidence to the writings of Mahan and to lesser figures such as Sir Edward Bruce Hamley. Hamley's *The Operations of War Explained and Illustrated* was first published in 1866. It went through numerous revisions and printings and was still being reprinted as late as 1923. Precisely because he was a lesser figure, without even the talent of Mahan, much less of such strategists as Jomini or Clausewitz, Hamley can stand for his times. He did not shape intellectual outlines, he reflected them. And what he reflected was the inductive method applied with confident and striking disregard for chance or human vagaries. His chapter headings are at once precise and revealing: "The Effect of Operating on a Front Parallel to the Line of Communication with the Base" (with examples from the Austro-Sardinian campaigns of 1849) or "Case of Combined Armies Operating from Divergent Bases" (Waterloo). And to make sure that the proper principles would stand out for the student of military affairs, these chapters closed with a special section, "General Conclusions from the Foregoing Examples."[7]

There is nothing mysterious or frightening about war in such treatments of the subject, nothing to suggest that events might spiral out of everyone's control. One learns definitions, principles, rules to be drawn from the principles, troop strength and disposition, and weapons capabilities; and one is ready to match wits with the enemy. So the Japanese made their preparations on one side of the multiple, twisting channels of the Yalu and Aiho rivers, and the Russians made theirs on the other side; and the correspondents who were accompanying the two armies filed local-color stories while they waited for the action to begin. (Russian troops required fresh black bread and hot soup. Rice cakes would sustain the Japanese.)

At daybreak on 1 May 1904, the Japanese attacked. Their elaborate efforts at concealment paid off handsomely. Until the last moment the Russians did not know the size of the force opposing them and thought it was much smaller than it was. Moreover, the persistent shelling of their right flank by the Japanese gunboats on the Yalu had convinced the Russians that the attack would be directed against their right. They did not anticipate a strike at their left. Even when two days before the main attack, the Japanese Twelfth Division crossed the Yalu some seventeen miles upstream and took up a position on the Russian left, the Russians interpreted this as a feint to draw off their troops and leave their right flank vulnerable. Their attitude throughout the days of preparation had been one of confidence in themselves and contempt for the enemy. They made no attempt to conceal their defenses, neither the entrenchments for their infantry nor the emplacements for their guns. Their intention was to teach the presumptuous Japanese an initial lesson in warfare and then retire upon their reserves where Japanese troops who were foolish enough to follow could be cut to pieces at leisure.

They quickly found themselves in trouble. The Japanese had bridged some of the river channels and, under cover of night, had conveyed howitzers to one of the islands and concealed them behind screens of driftwood and trees. These screens were thrown down before the attack, and the Japanese gunners found easy targets in the exposed Russian defenses. Because the channels had been bridged in several different places by the engineers, Japanese troops were able to advance in force all along the front. At the same time the Twelfth Division began to move downstream against the Russian left and the high ground of Tiger Hill. Throughout the morning the fighting continued and, little by little, the Russians were forced to give way. They abandoned one position after another and finally when their left flank was in danger of being turned, they withdrew their troops, covering their retreat along the single road that led to Feng huang-cheng and safety. It was not a rout, but it was a hasty and confused withdrawal that left two thousand dead and wounded behind. Twenty-one of the twenty-four guns in the three Russian batteries were captured by the Japanese, along with eight machine guns and nineteen ammunition wagons.

There was no gainsaying the extent of the Japanese victory. The world's press rang with praise for Japan, that little island nation that had routed the Russian bear. Military experts commented at length. The general staffs of the world gathered reports from their observers who were on the spot, following every move of the armies, sketching and measuring defensive installations, evaluating tactics and weapons performance. The Japanese themselves, after taking care of the wounded and burying the dead, called in the military attaches accompanying their army and explained to them how they had won.

The war continued for fifteen more months with a full complement of overland marches, sea battles, feints and sorties, one prolonged siege, and many pitched battles to be reported to the waiting world and studied by the general staffs. In many ways, though, the Japanese victory at the Yalu was the high point of the war. It was the place where the rules worked. (Military strategists could point out that the Russians had, among other things, neglected the basic principle of concentration of force.) It was the place where gallantry and planning actually achieved the desired ends, where the losses were not high in proportion to the number of troops involved, and where a remnant of chivalry softened the stark outlines of torn flesh and splintered bones. The officers among the Russian dead were given special treatment by the Japanese. They were separated from the other dead and buried with full military honors.

The rest of the war did not fit so neatly into the framework of war as an acceptable instrument of policy. To be acceptable, it had to be controllable, and for anyone with a bent for projecting current trends into the future, there were parts of the Russo-Japanese war that were downright frightening. There was first the matter of a formal declaration of war. Japan did not issue a declaration until 10 February 1904, two days after her torpedo boats had attacked the Russian fleet at Port Arthur. The attack might, of course, be taken as a kind of de facto declaration—one with obvious intent—but this was a little too much even for warlord states to stomach. Japanese authorities had an embarrassing number of European precedents for their undeclared strike, which they proceeded to cite, chapter and verse. So while being careful not to condemn or offend what was obviously a rising power, the states did agree at the second Hague Peace Conference (1907) that formal notice of some kind was desirable when starting a war, if only to give neutral states fair warning so that they could stay clear of the battle areas.

Then there were the battles fought after the battle of the Yalu. As the war went on and Russia was able to bring more troops into the field, the battles got bigger and messier. Often they were indeterminate affairs where the chief accomplishments seemed to be casualties. Finally in late February 1905 came the battle of Mukden. At the beginning of the battle more than six hundred thousand men faced each other from heavily entrenched positions. The opposing forces were about equal in number, and they were composed of veterans of months of fighting through Manchuria's bitter cold and mountainous terrain. On 21 February the Japanese began their advance. For two weeks the battle raged on a front two days' march in length. On 9 March the exhausted Russian troops began to withdraw. It was a masterly retreat right out from between the closing ends of a Japanese encirclement; but it was still a retreat, and Russian losses were heavy: sixty thousand killed and wounded, twenty-five thousand taken prisoner. The Japanese held the contested ground, but in this battle even victory had the flavor of defeat. The Japanese could not pursue the Russians and make victory decisive. They had strained their resources to the limit, and while they held the ground, it was theirs at the cost of seventy thousand dead and wounded. The high human cost of the battle of Mukden and the inability to fight without a reckless expenditure of lives were a foretaste of the slaughter of World War I.

Finally, there were the mines. Submarine mines had been used before the Russo-Japanese War but never in such numbers and not in the open sea. The Russians had used mines during the Crimean War of 1854–1856 to protect the harbor at Sevastopol, and the Confederates had used them off Mobile during the American Civil War. In the Russo-Japanese War, both sides laid mines extensively. The international waters around the Liao-tung peninsula, in particular, were filled with these deadly weapons. The mines were of the independent contact type: once laid, they required nothing to activate them but contact with a ship, any ship. The mines were anchored, but it was not at all uncommon for them to slip their moorings and drift.

The potential deadliness of the mines can be seen in the loss by the Russians of the battleship *Petropavlovsk* and by the Japanese of the battleship *Hatsuse*, both sinking within minutes after striking mines with the loss of most of their crews and, in the case of the Russian ship, with the loss of the admiral commanding the fleet at Port Arthur. Minesweeping was scarcely practical for the many neutral merchant ships whose crews and cargo were put at risk by these drifting, unpredictable weapons. It was another instance where the acceptable instrument of national policy had slipped out of the control of those who took it up and used it with such confidence. They did not mean for the innocent to pay the price but, increasingly, with the development and spread of modern weaponry, the innocent were doing so.

Feckless Pursuits

The international system was basically unchanged by the Russo-Japanese War. Japan's victory, shortly after the battle of Mukden, put one more major player into the arena, and that was about all it did so far as relations between the states were concerned. The states still spied on one another, still armed themselves to the limit of their borrowing power. They spoke in moderate tones of the balance of power and the national interest, all the while maneuvering ceaselessly for advantage and for an expansion of territory and influence. "The politics of cabinets" is what Léon Bourgeois called it in 1909. At fifty-eight, this French statesman and social philosopher had more than thirty years' experience in the politics of France and the world. He was not impressed with the cabinets' talk of peace while they pursued their own interests and sought to check the similar pursuits of everyone else.

They call this diplomacy "realist," observed Bourgeois. It is, in fact, a "diplomacy of force," and the outcome is war—but worse than that: "The result of their calculations and combinations is that it is almost impossible to localize a conflict—the conflict spreads until it takes in the entire civilized world."[8]

Bourgeois could hardly have known how prophetic his words would be as the world slipped from conflict to conflict after 1909 and finally, in 1914, into the conflict that could not be localized despite the "realists'" best efforts. World War I bore out the worst projections of certain trends in the Russo-Japanese War: the flouting of the rules of international comity, the enormous casualties, and a weapons-driven mode of war that made little distinction between combatants and noncombatants. As Thomas Hardy wrote about the war in one of his most savage poems:

> Herod howls: "Sly slaughter
> Rules now! Let us by modes once called accurst,
> Overhead, under water
> Stab first."[9]

The prescient had long seen this coming and even before the Russo-Japanese War had been able to predict the outcome of the states' actions. As early as 1889, William E. Hall, whose work was in international law, wrote of the war he saw coming: "Whole nations will be in the field; the commerce of the world may be on the sea to win or lose; national existences will be at stake. Men will be tempted to do anything which will shorten hostilities and tend to a decisive issue. Conduct in the next great war will certainly be hard; it is very doubtful that it will be scrupulous, whether on the part of belligerents or neutrals; and most likely the next war will be great."[10]

The Great War of 1914–1918 took longer to come than Hall had predicted. Otherwise, he was right on the mark. But Hall did not leave it there. He still had some of the optimism of the late nineteenth century and its faith that states, as well as individuals, could be bound by law. Hall pointed out that in the past when states had embroiled themselves in wars and disregarded the laws they claimed to uphold, there was always a reaction from that "towards increased stringency of law." His example was Europe, which, he said, would cast aside restraints and then, in a fit of penance, put "itself under stricter obligations than those which it before acknowledged."[11]

The first part of Hall's prophecy had been bitterly borne out by World War I. Events at the end of the war were to be a test of the second part of his prophecy. As the representatives of many of the world's governments gathered in Paris in late 1918 and early 1919 to write the peace treaty that would formalize the end of the war, they were asking themselves how such a war might be prevented in the future. There were vindictive voices in plenty at the conference, but there was also an undercurrent of alarm and, for the moment at least, a willingness to consider new approaches to each other. With nearly 8.5 million dead in the war and the heart of Europe devastated, the states represented at Paris were, at last, frightened enough to begin a search for a better world than the one they had made. Woodrow Wilson put this search on higher ground than many were willing to go, but he caught the essential impulse behind the states' efforts when he said, "What we are striving for is a new international order based upon broad and universal principles of right and justice—no mere peace of shreds and patches."[12]

2 The Ethical Heritage

As there are natural rights of man, so there are natural rights of nations. The inalienable fundamental right of every state is the right of self-preservation and self-determination.

German observations on the peace treaty
29 May 1919

One of the great dramas of the twentieth century began to unfold in Paris in January 1919 as the peace conference got under way. It is not the familiar story of President Wilson doing battle with the forces of reaction and revenge and being bested by them. That emphasis makes the conference little more than a morality play, and it focuses too much attention on one of the protagonists. Wilson was a part of the drama, but only a part. What happened was far more complex and difficult than a morality play and, in the long run, far more dramatic and interesting. At Paris in 1919 the states began to create an ethical framework for international affairs.

This effort by the states distinguishes the Paris conference from previous conferences, particularly from the 1815 Congress of Vienna, with which it is often compared. At Vienna, the big powers had been determined to restore order to a world that had been thrown into turmoil by the Napoleonic wars. They resolutely ignored or repressed the forces for change that had received an impetus from that turmoil. At Paris, a little more than a hundred years later, restoring order was also high on the list of critical tasks, but this was to be in the service of change. The goal was to create a new international system in which the forces for change would have a definite stake. So the tentative ethical framework that emerged from the pulling and hauling of conflicting interests at Paris was not just an exercise on paper. It was given material form in specific institutional structures through which decisions could be made and actions taken.

Four different strands of ethical thought came together at the peace conference:

—conflict resolution and control

—standards of social justice
—human rights guarantees
—fundamental principles of international life
All four strands of thought could be traced to antiquity if one were so inclined, but each had a different meaning in 1919 than it had had in earlier times. The context of the conference and the experiences of the participants were so different from any earlier period that words such as conflict, justice, rights, and peace had a meaning peculiar to the twentieth century. The greatest change with which people were struggling was the rapid increase in scope and intensity of relationships between the states of the international system. To understand and cope with this highly volatile and novel situation, they had institutions and habits of thought that had been formed when contacts between states were intermittent and when the great powers of Europe could dominate the system without great effort.

Implicit in all discussions of world affairs in this period was the question, "What does it mean to be international?" What did it imply, for example, for the national structures of trade and investment that had mediated contacts in the past? How did an empire, with its ideals of cultural pluralism and political unity, adjust to the wildfire spread of the ideals of nationalism and self-determination? What *was* a viable state? Who should decide?

The most confused parts of the discussions at Paris can be seen as attempts to answer these questions. The problems of blockades and reparations, for example, were comparatively simple in theory, if not in application. Blockades and reparations offered no conceptual difficulties. Long effort and experience had developed a complex set of rules of blockade. As for reparations, the Franco-Prussian War (1870–1871) and the Sino-Japanese War (1894–1895) offered recent examples of victorious powers imposing heavy indemnities on defeated powers. These problems fit easily into traditional ways of thinking about international affairs. The conceptual difficulties came in the attempts to work out new ways of thought and different structures for a world that had burst the seams of the old international system.

"How changed is our world!" wrote foreign correspondent Stephen Bonsal after watching the arrival in Paris of the delegation from Ethiopa—tall magnificent looking men, dark-skinned, in long white robes. "The once-secluded Ethiopians are right in the midst of things today. How our so-called civilized world has grown in space and how it has dwindled in transit time!"[1]

It was for this unprecedented world, this world that had grown in space and shrunk in time, that a framework of understanding had somehow to be devised. A rich heritage of ethical thought was available to help in the task, but it was a heritage of such complexity that bits and pieces could be appropriated by the advocates of almost any plan of salvation. Creating some sort of coherent scheme out of this moral hodgepodge was one of the major tasks at Paris in 1919, and the fact that one was created—crude and tentative though it was—was one of the major triumphs of the conference.

Conflict Resolution and Control

The Great War of 1914–1918 had taken most of the autumn of 1918 to come to its ragged, unsatisfying conclusion with the signing of the armistice with Germany on 11 November. The conclusion was ragged because victory for the Allied and Associated powers came piecemeal throughout the autumn months with first Bulgaria, then Turkey, then Austro-Hungary, and finally Germany forced to concede defeat. It was unsatisfying because the armistice did not bring peace but only the exchange of one kind of violence for another. Fighting raged among the ruins of the Austro-Hungarian empire, in parts of Germany, in Poland, in the Baltic states, and all around the borders of the revolutionary Soviet state that had seized the instruments of government in imperial Russia. The revolutionists introduced a new element into the traditional struggles for power and gain still keeping Europe in turmoil: a willingness to destroy society itself in order to create a new kind of state, and to support that kind of violence wherever it might be found.

This was the temporal setting for the peace conference. The emotional setting was a compound of utter weariness with bloodshed and suffering, and a determination that such a war must not happen again. The delegates, and the governments and people they represented, might—and did—disagree on the way to achieve that goal, but they did not disagree on the goal itself. Never again the mobilization of millions, to be sent marching across Europe to deaths undreamed of in the war plans of the various general staffs. Never again the bombing of cities from the air, or the mud-filled, lice-ridden, rat-infested trenches where yesterday's corpses shared quarters with the living. Never again.

"On the last day of the war," wrote Gilbert Seldes, a newspaper correspondent accredited to the American army's press section,

the fields still green, the sun shining brightly, four members of the Press Section drove into terrain which a few hours before had been a battlefield. In that scene of peace and beauty the torn and twisted bodies of human beings seemed so shockingly out of place; yesterday they were a commonplace of war; today they were murdered men. As we stood silent in the unharvested fields and uncovered our heads, the same thought came to all of us. Without questioning each other's feelings, we there pledged ourselves to tell the world, or the many who would read our newspapers, the "true facts" about this war, so that there would be no more wars.[2]

Seldes captures perfectly the mingled horror and determination with which people faced the task of creating a new international order. He captures also the faith in the public that animated the whole immense endeavor. If the public only knew, then all would be well. Once the facts were known, the public could hold their leaders accountable; and the crimes and deceptions of the past, which flourished in the dark of secrecy, could not be committed again.

This was the faith that Woodrow Wilson took with him to Europe. Before the negotiations at Paris had begun, he had made a tour of Europe to sustain and arm himself for the battles that he knew awaited him. The tour had turned into a triumph. Everywhere, he was cheered to the heavens and called the savior of humanity. Being Wilson, he did not take this as a personal triumph but as a sign that he had rightly heard and interpreted the will of the people and their passionate, if inchoate, desire for justice and peace.

It was, then, not faith in himself as such but faith in himself as the representative of the public that sustained Wilson in the struggles at Paris over various provisions of the peace treaty and that led him to appoint himself as the American representative on the committee to draft the Covenant of the League of Nations. Secure in this faith, he labored against and with other committee members to make the covenant the long-term guarantee for the peace that had been bought at so high a price.

Three different kinds of conflict threatened that peace: hostile encounters, wars of aggression, and revolutionary violence. Members of the Covenant Committee devised means that at least held promise of coping with the first two. The third kind of conflict introduced problems that the covenant did not even deal with and was a source of constant anxiety throughout the months of the conference and on into the years beyond.

The delegates could draw on some twenty years' experience with definite procedures for handling hostile encounters and seeing that they did not escalate into full-scale wars. As French delegate Léon Bourgeois never tired of reminding fellow commission members, the Hague Peace Conference of 1899 had given permanent form to the arbitration of conflicts. It had provided an institutional structure that could be called on at any time, instead of depending on the ad hoc arrangements that had served before 1899. As a member of the Permanent Court of Arbitration, the panel of jurists who had agreed to serve as arbiters in case of need, Bourgeois had a personal stake in the issue, but he also had a serious point to make. He insisted that some acknowledgment of the work of the two Hague conferences should be included in the League convenant, preferably in the preamble. "I renew my very strong protest against the preamble," he said when the vote had gone against such acknowledgment. "I consider it a serious matter to ignore completely, as if nothing had ever been done up to the present time for the organization of international law, what has been done and elaborated at the Hague in 1899 and 1907."[3]

Having made the point, Bourgeois drew breath and made it again. Once started, he was difficult to stop and almost impossible to sidetrack. He rode imperturbably over the diversionary tactics of his fellow commission members, tirelessly rephrasing points already made until everyone's patience was in tatters. Nor was he soothed by the soothing tactics of the chairman, Sir Robert Cecil.

"Nobody thinks of forgetting the work of the Hague Conference," Cecil told him. "It is a simple question of form, not an important matter."[4]

"To my mind it is a vital matter," Bourgeois shot back.[5] Then he was off again, reminding the delegates that the new order they were determined to create would have to depend in part on the old. They were all the beneficiaries of years of thought and effort by people from that old order, now to be pushed aside. In particular, he reminded them of the Dogger Bank incident, a potentially explosive international encounter that had been successfully defused through the procedures of the Permanent Court of Arbitration. The incident is an example of the kind of conflict that by 1919 the international system was learning to handle. As such, it is worth looking at more closely.

The surprise Japanese attack on the Russian fleet at Port Arthur in February 1904 had consequences far beyond the damage done to Russian ships and morale. The peaceful passage of ships anywhere on the sea depended on certain assumptions about behavior that were now uncertain, even thousands of miles away from the scene of the Russo-Japanese conflict. The result was disastrous for a British fishing fleet operating out of the port of Hull on the east coast of England.

Eight months to the night after the attack at Port Arthur, the English trawlers were on their usual fishing ground, the Dogger Bank in the North Sea. A light fog lay on the water. Despite the fog and a cloud cover that allowed only occasional glimpses of the moon, the thirty trawlers maneuvered easily on the port tack. The crews were accustomed to working together and following the orders of their fishing "admiral" in the lead boat. At about 1:00 A.M. on the morning of 9 October, a green rocket was fired from the lead boat to signal the fleet to begin to trawl on the starboard tack. Immediately the beam of a searchlight flashed through the fog. There was a burst of gunfire, then more searchlight beams, and more gunfire. The firing lasted for about ten minutes. Then several massive shapes that had borne down on the fishing fleet in the fog moved on past and disappeared into the night. Two British fishermen died in the attack. Six were wounded. The fishing boat *Crane* sank, and five other boats were damaged.

The massive shapes from which the firing had come were four new Russian battleships on their way to the Russo-Japanese war in the Pacific. They were part of the Baltic fleet that Russia was sending halfway around the world to try to break Japan's control of the seas in the battle area. This division, under the personal command of Admiral Z. P. Rozhestvenskii, commander of the squadron, was operating with what might be called a remember-Port-Arthur mentality.

Knowing what had happened to the Russian ships in Port Arthur when the Japanese torpedo boats raced in without warning, the crews of the Russian battleships were candidates for panic. While they had been getting ready for sea, they had heard rumors of unidentified boats, running without lights just outside the roadstead at Reval (Tallinn) on the Baltic Sea or hovering off the coaling station at Cape Skagen, Norway. As the squadron headed south, one transport, the *Kamchatka*, had to drop behind for repairs. When members of its crew sighted some neutral vessels, they opened fire (without inflicting any damage) and sent a wireless message to Admiral Rozhestvenskii saying that they were "attacked on all sides by torpedo boats."

The Russians now believed that there were hostile torpedo boats in their rear and that the boats could close the gap at about one o'clock on the morning of 9 October. Even then, the Hull tragedy was not inevitable. Five divisions of the Russian squadron passed through or near the fishing fleet, correctly identified the boats as trawlers, and continued on course. The sixth and last division arrived just as the lead trawler's rocket was fired for a course change, and the lookouts on the Russian battleships lost their heads. They saw, or thought they saw, a vessel with no lights bearing down on them. They threw a searchlight on it, decided it was a torpedo boat, and the order was given to open fire. After that, careful judgment was blown away along with the fishing boats, although all were showing the proper lights. Confusion was compounded because the Russian searchlights were used for two purposes: to see what was happening and to direct fire against a target vessel. The Russian cruiser *Aurora*, which had fallen behind earlier divisions, ended up in the midst of the melee and was hit by several forty-five- and seventy-five-millimeter shells from its own ships. The Russian crew was more fortunate than the British fishermen, and no one was hurt.[6]

Great Britain and Russia agreed to arbitration to determine how this incident should be handled without recourse to war. A commission of inquiry was appointed under the provisions of the Hague conference convention for the peaceful settlement of disputes. It did not, of course, open an inquiry into the international system itself, which legitimated war as an instrument of national aggrandizement. Its charge was the narrow one of the Dogger Bank incident, and this it fulfilled faithfully. Admirals from the British, Russian, French, Austrian, and United States navies conducted a two-month investigation and concluded that Russia should pay damages. Their investigation showed that there were no torpedo boats either among the trawlers or anywhere near the area and that therefore Admiral Rozhestvenskii was "not justified" in opening fire. (The single dissent to this conclusion came from the Russian representative on the commission of inquiry.) To help soothe national pride—which rejected the very idea that warlords could make mistakes—the commission noted that Admiral Rozhestvenskii's actions, while not justified, were also not "such as to cast discredit upon his military abilities or humanity or that of the personnel of his squadron."[7] Thus absolved of guilt, Russia agreed to pay the damages.

There were special circumstances that made this military encounter resolvable by inquiry and arbitration. Foremost was the fact that neither Russia nor Great Britain wanted war. Even though Great Britain was allied with Russia's current enemy, Japan, this was an alliance in reserve, so to speak, that did not demand Great Britain's participation in the war unless Japan were attacked by a second power. Relations between Great Britain and Russia were such that, although there was a public outcry in England over the attack on the Hull fishermen, it was not enough to force political leaders into a situation of threat and counterthreat in order to appease the electorate. Had *German* ships fired on British fishermen, the situation would have been entirely different. The tensions of a naval armaments race between the two powers were already creating a context in which the flashpoint for war was much lower than under ordinary circumstances. Since the firing was by Russian, not German, ships, an agreement to accept arbitration could be reached and arrangements could be made with a minimum of public posturing.

Acknowledgment of the contribution of the Hague conference arrangements was not written into the League covenant, despite the maneuvering and persistence of Bourgeois, but the arrangements themselves were kept and strengthened. Provision was made for the establishment of a Permanent Court of International Justice to supplement and extend the work of the Permanent Court of Arbitration. Also included was a series of steps for the investigation and reporting of disputes and an explicit acknowledgment that any state had the right to call the attention of the League to any situation that might threaten the peace. In this way the peaceful settlement of disputes was made a principal part of the ethical framework the states were creating at Paris in 1919; and two permanent courts were charged with helping in the task of settlement. They could only function effectively, however, in disputes of a certain kind. These were encounters that had the potential for war—given the latent hostility of relationships between warlords—but that, for one reason or another, the states were willing to see damped down. When that set of circumstances prevailed, here were the means to carry out the damping-down process.

And when those circumstances did not prevail? Then the best known of the provisions of the League covenant were to come into play, those designed to stop wars of aggression. An act of war against one member of the League was to be considered an act of war against all members, and the severance of all relations with the offending state was to follow automatically. The states pledged that they would support one another in isolating the aggressor through breaking off financial, trade, and personal relations, and would come to the aid of any state that might suffer from special measures directed against it by the aggressor. Further, they were to allow passage across their territory to any military forces of League members cooperating in efforts to protect the covenant of the League.

It has been pointed out ad infinitum that these provisions did not work and that in the 1930s the League failed to halt the aggressions of Japan, Italy, and Germany. This failure is used to discredit the whole idea of the League and to indict the framers of the covenant for their "naiveté." What is not often pointed out is that these provisions were never applied as intended because the support of the public, which was a vital necessity if such a widespread, coordinated effort were to be sustained, was not there. Without public support, government leaders waffled about, torn between the traditional warlord's attitude of seeing what could be gained from others' misfortunes and a dim, recurring notion that somehow the circumstances called for something more.

But these failures and uncertainties were in the future. In 1919, the antiaggression provisions of the League covenant were seen as part of the whole section dealing with the peaceful settlement of disputes. Aggression was only one kind of dispute to be dealt with, and all the preceding steps were designed to avoid ever arriving at the stage where the antiaggression provisions would have to be invoked. Being realists, the framers knew that this might occur despite all their arrangements. They had, after all, just emerged from a war of aggression that had escalated into the most terrible war in memory. So they put in strong provisions and then placed their ultimate reliance on the overarching, compelling power of informed public opinion. The extent of this reliance on the public will be dealt with in chapter 6. Here, it is enough to note that the restraining power of public opinion was an integral part of the League's measures for conflict resolution and control.

Revolutionary violence was very much the uninvited guest at the victory feast in Paris. With revolution in Russia, Germany, and Hungary, and the potential for such violence throughout areas where traditional authority was helpless against the rule of hunger and disease, much attention was given to the problems that this kind of conflict posed for the new international order. The attack was threefold: direct military action, as in the allied interventions against the Soviets; support for indigenous antirevolutionary forces, as in the Baltic states and, again, in Russia; and massive relief, rehabilitation, and state-building efforts to wipe out the breeding grounds for social upheaval. All of this effort absorbed a great deal of the attention of the political and military leaders in Paris, and it demanded resources and energy that the war had left in short supply. The efforts yielded success of a kind: revolution was, at length, confined to Russia, where it established itself despite fierce opposition from within and without.

The real failure came in the conceptual realm. This revolutionary violence did not spring from some perverse desire to spread destruction. Rather, it arose from grievances against a social order that was perceived as cruel, uncaring, and unjust, with intolerable inequities of opportunity and wealth. Violence against such an order was seen not only as a duty but a privilege, a boost along the way to a brighter, fairer future. In this formulation—which was the creed of the dedicated few and the marching anthem of thousands—a revolution anywhere became more than that particular revolution. It became The Revolution, the twentieth-century version of the just and holy war.

There was no way that this explosive concept could be accommodated in the arrangements for the peaceful settlement of disputes laid out in the League covenant, nor would it fit the allowable forms of conflict: self-defense, collective action against aggression, or the use of force when arbitration and adjudication efforts had failed. The delegates were uneasy at the challenge posed by revolutionary violence. Many of them, even those who were frightened by it, knew that repression was not a sufficient answer to the challenge, but conceptually they were at a loss. As it turned out, the long-range challenge of revolutionary violence was taken up most effectively not by the framers of the League of Nations Covenant but by a different group, the framers of another section of the peace treaty, the charter of the International Labor Organization.

Standards of Social Justice

So much has been written in a similar vein about the Paris Peace Conference that the proceedings begin to take on the quality of a tableau in which familiar images follow one another in a set sequence. Here is the top-hatted Wilson arriving at Brest and waving to the cheering crowds. Here is Clemenceau with his gray suede gloves worn indoors and out. Here is Lloyd George, his fly-away hair mirroring his restless temperament, and Orlando, who sometimes weeps as he pleads Italy's claims—to the great embarrassment of his northern colleagues. It is a pageant of the powerful and visible.

There was another side to the peace conference. It was made up of people who are mostly forgotten today and were not much remarked at the time. No one met them at the train with flowers and cheers. No one cared what they wore, whether their hair was short or long, their temperaments warm or cool. They simply came to the conference and provided the information, the documents, and many of the ideas that went into the making of the peace treaty and the shaping of the future international system. They flooded into a city still plagued by wartime shortages of food and coal yet giddy with release from wartime pressures and with excitement at the sudden influx of visitors. For the first six months of 1919, Paris was, said Samuel Gompers, "not a city but a cosmopolitan caravansery."[8]

Gompers, president of the American Federation of Labor, was one of the more prominent of those whose names rarely appear in accounts of the conference. He was there to work on what was usually called "the labor question." This innocuous term conceals the fact that this was one of the incendiary issues of the time, one of those issues that focuses the deepest passions of an age. So long as such an issue is unresolved, it stands as an affront to proclaimed values and a challenge to existing social arrangements. Thus "the labor question" ranked high on the list of problems to be addressed and helped contribute to the feverish and hectic atmosphere of the conference.

"'Everybody of importance' was there," said Gompers, reflecting on his experience in Paris, "and the many who hoped to achieve that distinction. There were thousands of those necessary to the machinery of treaty-making, thousands of onlookers and hangers-on. Nothing was normal—prices were appalling—there were apparently no restraints in living. The tension of work and responsibility was so intense that relaxation was in proportion. At no time in my life have I ever worked harder or against such tremendous odds."9

With his colleagues on the International Labor Commission, Gompers was attempting to direct and shape one of the hidden currents of history that, throughout Europe and Asia, were boiling violently to the surface in destructive and frightening eruptions. Whether the labor movement, with its rage and its grievances, was to smash old forms of polity and property or try to bend them to new uses was one of the most explosive questions at Paris, and the issue was very much in doubt. Even those workers who did not identify with socialist or communist tactics and goals were demanding changes in the political and economic systems that had excluded them from power.

Gompers knew exactly where he stood in all of this. He had learned his lessons in the school of poverty, and they had been learned for life. He had seen his father's skills as a cigarmaker made redundant and had seen, too, how his father and his father's friends had so little bargaining power that employers did not feel obligated to pay any attention to what they said. Organization, not destruction, was Gompers's answer to "the labor question."

Was labor powerless, relative to the great combines of employers and the governments that backed them up? Then let labor organize so that workers could act together in a great combine of their own. Was labor speechless amidst the clamor of special interests? Then let labor organize its own newspapers, elect its own representatives to legislative bodies, mobilize votes to defeat politicians in the pockets of the trusts. In Gompers's program to give labor an effective voice in the affairs of the world, the destruction of the means of production was worse than useless; it was self-defeating. Nor did he have any desire for the workers to own and manage the means of production, either by themselves or through the apparatus of the state. Let those who knew how to manage do so. All his efforts would be directed to strengthening labor's bargaining position, making labor an equal partner in negotiations in order to secure for workers a more equitable share of the wealth that their skills and sweat produced. Around this program he had built the powerful American Federation of Labor in the United States. With this program he came to Paris.

In Paris, Gompers came up against men who thought him entirely wrong. They granted his achievements in the United States but said that that was a special case with no applicability to the rest of the world. They had their own ideas on the role of the state and the kinds of legislation needed, and they were quite as prepared as Gompers to fight for what they believed to be right. These were the "tremendous odds" that Gompers spoke of in his reflections on the peace conference. As a courteous gesture to Wilson and the United States, the members of the International Labor Commission elected Gompers as chair and then moved to get their own program adopted.

Gompers found himself faced by quiet, dogged men such as George Barnes and Harold Butler of Great Britain. They had come fully prepared with a program that Gompers knew would never be accepted by his own American Federation much less by the U.S. Senate, which would have to ratify the peace treaty with its labor provisions. Yet he had to proceed with caution. These men were as experienced as he in the battles of the labor movement. They were veterans, too, of a thousand labor meetings, and they were not moved by Gompers's eloquent speeches, one of his greatest strengths in the rough and tumble of a union hall. Here, out of the public eye, he was at a disadvantage, and he moved with care. "He who sups with the Devil must needs have a very long spoon," was his motto on the commission; and, while it would take an overactive imagination to see the devil in these prosaic and decent men, their ideas had, in Gompers's view, to be taken with a very long spoon indeed.

What they had in mind was reflected in the official name of the labor commission: the International Commission for Labor Legislation. They wanted to turn the international labor organization that they were creating into a kind of world legislature in which governments, labor, and industry would all be represented. The labor regulations and standards approved by the oganization would, in their plan, become binding on member states through automatic ratification unless specifically rejected by whatever body had the treaty-making power.

It was a bold move and, Gompers believed, a futile one. Even though governments would be represented in the organization, they would still be sure to see this as an encroachment on their sovereign power. The U.S. Senate, in particular, was jealous of its prerogatives in foreign affairs, and the idea of trying to get such an arrangement through that body was almost ludicrous. The situation in the United

States was further complicated by a constitutional issue. The extent of the powers of both the federal and state governments to regulate labor under the Constitution was still a matter of great uncertainty, the powers being first extended and then curtailed under conflicting court decisions.

These were some of the problems facing the commission, but there were incentives as well. There was, above all, a determination to keep faith with all those workers who had sweated out their lives in poverty and hopelessness, waiting for the public conscience to become aware of their plight. The past pressed heavily on the task of creating an international labor organization, and the labor commission conducted its business in the midst of a crowd of ghosts. Their words, their faces, and the bleak records of their lives were preserved in the massive reports that the statistical bureaus of the industrializing countries had been issuing for some seventy years and in the publications of private organizations concerned by the high social cost of industrialization. Sometimes the ghosts had full names, sometimes only a first name, or initials. "Waylon _____, aged 11, has worked 9 months, earns 30 cents a day"—this from an investigation of a North Carolina textile mill just before the war. "Maggie _____, aged 12, has worked 1 year, earns 50 cents a day. David _____, aged 12, youngest of 5 children all of whom work, earns 25 cents a day."[10]

Report after report pointed up the urgency of the commission's task and laid out the evidence of the cost, in human terms, of the lack of power and the lack of effective state regulation. Here is Rose Brennan, textile worker in Massachusetts, testifying against the repeal of a state law mandating a maximum eight-hour workday for children. At age thirty-three, Rose Brennan is a veteran of twenty years in the mills. "I wanted an education. I went to night school just as long as I possibly could. The work I did all day robbed me of my strength of mind and body and I fell asleep at my desk many a night in night school, and I think eight hours a day is enough for the children. . . . They are never going to get an education in a cotton mill."[11]

The eight-hour day, not just for children but for all workers, was something that Gompers and Barnes and many on the labor commission could agree on. How it was to be achieved was a point of argument. How it could be applied in Asia where workers routinely labored far more hours a day than in the West was another problem and a serious one. In labor questions the difficulties caused by the rapid internationalization of political and economic relationships was brought sharply to the consciousness of those trying to plan a new international order. Nothing existed in isolation. If they took hold of a problem in Liverpool, they found themselves juggling New Delhi and Tokyo as well.

The whole idea of standards of social justice, which underlay the attempt to create an international labor organization, had from the first raised questions about the effect of national boundaries. No producer would or could introduce changes that might benefit labor but would put him at a competitive disadvantage with those who refused to make the changes. The standards had to be industrywide and, increasingly, that meant that they had to be international. National regulation alone would not serve, since the chief result might be to put national industry at a disadvantage in international competition. But what form were the international standards to take?

In the rational world of economic theory, this was not a problem. Jérome Blanqui, French theorist and economist, had found the perfect answer as early as the 1830s: "Treaties have been concluded between one country and another by which they have bound themselves to kill men; why should they not be concluded today for the purpose of preserving men's lives and making them happier?"[12]

Nothing could be simpler or more logical. But logic had a very low rank in the world of the warlord states, so the form that international standards were to take was a problem. They had to be effective, yet not intrusive; flexible enough to cover a wide variety of conditions, yet firm enough to function and withstand pressure. And the states were only part of the difficulty. There was organized labor itself. The Byzantine politics of the international labor movement assured that its ranks would be split over almost any tactic, while the cutthroat competition of many labor leaders for credit and power meant that their attention was always divided. It was left to the fifteen men on the labor commission and their expert advisers to devise arrangements that would work in the world as it was while also nudging things along toward the world that could be.

In this task, their differences and failings came to the fore. They haggled over commas and lost their tempers over adjectives. They often stood on national pride. They quarreled over petty details as often as over matters of principle. What they had in common was a conviction of the importance of their job and a determination to see it through. And see it through they did.

They wrote into the basic treaty that emerged from the peace conference the principle that "peace can be established only if it is based upon social justice."[13] Here was the premonitory sound of a trumpet outside the walled gates of national sovereignty, clear notice that in the future social justice was to be a matter of international concern. Nor was this a spongy, election-year kind of justice, thrown in at the last moment to sop up votes. In forty-two treaty articles plus a preamble and an annex, commission members spelled out what they meant by social justice and provided a plan to establish the institutional mechanisms and procedures through which justice could be pursued. In so doing they created the most successful part of the ethical framework being roughed in at Paris. As it turned out, they also provided a model for future efforts to establish international standards in areas other than labor, standards that states could aim for and by which they could be judged.

But that was an unintended consequence—and benefit—of their concern for the problems of labor. One of the strengths of the labor commission was the way its members concentrated strictly on the job at hand. They met head-on the problem of standards for countries at different levels of economic development by explicitly recognizing that the different levels "make strict uniformity in the conditions of labour difficult of immediate attainment." So Japan, India, China, and other newly industrializing countries could be brought within the new labor organization without stigma. But the commission also insisted that the basic principle "that labour should not be regarded merely as an article of commerce" applied everywhere, no matter what the level of development, and that from that principle could be derived methods to regulate labor conditions for the benefit of the Japanese no less than the Belgian worker.[14]

As for the eight-hour day, the commission did not make this demand a part of the basic structure of the labor organization, as some members wanted. That would have provided an excuse for some governments to boycott the organization from the start. Instead, the less challenging principle of the regulation of hours of work was included in the preamble, and the goal of a forty-eight-hour week was made part of a list of general principles, a "standard to be aimed at where it has not already been attained." Then, in a swift move for action, the application of that principle was put on the agenda for the first gathering of the delegates of the organization, the first Annual Labor Conference, to be held in the fall of 1919.[15]

It was, however, in the matter of the regulations and standards that might emerge from this first labor conference or from subsequent conferences that commission members showed best their ability to maneuver imaginatively toward their goals. Here was the sticking point between those who wanted to turn the Annual Labor Conference into sessions of a world legislature on labor problems and those who saw this desire as a fatal challenge to state sovereignty in

general and a slap at federal states, such as the United States, in particular. Meetings on this subject were interminable and were punctuated
with the outbursts of men taking their stands on principle. When the
gap between opposing principles was finally and painfully closed,
commission members had cut off at the ground one of the basic assumptions of the old international order. While acknowledging the
national base through which decisions had to be made in a world of
sovereign states, they provided a structure through which transna-
tional perspectives could be brought to bear.

This structure involved careful arrangements for representation
from governments, industry, and labor in each of the member states,
both in the annual conference and on the governing body that would
provide continuity in the periods between the meetings of the conference. As might be expected, the states appointed the delegates to the
conference. They appointed those representing industry and labor as
well as those representing the government. Here was a recognition of
the position of the states in the international system. In the final analysis, they would be the ones to take action on any standards for social
justice that might be set by the international organization. But there
were many different routes to that final analysis, and the members of
the labor commission picked one that encouraged state participation
but not state dominance.

They did this through two provisions. First, they stipulated that
state appointment of the delegates from industry and labor must be
done in consultation with the national bodies representing those interests. As a check on that, the Annual Labor Conference could refuse
to seat any delegate inappropriately chosen. Second, and most important, they devised a voting arrangement that discouraged the strictly
national view that most states were accustomed to adopt, no matter
what the question under discussion. Instead of requiring delegates
from each member state to vote as a bloc, the usual method in meetings of international bodies, commission members stipulated that
delegates could vote individually.

With this provision, the commission said, in effect, that the problems of labor transcended national boundaries and that the unitary
view of national interest implied in a bloc vote did not apply. Even
though each member state was entitled to two government delegates
to the annual conference while industry and labor had only one delegate each, the total state delegation did not have to speak and vote
with one voice, as if the merit of a question were somehow tied to a
single national view. This simple voting procedure uncoupled the linking of merit and national interest that was an all-but-automatic

assumption in most international bodies and allowed delegates to consider questions from other points of view.

Finally, commission members decided that the labor standards and regulations adopted by the conference could take the form either of a recommendation or a draft convention suitable for ratification by the member states. This approach got around the problem posed by those federal states, such as the United States, where the national legislature did not have the sole power to regulate labor. But in either case, recommendation or draft convention, the member states agreed that within a year (or eighteen months under special circumstances) after the close of the conference, they would "bring the recommendation or draft convention before the authority or authorities within whose competence the matter lies, for the enactment of legislation or other action."[16]

Here was the heart of the matter. Before the first Annual Labor Conference had even met, the states agreed that they would take action on any international standards adopted by that body. Not just take note, take action. And because representatives of labor and industry were involved in working out and adopting the standards at the international level, an attentive public was guaranteed right from the start—a public that had a stake in bringing pressure to bear on national governments. This arrangement could be supported by those, such as Barnes, who put their faith in legislation, and by those, such as Gompers, who believed more strongly in organization. It could include both the economically developed and the less developed states, and a wide variety of state-industry relationships. In fact, the tedious and undramatic business of working out matters of representation and voting had resulted in a structure with dramatic potential for channeling social conflict into cooperative social endeavor.

These untraditional structural arrangements were put to the service of traditional goals. The members of the labor commission drew on a long tradition of ethical discourse on matters of social justice. This ancient idea had, in the nineteenth century, taken on a new expression and a particular urgency in regard to labor. As Pope Leo XIII put it in his 1891 encyclical on the condition of labor, "The momentous seriousness of the present state of things just now fills every mind with painful apprehension; wise men discuss it; practical men propose schemes; popular meetings, legislatures, and sovereign princes, all are occupied with it—and there is nothing which has a deeper hold on public attention."[17]

The "apprehension" as to the outcome of labor unrest was even more painful in 1919 than it had been in 1891, but by 1919 there was more experience to reflect upon as people attempted to integrate labor and industry into a new international order. Various plans for workmen's compensation, unemployment and health insurance, and pension plans were being tried in several countries and in some of the states of the United States. These were local and national approaches. Internationally, by 1919, there was at least limited experience with the setting of international standards and their effect on national legislation and on actual conditions at the level where individual workers lived and died. Standards concerning the use of white phosphorus in the manufacture of friction matches provide the best example of a pre–World War I attempt to draw on a heritage of social justice and give it effective social expression. This method was to prove critical in the years after 1919.

By the latter portion of the nineteenth century it was known that workers in the match industry were at special hazard from the white phosphorus used on the tips of friction matches. Fumes from the chemical entered the workers' bodies through cavities in the teeth and in many cases caused extensive damage to the bones of the jaw. Medical authorities called this "phosphorus necrosis." The workers called it "phossy jaw." Under either name, teeth fell out as the jaw bones rotted. In some cases the jaw bones had to be removed entirely.

Manufacturers and governments searched for a way to remove the hazards without removing the phosphorus, the most economical chemical for this use. They tried increased ventilation in the dipping and packing rooms. They instituted strict sanitation procedures and mandatory dental examinations. These helped but did not solve the problem. Finland took the legislative lead in 1872 by outlawing the use of white phosphorus in the manufacture of matches and prohibiting their import or sale. Over the next thirty-one years, five more countries followed suit. In 1906 those five countries and two more signed a multilateral treaty, the International Convention Respecting the Prohibition of the Use of White (Yellow) Phosphorus in the Manufacture of Matches, and invited other states to adhere to the treaty. The stated purpose of the treaty was "to facilitate the development of the industrial protection of workpeople by the adoption of common provisions."[18]

An international standard had been set and a precedent established. The problem had not yielded to local, private efforts nor to national legislation. Only a concerted, multinational endeavor could make worker protection in an international industry more than mere talk. The difficulty of achieving this has been mentioned in general terms. In specific terms, we have the complete willingness of Austria and Hungary to sign the convention if only Japan would do so. Great Britain was willing if Austria, Hungary, Belgium, Spain, Portugal, Sweden, Norway, and Japan would sign; and Sweden was willing if all those countries including Great Britain adhered. Portugal explained with regret that the Portugese government had recently granted a match monopoly for thirty years and so could not possibly sign.[19]

But still, a standard had been set. Over the next several years, the effect of that standard worked away undramatically, like the proverbial leaven in the great unleavened mass of competitive jealousy that constituted the international norm. Austria, Great Britain and Ireland, Hungary, and Spain swung into line with the original seven states: Denmark, France, Germany, Italy, Luxemburg, the Netherlands, and Switzerland. Then blocks of British and French colonies, and Australia, as a member of the Commonwealth, followed suit. Movement was slow, but there was movement.[20]

While the international system was adjusting itself to the idea of common standards for a common good, workers in many areas continued at risk. They appear in the records as abbreviated names in abbreviated accounts of the lives being used up during the slow processes of social and political change. "Maria O., a strong and healthy girl, had worked for several years as a packer in a match factory." This glimpse is in a prewar report on phosphorus poisoning in the match industry in the United States. Maria O. lost most of her teeth and several inches of both jawbones. "When the writer saw her in December, 1909, she was scarcely able to open her lips enough to speak and could not separate her upper lip from her six remaining lower teeth."[21]

Such glimpses give human meaning to the labor statistics that provided the driving power for Samuel Gompers and George Barnes and for experts on the labor commission, such as James T. Shotwell, who helped work out the compromises that made agreement possible. They knew that statistical tables of the incidence of disease, poverty, and occupational mortality were the aggregate descriptions of workers such as Bridget D. "a proud-spirited girl," who would not admit, even to her dentist, that she worked in a match factory. In the end, she had to have her entire lower jaw removed but, before it came to that, she tried to cure herself at home. To gain relief from the pain, she would sit behind the kitchen stove with her face pressed to the warm wall. Her mother kept hot poultices on her daughter's face, but there was no cure short of surgery. "My work was all for nothing," said the mother to the interviewer from the Labor Bureau. "Poison it was that was there."[22]

By 1916, Mexico, the United States, Norway, and India had joined the ranks of those who had either adhered to the 1906 convention or had passed national legislation to achieve its purposes. This process was eased by the development of workable substitutes for white phosphorus in the manufacture of matches. The new materials were more expensive, but widespread adoption plus increasing prohibition of the use of white phosphorus helped make the changeover possible and offered hope that future factory workers would escape the fate of Maria O. and Bridget D. Then in 1919 the labor commission at the peace conference moved to build on the foundations already laid. One of the items on the agenda for the first meeting of the fledgling International Labor Organization was the "extension and application" of the convention on the prohibition of white phosphorus in the manufacture of matches.[23]

In this way, an obscure international instrument, of immediate interest to only a few, became a part of the new international order being created at Paris in 1919. More importantly, the phosphorus convention provided a model for a way to outflank the ritualistic insistence of sovereign states that what went on within their own borders was not a matter of international concern. By many different routes and procedures, forty-five different states and colonies had by 1916 come to the conclusion that social justice for workers required that certain international standards be observed in the manufacture of matches. Beginning with that recognition, the International Labor Organization took up its long struggle for the setting of similar international standards for hours of work, employment of women and children, and protection against sickness, accident, infirmity, and disease. The idea of universality was thus, right at the start, built firmly into the ethical framework that the states were constructing at Paris.

Human Rights Guarantees

In the midst of the varied activities of the peace conference an embarrassing moment occurred on 11 February at a meeting of the commission to draft the Covenant of the League of Nations. Despite private efforts at dissuasion, the Japanese delegates on the commission brought up for discussion and vote an amendment to the preamble of the covenant. The covenant preamble was not an elaborate statement of principle. It set out, simply and briefly, the rationale for the League. Its purpose was "to promote international co-operation and to achieve international peace and security." The states were to proceed toward this goal by agreeing not to resort to war; by conducting their relations with each other openly and honorably; by taking the understandings of international law as their "actual rule of conduct"; and by maintaining justice and respecting their treaty obligations. To these four pledges, the Japanese wanted to add a fifth: "by the endorsement of the principle of the equality of Nations and the just treatment of their nationals."[24]

Their proposal was clear and direct and wholly within the spirit of the new international order that was being established. It was also unsupportable by most of the states represented on the commission and at the conference itself. Immigration restrictions based on racial criteria were a part of the domestic policy of many countries, including the United States, and the criteria were often especially applied to Asians. This situation was difficult enough, but worse difficulties yet resided in the seemingly simple amendment. Even though the principle asserted was "the equality of Nations," the principle evoked was the much more inflammatory one of the equality of races. Japan, being for the most part racially homogenous, could reasonably draw the second principle from the first, as was made clear in the statement of Nobuaki Makino, one of the Japanese delegates.

Makino and his fellow delegate Sutemi Chinda had not spoken much during the discussions on the covenant. In this they were typical of the entire Japanese delegation to the conference. This meeting was the first major international conference that the Japanese had attended as one of the great powers, and they seemed to be trying to make it easy for the Europeans to treat them as diplomatic equals. They spoke little on European questions and made it clear that their chief concern was Asia, where they unhesitatingly asserted a position as the dominant power. It was, then, an obvious departure from the routine when the quiet Makino, despite the embarrassment of his colleagues and their attempts to sidetrack the whole issue, insisted on raising the question of the racial equality amendment and pressing for a recorded vote. His accompanying statement was filled with thoughtful observations to which his colleagues, as private individuals, might or might not have taken exception but which, as political representatives, they could in no way support.

He spoke first of the League as an attempt to hold nations and peoples to a "higher moral standard" than in the past. He spoke of the intense national feelings stirring among long-suppressed peoples and how their longings for freedom were at last going to be satisfied. He then pointed out that oppressed nationalities were not the only ones who had suffered wrongs:

In close connection with the grievances of oppressed nationalities, there exist the wrongs of racial discrimination which was, and is, the subject of deep re-sentiment on the part of a large portion of the human race. The feeling of being slighted has long been a standing grievance with certain peoples. And the announcement of the principle of justice for peoples and nationalities as the basis of the future international relationship has so heightened their legitimate aspirations that they consider it their right that this wrong should be redressed.[25]

Lest the implications should not be understood, Makino then pointed out, with impeccable courtesy, the possible outcome of a failure in this sphere. In so doing he provided a clear exposition of the connection between principle and policy. For his policy example, he chose the collective security arrangements of the new international order. What do you suppose would be the reaction, he asked his hearers, if a nation discriminated against because of race was called on for a military contribution to defend another state against aggression? He answered his own question in terms that, gentle and oblique as they were, still constituted a refusal: "It will not be easy for people to reconcile themselves to the idea of submitting to a call for heavy and serious obligation, perchance in defence of those at whose hands they are refused a just treatment."[26] In other words, you cannot expect us to come to the defense of a state that discriminates against us.

There is an authentic ring to Makino's words that is the more impressive when placed against his habitual reticence and reluctance to bring painful subjects into public view. This uncharacteristic frankness said bluntly to the other delegates, "The shoe pinches here. What do you propose to do about it?" There was, in fact, not much that the delegates could do, since their actions were constrained by the strength of racial feelings in their own countries. As Wilson remarked, in one of those observations showing his political experience and hard-headedness, "How can you treat on its merits in this quiet room a question which will not be treated on its merits when it gets out of this room? It is a question altogether of the wisest thing to do, not a question of our sentiments towards each other or of our position with regard to the abstract statement of the equality of nations."[27]

Makino had brought briefly into view the wounded national and racial pride that would, on a world scale, make it difficult to create a new international order, but his statement was more than just a reminder of that bitter fruit of European arrogance. It was also a timely demonstration of the complications in the uses of morality. The League covenant spoke of justice, and everyone replied, "Oh, yes indeed." No sooner had they agreed with the moral principle than they found themselves in a procedural swamp: What kind of justice? For whose benefit? At whose expense? Who will decide? None of these questions would go away when the sword of justice was waved at them. They only multiplied. Meanwhile, Makino had to be answered and some decision made on the Japanese amendment. Wilson devised an answer that moved the proceedings safely through the reefs of unusable abstractions without abandoning principle altogether:

This League is obviously based on the principle of equality of nations. Nobody can read anything connected with its institution or read any of the articles in the Covenant itself without realizing that it is an attempt—the first serious and systematic attempt made in the world—to put nations on a footing of equality with each other in their international relations. . . . It is a combination of moral and physical strength of nations for the benefit of the smallest as well as the greatest. That is not only a recognition of the equality of nations, it is a vindication of the equality of nations.[28]

Wilson's statement provides a clue to the kind of ethical framework being constructed at Paris. It was not a framework of abstract principles; it was a framework of institutional arrangements that *embodied* certain principles and allowed actions to be taken. Thus, in the matter of human rights guarantees, there was no abstract statement about fundamental rights to be secured regardless of national, racial, or ethnic origins, just as there was no abstract statement about the equality of nations. There were, however, institutional structures and procedures based on these principles.

So, while the Japanese amendment was left out of the covenant (along with a statement on religious toleration that Wilson very much wanted), the principle of the equality of nations was resoundingly affirmed, as Wilson had pointed out, in the very structure of the League. What it boiled down to was this: the Japanese had asked for a symbolic statement on racial equality that they could use to placate the government, the press, and the public in Japan. What they got instead was a substantive embodiment of the principle of the equality of nations, the principle on which they had taken their stand. It did not serve immediate Japanese purposes, but it did serve the long-range purposes of the new international order.

This little wrangle with the Japanese illustrates the approach of the delegates in Paris to the whole subject of human rights and human rights guarantees. The approach was more political than philosophical, as can be seen in the human rights guarantees written into six different treaties that came out of the work of the Paris Peace Conference and signed by the end of the year. The treaties were between the principal Allied and Associated powers on the one hand, and Poland, Austria, Czechoslovakia, Yugoslavia, Bulgaria, and Romania, on the other.

In no other portion of their work did the delegates draw so heavily and consciously on precedent as they did in the area of human rights guarantees. They had a pressing reason to emphasize precedent in this matter. International guarantees of civil, political, and religious rights for certain groups within the borders of an independent state were, by anyone's definition, encroachments on the sovereign power of that state. Yet that was exactly what the six treaties did. The treaties, both with former enemy powers such as Austria and Bulgaria and with newly constituted states such as Poland and Czechoslovakia, made the League of Nations the guarantor of stipulated rights for minority groups within the respective states. Further, the treaties declared that the clauses specifying the rights and the groups were part of the fundamental law of that state and could not be changed without the express permission of the League.[29]

In the political climate of 1919, this remarkable interference in the internal affairs of sovereign states could not be justified on the general grounds that the international community had a responsibility to see that even sovereign states met certain minimum standards in the treatment of their own nationals. To do so would have opened such a Pandora's box of politically motivated interventions as to make the most internationally minded leader blanch with horror.

On the other hand, neither could a new international order tolerate the kinds of abuses that had in the past shocked the consciences of even warlord states: the massacre of subject populations, such as the Bulgarians in the Ottoman Empire in 1875; the lack of all legal protection for the Jews in Romania, Russia, and the eastern section of what had been Poland; or the government-sponsored pogroms that had sent thousands of Jewish survivors fleeing through Europe or across the ocean to the New World. Such abuses had to be avoided in the future, but general abstractions about international responsibility for human rights would not serve. The abstractions could too easily be turned against the victor states themselves, and they were not about to offer any other state such convenient justification for intervention.

The way out of this impasse, the way to protect the basic principle of sovereignty and yet also protect minority groups in central and eastern Europe, was to call on precedent: "We are not doing anything new." This was the defense and the justification offered by the Allied and Associated powers to the objections raised by the six treaty states—and there were prolonged and vociferous objections. The Poles and the Romanians, in particular, objected to the special protection afforded the Jews within their borders, protection that was included specifically because of the record of persecution in those countries and the open disdain expressed by influential leaders. "We have too many Jews," said Roman Dmowski who, with Ignace Paderewski, officially represented Poland at the peace conference. Dmowski was considered a moderate on the subject. He did not advocate getting rid of the Jews. He only said that those who were allowed to remain in Poland must change their ways. "The Jew must produce and not remain devoted exclusively to what we regard as parasitical pursuits. Unless restrictions are imposed upon them soon, all our lawyers, doctors, and small merchants will be Jews."[30]

Clemenceau was the man to deal with this situation in the chosen context. He downplayed talk of rights and founded the case for the victor powers firmly on precedent. These kinds of stipulations are not new, he told the Poles in a note that accompanied a copy of the treaty they would be asked to sign. For a long time it had "been the established procedure of the public law of Europe" that when a state is created—or re-created, as in the case of Poland—or a large accession of territory made, then recognition by the great powers is accompanied by a binding international convention on the part of the new or enlarged state that it will "undertake to comply with certain principles of government."[31]

"Certain principles of government" was as far as Clemenceau would venture in this matter onto the treacherous ground of abstractions. He immediately launched into a lawyerly review of the work of the Congress of Berlin, which in 1878 had made recognition of the independence of Serbia, Romania, and Montenegro dependent on the new states' agreeing to equal treatment for all the ethnic and religious groups within their borders. With this precedent safely established, he then moved the discussion to 1919 and took his stand on the high ground of duty: "There rests, therefore, upon these Powers an obligation, which they cannot evade, to secure in the most permanent and solemn form guarantees for certain essential rights which will afford to the inhabitants the necessary protection whatever changes may take place in the internal constitution of the Polish State."[32]

The essential rights to be secured in the Polish treaty, as in the other treaties, were the protection of life and liberty, the free exercise of religion, equal standing before the law, equal access to public office, the retention and exercise of cultural attributes such as language, and, in the case of nationals of other countries now included within the borders of the state, the right to become a citizen without the requirement of any formality. Where the Jews were mentioned specifically, it was to guarantee them the rights of the observance of their Sabbath without penalty if, for example, they refused to conduct any legal business or to appear in court on that day. The state also was not to make an issue of Sabbath observance by calling an election or holding voter registration on Saturday—thus deliberately excluding the Jews. The Jews also were to receive a proportional share of public funds for their schools, which they could manage themselves (under the general supervision of the state) through locally appointed educational committees.

The human rights guarantees that were made a part of the ethical framework of the new international system in 1919 were, as can be seen from these examples, specific to certain groups within certain states. This practice was continued over the next several years as other states, either by treaty or declaration, agreed to maintain those specified rights for minority groups within their borders, the agreement being a condition of their recognition by the great powers and their admission into the League of Nations. The states of whom this was demanded were not slow to point out that more was being asked of them than of other states where the treatment of minorities, such as blacks in the United States, for example, or Koreans by the Japanese, was not considered anyone else's business.

The fact that the human rights guarantees applied only to particular groups in particular states should not, however, be allowed to obscure the fact that the rights had been given international recognition and placed under international guarantees. In this latter respect there was a departure from the precedent on which the victor states had relied for their justification. In the past, the great powers had been the guarantors of any such stipulations. This had not worked very well. As Clemenceau pointed out, "Experience has shown that this was in practice ineffective, and it was also open to the criticism that it might give to the Great Powers, either individually or in combination, a right to interfere in the internal constitution of the States affected which could be used for political purposes."[33]

Not only "*could* be used for political purposes" but *had* been used that way many times, as even the most superficial student of European affairs well knew. Now the League was to be the guarantor. Collective wisdom was to take the place of separate, competing national policies, and this, it was hoped, would take the question of human rights out of the political sphere entirely. The wisdom of the group was to be expressed through the organs of the League. This meant the Council and, when necessary, the Permanent Court of International Justice—an essential component of the new international order. The court was not established during the negotiations at Paris, but it was called for in the League covenant; and steps were taken for its establishment in the near future.

All of this is a far cry from trumpet calls and manifestos that can stir hearts and mobilize public opinion for a great leap forward. There is little that is memorable in treaty articles that begin "Poland undertakes to put no hindrance in the way of" or "Austria undertakes to assure full and complete protection of," but they address human rights issues nonetheless, and address them in practical, enabling terms. Aesthetically speaking, it would be far more satisfying if human rights guarantees had not been built into the framework of the new international order to the accompaniment of furious protests from those being forced to grant them, but the rights were just as much a part of the framework as if their inclusion had been more glorious. The years ahead would tell if this insistence on certain human rights standards was just an aberration, or if the states would build on this beginning and make it into a continuation of what Nobuaki Makino had called "the present worldwide moral renaissance."[34]

Fundamental Principles of International Life

Underlying much of the work of the peace conference was a body of thought about the states in the international system, their rights and duties, and their relationships to each other. When the German representatives objected to the terms of the peace treaty on the grounds that there were "natural rights" of states as there were of individuals and that the treaty violated those rights, they were basing their argument on this substantial body of thought about the fundamental principles of the international system. The quotation from the German statement is put at the head of this chapter because this particular strand of the ethical heritage being drawn on at Paris was, in the long run, the most influential portion. It will receive fuller treatment in later chapters when the power and implications of its assumptions became clearer than they were at Paris. Here it will be enough to sketch the broad outlines of the body of thought and suggest its influence on the work of the conference.

The influence was profound, but it was indirect. Nowhere in the League covenant or in the rest of the several peace treaties is there a list of fundamental principles similar to those that became common in international instruments of a later period. At Gompers's insistence, a list of principles was included in the section of the treaties that dealt with the new labor organization, but the "General Principles" of part 13, section 2, apply specifically to labor, not to the international system as a whole. Attempts were made by the Italian delegation and by two technical advisers to the American delegation to preface the League covenant with a list that would set out fundamental principles for the whole system, but these suggestions never emerged from the preliminary meetings where the many different versions of the covenant were being considered.

The reasons that such a list never saw the light of day are not spelled out in the record but can be speculated upon with some assurance. Statements of abstract principles of international relations held as little interest for most of the delegates as did abstract statements about human rights. James Brown Scott, one of the technical advisers to the U.S. delegation, and Secretary of State Robert Lansing were exceptions to this rule, but they were very much outsiders at the conference. Wilson sought advice from his friend Edward M. House rather than from his secretary of state and, in fact, often did not let Lansing know the progress of deliberations on the League.

Then, too, the delegates already had Wilson's Fourteen Points as guidelines for their actions. There were also his subsequent statements, which with the Fourteen Points were the basis for the armistice that had brought the fighting with the Germans to a close. Here were principles enough to act on, and it was action that concerned the delegates at Paris, not statements of principle. The establishment of new states, the reconstitution of old states, the elaborate machinery of mandates for administering territories not deemed ready for statehood— this was the business of the conference. It was also a practical working out, through the adjustment of boundaries and peoples, of the fundamental principle of self-determination. The principle was neither questioned nor analyzed nor was it placed within a context that would relate it to other fundamental principles of international life. It was simply acted on.

As for the body of thought from which the principle of self-determination was derived, that was so much a part of the intellectual and emotional milieu of 1919 that its propositions seemed not so much self-evident as natural. *In the beginning was the nation-state, which people saw as good.* From that, the rest followed: the very structure of the League as an association of independent states; the establishment of new states; the preparation of mandated territories for eventual statehood; the guarantees of the political independence and territorial integrity of existing states. The list exemplifies the absolute dominance of the idea of the state as the highest form of collective expression and fulfillment. Every arrangement for the new international order was grounded on the fact of the state and shaped by consideration of the rights that flowed from its very existence. These rights were not, and did not have to be, enumerated to be influential. They were, as was much else at Paris, simply assumed and then given institutional form.

Peace? That was certainly the goal of the delegates at Paris. And justice, too. But this justice and this peace were through and for the states of the international system—armed as ever, suspicious as ever, and only temporarily frightened by the consequences of their own warlordish behavior. In Paris they had managed to put together the beginnings of an ethical framework that could guide their actions and provide standards for judging them. They had worked four strands of thought from their ethical heritage into the framework: conflict resolution and control, standards of social justice, human rights guarantees, and fundamental principles of international life.

From the standpoint of systematic thought there was not much to celebrate. The framework was not consistent, the parts were not related in any rational way, and they were filled with contradictions. Moreover, the structure bore clear marks of the many political maneuvers and compromises that had brought it into being.

But—it existed. That was the important point. In philosophy, the tensions and contradictions would be cause for dismay. In politics, they were cause for hope because in them lay the possibilities for change and for the choice of different alternatives—all within the basic ethical structure. The states had, with great effort, brought this structure into being. It remained to be seen what, if anything, they would do with it in the years ahead as they worked to establish their new international order.

3   New International Approaches

The world has had far too little practice in international activity. To be sure we've had the Universal Postal Union and the International Bureau of Weights and Measures and the International Sugar Commission, and during the war we had the successful operation of such cooperative ventures as the Allied Maritime Transport Council. But we never had a systematic international approach to problems where everybody has everything to gain and nothing to lose.

Raymond B. Fosdick
Under Secretary-General
League of Nations
15 August 1919

From the perspective of the present, it is easy to see the years from 1919 to 1939 as little more than an ill-fated runup to World War II. The sheer scope of that conflict casts its shadow back over the negotiations at Paris and throws a pall of apparent futility over all subsequent proceedings. It is, then, important to be reminded of the obvious fact that those who took up the task of building a new international order did not know that they were living in what would come to be called the interwar period. They saw the first ten of those years as a time of promise and excitement, and they worked doggedly to the very end of the second half of the period to avert the catastrophe that eventually overwhelmed them.

When they *were* overwhelmed by that catastrophe, they were not at the same place, ethically speaking, that they had been in 1919. During those twenty years they had managed to establish institutions and habits that departed from the past and set patterns for the future. There were later, better-known efforts to control conflicts, articulate standards for state behavior, specify rights for states and individuals, and make the international system responsive to states with widely different traditions and needs, but more often than not, these later efforts followed paths that had been marked out between the wars.

The twenty years following the close of the Paris Peace Conference were, then, years of development of the ethical framework that the states had devised in those negotiations. Much of this development took place in the midst of events that overshadowed the work of the international bodies concerned with ethical matters. The overshadowing is easily understood. When a committee report or a speech in Geneva had to compete for the attention of press and public with a general strike, the fall of a coalition cabinet, the seizure of territory, or the assassination of a king, there was no question where attention would be directed.

Despite the difference in dramatic impact, there was a close relationship between ethical development, with its slow and quiet pace, and the spate of daily happenings in the world. The events just mentioned and the many others that occurred between the two world wars were not simply a backdrop for the development of the ethical framework. They were the turbulent context within which development took place; and there was a ceaseless interaction between context and ethical evolution. The events helped to determine what was thought possible or desirable in the standards that the states were trying to develop and maintain. The standards, in turn, provided guidelines for the conduct of states involved in the turbulence of the times. State actions frequently did not conform to state standards, but that did not negate the potential value of those standards as agreed-upon alternatives to self-interest as the chief measure of conduct in the international sphere.

During the twenty years, conflict resolution and control continued to occupy much of the attention of national leaders both within and outside the League of Nations. The Paris negotiations had not, of course, resolved all the old points of contention between states, and the efforts to sort out past problems for a fresh start had inevitably created new points of contention. Nor had the negotiations changed the states' propensity to maneuver for advantage. Even in the first postwar years when the desire for a new international order was still strong, it became clear that the desire for order was offset by a determination on the part of states old and new to secure for themselves as favorable a place as possible within that new order—or any other order that might be established.

Despite their lack of experience in cooperative international activity, and despite their own constant maneuvering for advantage, the states managed to achieve a great deal in the interwar period. The accomplishments were important at the time. They also served as a foundation on which to build when the opportunity came again after World War II. One of the major achievements of the 1920s, and one that is taken for granted today, was the creation of habits of consultation and institutional forums and machinery for addressing international problems. This was particularly true in the relatively nonpolitical areas of disease control, refugee relief and settlement, abolition of slavery and forced labor, and curbs on international traffic in drugs, arms, women, and children.

If not quite the systematic international approach to problems that League Under Secretary-General Raymond B. Fosdick had had in mind when he made his comment about the lack of practice in international activity, it was still a step in that direction. The mere existence of the League of Nations meant that such activities had an organizational center and focus that had been lacking in the past. And as Nicolas Politis, Greek delegate to the League, reminded his fellow delegates in 1927, the evolution of new ways of thought and action was a slow process. He counseled patience, but he also noted that the process of change could be affected by the states whenever they chose. "Those who are impatient because the League falls short of their ideals should blame not the League itself but the nations which are not yet sufficiently advanced to demand from it greater activity and power; when they are, these will not be refused them."[1]

This period also saw the emergence of an inter-American states system that began to play an important part in the development of international ethics. Prior to World War I there had been several continentwide conferences of the states of the Western Hemisphere (excluding Canada), but they had not provided the institutional means for sustained action. Beginning with the Fifth International Conference of American States, held in Santiago, Chile, in 1923, the American states' activities gradually began to cohere into an effective international organization that in 1948 became the Organization of American States. During this period of organizational development, the Latin American states were much concerned with defining their relationship with the United States. It was out of this concern, and out of a strong oratorical and declaratory tradition, that the American states' contribution to international ethics came. This was especially true in the 1930s, when much of the League's energies were devoted to attempts to halt great power aggression.

The American states did not add a new element to the ethical framework that had emerged from the Paris negotiations. Rather, they took tendencies that had been implicit and made them explicit. Their focus was on fundamental principles of international life. Through these, the Latin American states hoped to define their relationship with the United States more advantageously than in the past. The individual concerns of all the states involved, including the United States, meant that some latent tendencies in the tradition of fundamental principles were picked out of that context, articulated separately, emphasized, and written into specific international instruments. The long-term outcome of the short-term concerns of the American states in the inter-war period was an extreme assertion of the rights that a state could claim by the simple fact of its existence.

The relationship between the United States and the other states in the inter-American system also generated a tension that would become particularly important for international ethics after World War II. That kind of tension will be dealt with in more detail later; but it is mentioned here to show the continuity between the two periods in terms of the international problems that had to be addressed and—the reverse of that coin—the influences brought to bear on the developing ethical system. The tension arose from what would later be called the North/South problem: disparities in military power and political stability and in the development of economic resources and internal markets.

During the interwar period, the international conferences of the American states provided a means for the Latin American countries to bring their particular North/South problem onto the international stage. The traditional diplomatic means of address were not replaced: bilateral negotiations between the United States and Mexico, for example, over control of Mexican land and subsoil mineral rights, continued throughout this period. The conferences did, however, begin to shift the context of negotiations from the strictly bilateral—where the less-developed country was at a negotiating disadvantage—to the international. The shift would not be complete until after World War II. Then the Latin American states would join with the newly independent states to make demands upon the international economy. This call for restructuring on the part of the developing countries is another instance of the many new international approaches that had their start in the period between the two world wars.

Laboratories of the League

In 1941 when the British statesman Sir Robert Cecil looked back at his years of work within and on behalf of the League of Nations, which he had helped to found, he recalled the organization as a "Great Experiment."[2] A similar view was expressed by Sir Arthur Salter, who served in the 1920s as director of the Economic and Financial Section of the League Secretariat. In his autobiography he wrote of his years with the League, "I was not only a spectator but a participant in the most interesting experiment in the world."[3] And Nicolas Politis, the Greek delegate to the league mentioned earlier, looked at the organization in the same way. Few people outside of the Secretariat had devoted more time and effort to making the League an effective guarantor of peace than had Politis, and no one knew better than he how few guidelines there were to follow. Yet, as he pointed out, this lack did not mean paralysis. It only meant experimentation. After cautioning fellow delegates in 1927 against the extremes of too-great expectations or premature despair, Politis reminded them of the many projects being undertaken in "the ever-active laboratories of the League."[4]

Any attempt to trace the development of ethical standards by the states of the international system must take into account some of the activities of the League, particularly in the 1920s. The efforts that were made to solve the problems of the times, the institutions that were established, the ideas that were expressed in debates in the Assembly, in meetings of the Council, and in the voluminous reports issued by sections of the Secretariat and by special committees—all are important in understanding the ways that the standards developed. Light is shed also on those areas, such as human rights, where development by the League was minimal because the subject became so entangled with the political tensions of the day that little could be done.

By 1927, then, experiments—to use Politis's apt metaphor for the activities of the League—had been conducted in laboratories that extended from the Black Sea on the east to the Atlantic on the west and north to the Baltic Sea. Epidemics of typhus, dysentery, cholera, and enteric fever had been brought under control. More than four hundred thousand prisoners of war had been brought out of the Soviet Union and returned to their homes. Jurisdiction over the Aaland Islands had been decided, removing the dispute between Sweden and Finland as a source of international tension. Austria and Hungary had been rescued from financial chaos. The resettlement and repatriation of more than a million Greek refugees was well under way. League administration of the disputed areas of Upper Silesia and the Saar Basin was functioning successfully. Fighting between Italians and Greeks, Yugoslavs and Albanians, and Bulgarians and Greeks had been brought to a halt, and the League had made the arrangements by which peace was established and maintained.

If this were a general history, these successes would have to be set off against the failures of the League in the 1920s, in particular, its inaction in the face of the French and Belgian occupation of the German Ruhr and its inability to come to any disarmament agreement or even to get a disarmament conference under way before the end of the decade. It was the League's successes, though, that were important for the development of the ethical framework that the states had devised at Paris. They were important for the problems actually solved and the relaxation of tensions that this provided, but they were also important for the experience gained in international cooperation and the management of potentially dangerous situations. It needs to be emphasized that these were experimental undertakings, with no guarantees of success. They were experiments in solving the problem at hand, but they were also experiments in the coordination of international effort to address problems affecting the international community, particularly the community in Europe, which had for many years been a breeding ground of conflict.

This was not, of course, the first time that states had pooled their efforts to address common problems. The disorders of post-Napoleonic Europe, the breakup of the Ottoman Empire, and the clash of European colonial interests, especially in Africa, had brought the great powers of Europe together in various congresses and conferences throughout the nineteenth century. But those meetings were set only when the several foreign offices of the powers agreed that the occasion seemed to demand it, and any of the powers could nullify a joint effort by refusing to attend or by obstructing agreement.

Even the Hague Peace Conferences of 1899 and 1907, which are sometimes cited as the forerunners of and models for the League, were more reflections of the past than foreshadowings of the future. What Léon Bourgeois kept reminding the delegates to the Paris Peace Conference in 1919 was true: the Hague conferences did indeed build upon years of work by private individuals, peace groups, and professional associations of lawyers, teachers, and legislators. This was especially evident in the two Hague Conventions for the Pacific Settlement of Disputes with their detailed provisions for mediation, commissions of inquiry, and arbitration.

What Bourgeois did not say was that many of the most powerful states at the Hague conferences—Germany, for example, and Great Britain and the United States—were determined to preserve for themselves the greatest possible freedom of action in the international sphere. Nothing that threatened that freedom was allowed to disturb the proceedings of the conferences. Above all, and unlike the League, the Hague conferences did not set out to change the very context within which states of the international system dealt with each other. Modifications might be allowed but the system itself was to remain unchanged, and even the modifications had to be minor.

Certain aspects of the Hague conference proceedings are important, however, for the light they shed on ethical development by the states. Reaction against this type of development also helps to explain the League's emphasis on action rather than declaration. A brief look at the Hague conferences will show the influence of a highly abstract approach to ethics, an approach that was evident in the preambles to the two Hague Conventions for the Pacific Settlement of Disputes. One preambular statement asserted that solidarity was the basis for relationships between states in the international system. Another statement set out two bases for international society: "the principles of equity and right on which are based the security of States and the welfare of peoples."[5]

Such confident assertions of principle are notably absent from the Covenant of the League of Nations. Although the authors of the covenant were engaged on a much more ambitious task than the delegates to the Hague conferences, they were not inclined to give that task a philosophical base. This fact, which has been noted previously, is repeated here to set League activities within a frame of reference where its similarities to the past and departures from the past may be seen more clearly. The departure in this case was from a tradition of international thought that the framers of the Hague conventions were following when they set down their general principles regarding solidarity, equity, and right. The principles were not presented as philosophical assumptions. They were presented as statements of obvious fact.

The term *solidarity,* for example, could have been treated as a goal to be sought or as a standard by which to judge state actions. Instead, the framers of the Hague conventions used *solidarity* to describe current relations between states. "Recognizing the solidarity uniting the members of the society of civilized nations," was the way they put it[6]— a statement that managed to ignore the recently fought Russo-Japanese War, the ongoing Anglo-German armaments race, the recurrent crises over great power competition in Morocco, the secret undertakings that were dividing the Continent into two armed camps, and the determination of the United States to stay an ocean away from the bloodletting that so frequently masked the solidarity "uniting" the civilized nations of Europe.

This kind of thinking brought international law into disrepute and excited the scorn of people such as Alfred Mahan and Theodore Roosevelt and later Woodrow Wilson. This language of the fervent wish, decked out in legal dress, was what the framers of the League covenant were determined to avoid. For the most part, they managed to do so despite efforts to have it included. Their philosophical presuppositions were expressed as obligations—obligations that were undertaken by all the signers of the Versailles treaty and subsequently by those states admitted to the League. Obligations not to resort to war, to respect treaty commitments, and the like, are far removed from the Hague assertion that equity and right are the basis of the security of states and the welfare of peoples. The covenant sidestepped the vagueness and ambiguity of such statements by converting the whole field of argument into an obligation. The states agreed to make the understandings of international law their actual rule of conduct.

This emphasis on action rather than on declaration was carried over from the framing of the covenant into the early years of the League. During those years, the field where action was required seemed to be coextensive with the globe itself, considerably beyond the resources of the League, and it concentrated its actions in the more restricted area that has already been described. Much of this early work attempted to do more than meet a current crisis and make possible a return to everyday life. It also tried to address some of the root causes of conflict. In this, the League was indispensable. The destruction and upheavals of World War I, on a scale unknown within living memory, had left a trail of needs that no single state could handle. By the time the worst of the problems associated with disease, population displacement, and financial instability had been brought under control, institutional means of address had been devised by the League and tested under the harsh and uncertain field conditions that were the only laboratories the League ever knew.

Because members of the League were not the only states that took part in these experiments, the effects were more widespread than might at first appear. The Soviet Union, which was not then a member and at the time was hostile to the League, worked unofficially with the League's Health Organization to control the epidemics within its borders, while the United States, also not a member, coordinated its refugee relief and resettlement activities in Greece with those of the League. As these examples suggest, formal organizational boundaries do not tell the whole story of the influence of the League on the habits and institutions of consultation and cooperation that were an important part of ethical development in this period. No matter what the official policy of the various governments—both members and nonmembers of the League—and no matter how much foot-dragging on the part of some professional diplomats, there was a gradual buildup of confidence in the 1920s in the League's ability to handle problems requiring technical skills and coordination across state lines. By 1927,

Jonkheer van Blokland, Dutch delegate to the League, could say with pride, "During the seven years of its existence the authority of the League of Nations has steadily grown, and the place it occupies in international life has become more and more important."[7]

Three methods of League operation deserve particular mention for their institutionalization of cooperation and impartiality. The first was the rapporteur system of handling Council business. On any question that came before the Council, the League Secretariat prepared a statement of the facts of the case. One Council member was then appointed as rapporteur for the issue. The rapporteur was responsible for hearing the disputants in the case, conducting investigations and negotiations, and making recommendations for Council action. The system helped to establish the League's reputation for even-handedness and competence, particularly when the disputes did not involve the great powers. Some Council members, such as Kikujiro Ishii of Japan and Paul Hymans of Belgium, performed outstanding service as rapporteurs on questions that were at the least divisive and at the most carriers of potential warfare.

The second method was that of the dispatch of multinational groups under the auspices of the League to areas of actual or potential conflict in order to determine facts, separate combatants, keep the peace, or ensure fair play. Thus, military commissions, commissions of inquiry, boundary delimitation commissions, and plebiscite commissions went out from the League in response to the crises and conflicts that erupted with regularity throughout its brief existence. Such groups were instrumental in solving the Aaland Islands dispute (1920) and the question of sovereignty over the port of Memel (1919–1924), and they achieved what success there was in the Vilna dispute (1920). They also helped to keep the peace and resolve controversies between Albania, Yugoslavia, and Greece (1921); Greece and Italy (1923); Iraq and Turkey (1924–1925); Greece and Bulgaria (1925); and Columbia and Peru (1932–1935). The most notable failure of the method was, of course, in Manchuria in the early 1930s. The most outstanding success was in the Saar in 1935 when, throughout an extremely tense situation, an international military force of more than three thousand kept order during the plebiscite that returned the area to Germany.

International administration of trouble spots was the third League method that deserves special mention. League adoption of the method was involuntary. The peace treaty of 1919 had assigned to the League administrative responsibility for the Saar Basin, a heavily industrialized area on Germany's south border with France. Saddled with this thankless assignment, the League fleshed it out with the necessary administrative structures and made it work for fifteen years despite the running objections and obstacles thrown up by France and Germany.

A different kind of administrative solution was worked out by the League for Upper Silesia. In its long term effects, this administrative procedure may have been the most important of the League's innovations. By August of 1921, the contending claims and passions of Poles and Germans had turned the drawing of a Polish-German boundary through Upper Silesia into an international minefield. The favorite political device of the period, a plebiscite, had only complicated matters. The Polish and German populations were so intermingled throughout the rich industrial area that any boundary line would leave large minority blocs of one nationality inside the borders of the other state.

Nevertheless, the line had to be drawn and, so far as possible, in accordance with the results of the plebiscite. When members of the Supreme Council of the Allies, which was still dealing with problems remaining from the Great War, could find no solution to the problem, they put it into the hands of the League and agreed to abide by whatever solution the League could find to this obviously dangerous and apparently hopeless situation. The League proceeded to draw the necessary boundary but directed the bulk of its efforts to dealing with the results of the boundary division. It managed to work out acceptable arrangements for a joint commission and joint tribunal to protect minority rights and handle political and legal disputes, while still preserving the economic integration of the politically divided area.

The success of this experiment in Upper Silesia had a profound effect on the thinking of a young deputy secretary-general of the League, and that in turn was to have a profound effect on the future of the international system and on what people saw as possible forms of international association. For Jean Monnet the lesson of Upper Silesia was clear, and the more he reflected upon the experience, the clearer the lesson became. As one of the deputies to League Secretary-General Eric Drummond, Monnet was deeply involved in the intense, behind-the-scenes activities that produced the public agreement on the division of Upper Silesia. In later life he noted that, at the time of the activity, League personnel were not thinking in abstract terms but in terms of the immediate problems that had to be solved:

What we had to do was identify and organize the common interest. Polish steel needed German coal; Polish workers needed to keep their jobs in German factories. People and products must therefore be free to cross the frontier. To that end we had to devise a certain number of practical measures which for the Germans and Poles would become rules accepted by both States, jointly administered under the supervision and final authority of an outside arbiter.[8]

The technical difficulties were formidable, but as Monnet noted when thinking back on this experience, when these problems were set within the common economic interests of the people in the area—no matter what their ethnic identification—then the problems became solvable. "Solutions which had seemed inconceivable the previous day became natural in the broad new context worked out for them."[9]

The lesson of a changed context was one that Monnet never forgot. He was to draw on this experience again and again when, after another devastating world war, Europe again faced the task of rebuilding. The Upper Silesian experiment was for Jean Monnet a seedbed of ideas for the European Coal and Steel Community and the European Economic Community. These developments would not constitute the new international order that the delegates in Paris in 1919 had had in mind when they looked to the future, but they would surely have seen them as a step in the direction of their vision. Above all, the delegates would have recognized Monnet as one of their own for his quiet and unpretentious approach, his lack of resounding declarations, his emphasis on the shaping effect of institutions, and his motto that the key to action was to "look at the problem as a whole and in the light of the general interest."[10]

During the early years of the League of Nations, this pragmatic approach was firmly built into the structure of the developing system of international ethics.

Hard Cases

Most of the situations in which the league was involved in its early years were difficult ones. The greater the degree of difficulty and the more intractable to the usual means of settlement, the more likely it was that the problem would be turned over to the League. Two cases among the many will serve to show how certain abstract principles of international order actually functioned in a particular historical context—in this case, the early 1920s—even in the exceptionally difficult circumstances that gave rise to League involvement.

The first principle is self-determination. As noted earlier, no principle was more basic to the new international order sketched out at Paris. True to their nondeclaratory stance, the framers of the Versailles treaty had not proclaimed self-determination. They had simply acted on it in making arrangements for the creation of new states, the operation of the mandate system, the holding of plebiscites, the temporary international administration of disputed territories, and other dispositions of territories once held by the defeated powers. The clearest statement of this principle was, in fact, made in a reply by the victorious powers to an objection that Germany had made regarding one of these territorial dispositions.

The reply asserted the principle in no uncertain terms: "There can be no doubt as to the intention of the Allied and Associated Powers to base the settlement of Europe on the principles of freeing oppressed peoples, and redrawing national boundaries in accordance with the will of the peoples concerned, while giving to each facilities for living an independent national and economic life."[11]

In 1920 a small group of people on some rocky islands in the Baltic Sea attempted to apply the principle of self-determination to their own affairs. In so doing, they provided a test of the principle's potential as a base on which to build an international order. They also provided a clear example of the possibilities and limits of an abstract principle as a guide to action in the shifting circumstances of daily life. Since the League of Nations, which had the responsibility of decision in this case, explored the issues thoroughly, it is worth looking more closely at what happened when some twenty-five thousand Aaland (Ahvenanmaa) Islanders sought to dissolve their political bonds with Finland and join with Sweden.

The Aalanders' argument for incorporation with Sweden was a strong one. They could in all honesty rely on the very standards being used elsewhere in Europe to determine the disposition of territories and populations: ethnic identification, language, religion, culture. All of these pointed east toward Sweden rather than west toward Finland. Through all the vicissitudes of European wars and territorial transfers, the inhabitants of the Aaland Islands had maintained their linguistic and cultural ties with Sweden. The League commissioners who visited the islands during the course of their investigations noted that the houses "are built of wood and painted in vivid colours in the Swedish fashion. . . . In the primary schools the instruction is in Swedish; in the others in Swedish and Finnish, and the study of the Finnish language has been compulsory for the past two years. Swedish is the language for purposes of administration, justice and religion."[12]

In hostile hands, the islands could constitute a threat to Sweden, since they extend westward from the southwestern tip of Finland in an arc that ends not far off the eastern coast of Sweden. During the Aaland Islands controversy, the Finnish government, which had declared its independence from Russia in 1917, offered to negotiate to relieve any fears that Sweden might have about the military uses of the islands. The Swedes replied that security was not their chief concern. They were concerned with the desire of the Aaland Islanders to be united with Sweden, a desire that had been expressed in 1917 when the Finns declared *their* independence.

The Swedish reply pointed out that the islanders had sought outside support at that time by sending a delegation to the king of Sweden and a delegation to the Paris Peace Conference expressing the same desire. They had held a referendum in which a majority of the adult population had favored union with Sweden. For Sweden and Finland to negotiate as if Sweden's military concern were the only interest at stake would be to put the subject in the wrong light. As far as the Swedish government was concerned, "the main point of the question was the claim made by the Aalanders to the right of self-determination: a just claim based upon the right of all nations to decide as to their own lot."[13]

There could hardly be a more direct reliance on a principle as a justification for action. Nor were the Swedes the only ones to make this connection. The Aaland Islanders themselves in their message to the peace conference referred to Woodrow Wilson's public statements that peace would be made on the basis of people's right of self-determination. This right, said the islanders, was not reserved for the Allied powers but was a right "for all the rest of the world as well, and constitutes one of the conditions of a durable peace between nations."[14] They had, then, in all good faith, availed themselves of this right and had decided that they wanted to be separated from Finland and united with Sweden.

At a certain level of abstraction, the islanders' position was unassailable. They were relying on a principle that was by 1920 an article of faith and, furthermore, one that still carried the emotional weight of the war. Self-determination had been a rallying cry. Nations had been mobilized and lives lost in its name. Was it now to be denied to a people, indisputably Swedish by background, who were by an accident of history attached not to Sweden but to Finland—a people, moreover, who had taken pains to show that their self-administered plebiscite was truly representative of the wishes of the inhabitants of the islands?

The situation was full of difficulty. Not only were there the tensions to be expected when opposing nationalisms collided—Finland was as determined to retain sovereignty over the islands as the islanders were determined to put themselves under Swedish sovereignty—there was also the revelation of the disintegrative power of the principle of self-determination. The islands had been administratively attached to Finland for centuries: first when both the islands and the mainland had been part of Sweden, next when both had been transferred to imperial Russia early in the nineteenth century as one of the prizes of war. Wherever the League commission turned in its investigation, there yawned before it the abyss of self-determination unrestrained. If the Aaland Islanders, then why not the Welsh in Great Britain or the Tuscans in Italy? Why not any group with a grievance and a petition? Clearly, if the international system were not to dissolve into an unstable congeries of ministates, limits would have to be set.

The report to the League Council by its three-member investigative commission managed to do just that without at the same time destroying the underlying principle. The report was a model of casuistry, taking the word in its original, unpejorative sense of applying a general principle to a specific set of circumstances and deciding how much weight to give to each. The commissioners recommended against the union of the Aaland Islands with Sweden, despite the islanders' appeal to the principle of self-determination, and they based their recommendation on two grounds. First, they set over against the principle of self-determination another general principle, that of sovereignty. This was one of the oldest principles in the international system—considerably older than that of self-determination—and it had the states' unqualified support. Next, they looked at what it was that self-determination was supposed to achieve and asked if that could be secured for the Aaland Islanders without political separation from Finland.

The commissioners noted that Finland had existed as a state with the same frontiers for at least a century. Until the final years of formal Russian rule, Finland had existed as an autonomous grand duchy within the Russian empire under a sovereign who was both emperor of Russia and grand duke of Finland. Further, Finland

has given striking proofs of her national strength and solidarity. Is it possible to admit as an absolute rule that a minority of the population of a State, which is definitely constituted and perfectly capable of fulfilling its duties as such, has the right of separating itself from her in order to be incorporated in another State or to declare its independence? The answer can only be in the negative. To concede to minorities, either of language or religion, or to any fraction of a population the right of withdrawing from the community to which they belong, because it is their wish or their good pleasure, would be to destroy order and stability within States and to inaugurate anarchy in international life; it would be to uphold a theory incompatible with the very idea of the State as a territorial and political entity. . . .

In the acute phase which has been reached in this question, a final solution cannot be deferred, and it can only be based on the maintenance of the sovereignty of Finland.[15]

As to what it was that self-determination was supposed to achieve, freedom from oppression was one of the main goals. It had been linked to that goal in the reply of the Allied and Associated powers to the German observations on the peace treaty, and it was the rationale for the various plebiscites and the establishment of new states. The Aaland Islanders could cite no instances of Finnish oppression that went much beyond the requirement of instruction in Finnish in the secondary schools and restrictions on smuggling. Two of the leaders of the separatist movement had been arrested by the Finns, but they had been released pending the outcome of the League's investigation. Meanwhile, the Finnish legislature had passed a law granting the islanders considerable autonomy.

Still, the islanders were worried that they would eventually be forced to give up speaking and conducting business in Swedish, and they were alarmed by the fact that ethnic Finns were settling in the islands in increasing numbers. The commissioners addressed these concerns with sympathy but suggested that nothing so drastic as separation was necessary "to preserve and protect the language and the culture which are so precious to the Aalanders." Separation from a state of which the minority was a part "can only be considered as an altogether exceptional solution, a last resort when the State lacks either the will or the power to enact and apply just and effective guarantees."[16]

With this, the commissioners completed their careful delineation of the uses of general principles as guides to action in specific situations of conflict. They had pointed out that more than one principle was involved and that in this particular instance the second principle took precedence over the first, for reasons that they specified. They then turned their attention to the first principle, self-determination, and sought to make of it a useful tool of analysis and guide for action rather than simply a battle cry. They did this by setting it within both a situational and a functional context. In what situations was it intended to operate? In situations of oppression. What was it supposed to achieve? The protection of an oppressed minority.

These conclusions from the commissioners' report are of interest because they are sufficiently general to be transferrable to other situations where the problem is the same: the application of a broad principle as a guide to action in a set of particular historical circumstances. The commissioners were aware that they were in a precedent-setting position, and this helps to explain their exhaustive investigation and the care with which they formulated their conclusions. They saw the issue as critical. How was the principle of self-determination to be reconciled with the need for stability in the international system and still achieve its purpose of justice for the oppressed? In this specific case, by further guarantees to the Aaland Islanders, especially in regard to the use of the Swedish language and the ownership of land on the islands. In general, and in the future, reconciliation would be by just such a careful examination of the uses of principle as they had conducted, taking both the use and the principle not in isolation but in connection with other commonly accepted principles that might also bear.

The Aaland Island case yields one other important point, one that bears on the next case to be examined, the Polish-Lithuanian conflict over Vilna (Vilnius). When the Aaland Islands dispute was brought before the League Council by Great Britain, under article 11 of the covenant, which gave any member a right to call the Council's attention to a situation that was a possible threat to peace, the question of the Council's competency was immediately raised. Was this dispute an international concern? Or was it, as Finland claimed, an internal matter of legitimate concern to no one but the Finnish state and its citizens?

Later in this period, the Council would have asked the Permanent Court of International Justice for an advisory opinion, but in June of 1920, when the question came before the Council, the court had not been organized. The Council's solution, to which both Sweden and Finland agreed, was to appoint a special panel of international lawyers to investigate the question. The fact that the panel did find the League competent "to make any recommendations which it deems just and proper in the case"[17] meant that right from the start all sides conceded the League's right to investigate and all sides agreed to abide by the League's decision. The case could then be decided on the merits as seen by the investigative commission and, later, by the League Council. The clarity of this aspect of the Aaland Islands case was unusual among the problems with which the League had to deal. More commonly, there was the uncertainty to be expected in any new undertaking when paper powers are being translated into functioning powers.

In the early days of the League this uncertainty was compounded by the existence of an alternative body to which disputants could appeal when they did not like what the League was doing. This alternative body was the Conference of Ambassadors, composed of representatives of Great Britain, France, Italy, and Japan, and charged by the Supreme Council of the Allies with overseeing the execution of many of the provisions of the several peace treaties. (After 1921, a representative of the United States sometimes sat in as an observer.) Considering the scope of the peace treaties, it did not take much imagination for any disputant to claim that the Conference of Ambassadors, and not the League, was the proper judge of their particular situation, or to make the reverse claim if the League seemed the more advantageous venue.

In the Vilna dispute, Poland appealed to the League in September 1920 but then in 1923 fell back upon the Conference of Ambassadors when League proceedings were stalled, first by the actions of Poland itself and then by Lithuanian intransigence. If all this makes it more difficult to draw conclusions about the application of a general principle to a specific situation, it does at least have the merit of demonstrating a common feature in international disputes, the influence of extraneous factors, such as jurisdictional competition, on actions that are taken and decisions that are made.

The general principle involved in the case of Vilna was that of the peaceful settlement of disputes. One of the chief purposes of the League of Nations was "to achieve international peace and security,"[18] a goal that was to be accomplished by the pledge of the members not to resort to war. To help states honor this pledge, specific procedures for the peaceful settlement of disputes were stipulated by the covenant, the procedures to function under the direction and auspices of the League. Members were formally bound to seek satisfaction of their claims through League procedures for peaceful settlement. Only if these failed and only then after a three month cooling off period could they resort to force without violating their pledge.

The city of Vilna was claimed by both Poland and Lithuania, and the dispute was bitter. However, since Poland had asked for the good offices of the League and Lithuania had made no objection, everything seemed set for negotiations to proceed along the lines laid down in the covenant. The outlook was promising, despite the complications that arose not only from the sporadic fighting between Poland and Lithuania but from the fact that Poland and Russia were engaged in a war that raged back and forth across the territory in dispute. Vilna itself changed hands five times during 1920. In the fluid and dangerous conditions that prevailed in eastern Europe after World War I, where boundaries were still unsettled and animosities still unquenched, the confused status of an area such as Vilna was not unusual. What was unusual was the extent and effectiveness of the League's involvement—effectiveness up to a point.

That point was reached at the peak of the League's success in the matter. Poland and Lithuania had been persuaded to stop fighting and to withdraw their forces to either side of a neutral zone under the authority of a League military commission. Arrangements were then to be made for determination of the final boundary between Poland and Lithuania, a boundary that would settle the question of the possession of Vilna and remove it as a source of international tension. Without warning, a Polish armed force crossed the neutral zone, marched on Vilna, drove out the Lithuanians, and occupied the city. The Polish government disavowed this breach of the agreement, saying that the commander of the occupying force had acted on his own; but since the Polish high command was sending supplies and men to the troops occupying Vilna, the disavowal was more impressive for effrontery than for credibility.

There is no need here to go deeply into the many efforts made by the League to solve the problem after it had reached this stage. Meeting after meeting was held with the disputants, but each small move toward agreement fell victim at length to national pride. At one point the Poles agreed that an international force could replace Polish troops in Vilna while arrangements were made to hold a plebiscite. Nine states promised contingents for the force, which was to be led by General Ferdinand Foch, commander-in-chief of the Allied armies in France during World War I. Transportation and supply arrangements were already under way when Russia served notice that it would regard as a hostile act the occupation of Vilna by an international force under League command. This plan, too, had to be abandoned. The seesaw of promise and failure came to rest finally when the Conference of Ambassadors cut off further attempts at compromise by granting Vilna to Poland.

There were many private protests at the League at this intrusion into the matter, and many questions were raised about the legality of the action taken by the Conference of Ambassadors. There was, however, little that could by done by League officials or by representatives of those states involved in earlier negotiations except to grumble privately. The League was dependent on the support of the great powers whose representatives made up the Conference of Ambassadors. Geneva officials could scarcely say aloud what many were thinking, and that was that the ambassadors' decision to grant Vilna to Poland smacked more of French policy than of impartiality. Lithuania had been suspicious from the first of any French involvement. Not only was Poland allied with France, it was an essential part of the French plan to strengthen the central European states as a bulwark against Soviet advancement and the possible resurgence of German expansionism.

If all of this has a familiar ring, it is because it was indeed the old familiar game of power balancing, the very game that the League system was designed to replace. Throughout its eleven-year existence, the Conference of Ambassadors served as a center for old ways of thought and old approaches to international problems. Here the representatives of the great powers sat down and balanced their competing interests—suspicious, always, of each other's motives; watchful, always, for the turn of phrase that might mean success or failure down the road; careless, too, of the resentment of the smaller powers who were affected by decisions in which they had no say. This was the antithesis of the approach being worked out by the League in the same period, an approach that relied on the impartiality of third-party states not involved in the matter at hand. Citizens from Belgium, France, the Netherlands, Switzerland, and the United States had contributed to the settlement of the Aaland Islands dispute, and League delegates from Belgium, Japan, and Spain had labored to secure what agreements there were in the Vilna conflict.

Even at Vilna, peaceful settlement might have been possible despite the unyielding animosity of the two states and despite Poland's attempt to take by force what it would probably have won anyway in a League-administered plebiscite. Those who were concerned with the application of the principle of peaceful settlement could point out that, difficult as the situation was, League procedures were working until a great power—Russia—intervened. Operating on traditional sphere-of-interest principles and out of a dogmatic hostility to the League, Russia provided an early example of the fatal weakness of this league of sovereign states: in the face of great power opposition, it could do nothing. The action of the great powers on the Conference of Ambassadors, also operating out of traditional principles, underlined the point that had already been made and showed the effect on peaceful settlement procedures of an alternative body to which dissatisfied states might appeal. The situation kept alive tensions that might otherwise have been allayed. Lithuania never accepted the ambassadors' decision and maintained closed borders and a formal state of war with Poland for the next fifteen years.

The League made many other attempts to bring about a peaceful settlement of international conflicts, some of which have been mentioned earlier. One that deserves a closer look was notable for the complications resulting from the shifting of authority back and forth between the League and the Conference of Ambassadors: the conflict that arose between Italy and Greece after the murder of an Italian member of a boundary commission in 1923 and the subsequent bombing and occupation by the Italians of the Greek island of Corfu (Kérkira). The dispute was eventually settled and Italian troops evacuated from Greek territory, but not before Italy had shown itself particularly adept at playing the ambassadors off against the League, and vice versa, to its own advantage.

Two general attempts to tighten League covenant procedures for the peaceful settlement of disputes need to be mentioned in the discussion of this principle. The draft Treaty of Mutual Assistance, presented to the League in 1923 and referred by the Assembly to the member governments, served as a basis for the more comprehensive and almost-successful Geneva Protocol of 1924. The drafting committee had taken into account the comments of member states on the 1923 draft treaty and had brought in a proposal that enjoyed widespread support.

In the ordinary course of Assembly sessions, tedium was a frequent companion of the delegates as they threaded their way through parliamentary procedures and sat through speeches of predictable content. When the Geneva Protocol was presented to the Assembly in 1924, the atmosphere changed from one of tedious routine to one of excitement. The feeling was general that, at last, the League was about to close the loophole in the covenant that allowed recourse to force. By linking the arbitration of disputes with national security considerations, and those in turn with the reduction of armaments, the authors of the protocol seemed to have removed all the roadblocks that remained on the path to peace. And when the protocol was adopted by a unanimous vote of the delegates, the feeling of excitement approached exhilaration, as if an implacable enemy had been slain: "Our purpose was to make war impossible, to kill it, to annihilate it."[19] Thus, Eduard Benes, foreign minister of Czechoslovakia, who had worked to exhaustion on the protocol so that it could be ready for presentation to the Fifth Assembly.

The statement reveals the ardent hopes of the period. So ardent were the hopes for peace, that when the protocol failed adoption by the member states—primarily because of a change of parties in the government of Great Britain—those hopes made a full 180-degree turn and clung to the Kellogg-Briand Pact of 1928. The purpose of the Kellogg-Briand Pact was also to annihilate war, but this was to be done by outlawing it rather than, as in the protocol, by providing for compulsory arbitration, sanctions against states that refused cooperation, and gradual multilateral disarmament. The longing for peace was the same in 1928 as in 1924, but the method was different, and the difference was significant. As Greek delegate Nicholas Politis had warned a year earlier when the Assembly had considered declaring all wars of aggression illicit, such a declaration would be meaningless without provisions for compulsory arbitration and for sanctions. Politis's cautionary words applied to the Kellogg-Briand Pact as well. A declaration of such nature, unsupported by any backup provisions, was not only meaningless; it might even be dangerous:

Public opinion must not be allowed to believe that such a declaration would in any way serve as a practical guarantee of security. The question of security would be untouched; it would remain just where it stands today, under the Covenant and the regional agreements, with just the same guarantees and just the same uncertainties. Nor could we, on the strength of such a misunderstanding, ask the States to make concessions to which they would readily agree if real practical guarantees of security were forthcoming.[20]

But real, practical guarantees of security for the states were never forthcoming. Difficult cases continued to come to the League for settlement until at last the cases were too hard and the situations too difficult for the evolving but still fragile procedures of the League to handle.

A Discourse of Rights

A discussion of rights in the interwar period must begin with a disclaimer and an explanation. Anything resembling the 1789 French Declaration of the Rights of Man and the Citizen, or the post–World War II Universal Declaration of Human Rights should be put out of mind. The point of reference for most of the activity regarding rights in the interwar period was not the individual. It was the state. Even when the activity centered on the rights of minority groups under the guarantee of the League of Nations, the concept of the state was at the core. For those on what might be called the internationalist side of the minority question, the problem was, how can the cultural identity of the minority groups be preserved without undercutting the authority of the state in which they live? For those on the nationalist side, the question was either how to assert the authority of the state successfully, or—in the case of states that had lost territories and peoples—how to get back what the peace settlement had taken away.

From the internationalist point of view, it was thus a cause for great unease when German foreign minister Gustav Stresemann remarked in 1929, "Frankly, I do not think that we have in the present century established a condition of affairs which is eternal."[21] The context for his remark made it even more alarming. The occasion was a Council debate on League procedures for handling minority complaints. Since the League had had to spend a great deal of time investigating the complaints of German minorities in Poland, Czechoslovakia, and the Polish portion of Upper Silesia, the implication of Stresemann's remark was that Germans did not consider the peace settlement boundaries permanent—even Germans such as Stresemann, who was a good friend of the League. The alarm stimulated by this reading of Stresemann's remarks was an accurate reflection of the primary orientation of the states of this period: concern for the territorial integrity and political independence of states. Insofar as minority rights were a part of the whole system of post–World War I treaty arrangements designed to preserve that integrity and independence, they, too, were a matter of concern.

This said, some qualifications need to be made; and it is the qualifications that make the period interesting from the point of view of the development of ethical standards by the states. The 1919 treaty arrangements that had put minority groups in certain countries under the protection of the League had, by that act, introduced a dynamic and unpredictable element into the international system. Not only did the victor states say to most of the new or defeated states, "We now have a right to oversee your treatment of some of your own citizens," they also gave those citizens a right of petition and established procedures for the petitions to be heard by internationally constituted bodies. The paradox at the heart of this effort to strengthen the new and weak states of eastern and central Europe by heading off minority unrest was that the arrangements for heading off that unrest had, in themselves, the potential for undermining the very authority they were intended to preserve.

It is as easy to make too much of this potential as it is to ignore it altogether. In actual practice, the Council worked closely with the states against which complaints were laid. The procedure was to appoint a three-member committee, which after investigation tried to work out arrangements with the state to remedy the situation and prevent its recurrence. These Committees of Three were made up of delegates from states with no direct interest in the dispute, an effort at impartiality that was about the extent of the League's power in minority matters. It had no choice but to use methods of persuasion and conciliation, since an international military force—even were one available—scarcely seemed the appropriate response to a question of language instruction in the primary grades or the prompt issuing of visas for religious pilgrimages. It is a tribute to the reputation of the League and to the persistence of minority recourse to outside authority that more than 150 Committees of Three were appointed and functioned from 1921 to 1929.

And what was their function? The preservation of civil, political, and religious liberties specified in a number of peace treaties and in stipulations imposed on several states as a condition of membership in the League. Here on a small scale was the setting of international human rights standards that was to become so prominent a part of state activity following World War II. The setting of those standards was not the primary intent of the framers of the treaties and the stipulations, but the framers could not control either the consequences of what they had done or the interpretations that others put on their actions. The setting of standards, the international guarantee, and the provision of recourse outside the borders of the state that had minority obligations, were small departures from assertions of the primacy of the sovereign state; but departures they were, and they provided handholds for those who wanted to make use of them.

Some did. It is instructive to look at the uses made of what would appear to be simple and straightforward assertions of human rights: "All Polish nationals shall be equal before the law and shall enjoy the same civil and political rights without distinction as to race, language or religion."[22] One response to this statement of rights was apparently as simple and straightforward as the assertion itself: Why should this equality be limited to Poles, or Hungarians, or, for that matter, to Europeans? And so there was a push to universalize the human rights standards that had been put into the treaties chiefly to ward off irredentist movements against the treaty states, and by so doing to preserve the political stability without which peace would surely fail.

To do justice to the complexity of human action, however, this apparently simple response must be viewed through two different lenses. The push for the universalization of human rights standards took two different forms, a strong form and a weak one. The weak form is of particular interest because it came from the non-European members of the League, and their statements resonate both backward and forward in time: backward to the Japanese attempt to include a racial equality clause in the League covenant, forward to the time when non-European states would become a majority in the international system. In 1926 when the League Council was being enlarged to provide a permanent seat for Germany and greater representation for smaller states, the delegate from Persia (Iran) warned that a Council "from which Islam and the great Asiatic civilizations were excluded" would cause alarm among non-European member states. He went on: "We proclaim here the absolute equality of races and peoples of whatever colour, religion or importance. The League of Nations can only work effectively for peace by keeping this equality in view. Privileges, exceptions, combinations, and attempts at domination have always been the cause of those wars which have exhausted our poor world."[23]

In the League of Nations of 1926, dominated by the traditional great powers of Europe, there was not the slightest chance that such a statement would have much effect. The lack of power of the states making this kind of claim is why this response has been characterized as the weak form of the push for the universalization of human rights standards. The relative powerlessness of these non-European states did not prevent their keeping the issue alive, however, and demanding that the League make the particularistic minority protection clauses of the peace treaties into a general guarantee for minorities in every state. In 1933 the delegation from Haiti prodded the League "to embody amongst its fundamental principles the obligation of states to give equal protection to all inhabitants of their territory, and a fortiori to their own nationals without distinction of race, language or creed."[24]

Almost the same vocabulary was used in the strong form of the push for universal standards, but the words were used for a completely different purpose. When the delegation from Austria argued that "certain duties towards its minorities devolve on every civilized State, that these rules are consequently universal in character, and that they must be enforced irrespective of the provisions of existing treaties,"[25] it was not because Austria, like Haiti, wanted "equal protection to all inhabitants" of its territory—to use the Haitian formulation. It was because Austria, like the other minority-group treaty powers, wanted release from obligations that bore on their states and on theirs alone. By saying that they were willing to conform to truly universal standards, Austria and Poland and the other treaty states were setting a condition that they knew was impossible to fulfill, given the temper of the times. They used the vocabulary of human rights to put a good public face upon their determination to free themselves of their particular treaty obligations. By the mid-1930s, the whole structure of minority protection was in shreds.

Before that happened, however, an attempt was made by Germany to use the minority treaties for yet another purpose, again one that had not been contemplated by the framers of the treaties. In this instance, the guarantees of civil and political rights and the grant of the right of petition to international authority were used systematically by one particular minority group to try to force a change in the League's procedures for handling complaints. The change would have had the effect of making impartiality a dead letter, and that was exactly the result intended. The German minority in the Polish-governed portion of Upper Silesia wanted Germany to be their active advocate at the League of Nations. It was a role that Germany was eager to play, since not even internationalists such as Foreign Minister Stresemann were resigned to the loss of territory or people.

Accordingly, in 1929 Stresemann proposed that the Committees of Three be enlarged so that the states most interested in the complaints of ill treatment of their ethnic nationals could participate in the investigation and have a voice in the outcome. His argument was a masterly one that addressed the fears of those for whom stability was the sine qua non of peace. With the calm voice of reason, Stresemann spoke of duties first and then of rights—the rights of the minorities, but also, and in addition, the rights of interested states. To those who did not know of the constant irredentist agitation of the *Deutsche Volksbund* in Polish-governed Upper Silesia, Stresemann's request for German participation might have seemed eminently reasonable:

The provisions for the protection of minorities imply a duty which it is neither impossible nor beneath the dignity of a Sovereign State to fulfil. The fact of belonging to a minority and the special position resulting from that fact are certainly in no way incompatible with the accomplishment of the duties of a loyal citizen toward his State. This being so, it equally follows that the interest taken by a country in the minorities of another country, an interest which may take the form of an appeal to the guarantee of the League of Nations, cannot be regarded as an inadmissible political interference with the domestic affairs of a foreign Power.[26]

Everyone in the Council chamber may have suspected that "inadmissible political interference" in the affairs of its neighbors, and particularly in Polish affairs, was exactly what Germany had in mind, but this could hardly be said if amicable relations were to be maintained. It was left to Aristide Briand, Stresemann's old friend and antagonist, to answer this self-interested German argument. The two foreign ministers, Stresemann for Germany and Briand for France, had shared a Nobel peace prize for their efforts at international cooperation, and when Germany had finally been admitted to the League in 1926, their eloquence had brought tears to the eyes of the listeners in the Assembly Hall. "If you are here as a German and only as a German," Briand had said on that occasion, "and if I am here as a Frenchman and only as a Frenchman, agreement will not be easy. But if we come here, not forgetting our respective countries, yet as citizens sharing in the universal work of the League, then all will be well."[27]

In 1929 when Stresemann and Briand faced each other again, this time over the issue of minority rights, it was hard to see Stresemann as anything other than a German and only a German. Briand made no accusations. He simply pointed out that it was the lamentable habit of some human beings to turn to their own advantage the best-intentioned procedures and institutions, and this being so, arrangments had to be made accordingly:

Judging from his speech of this morning, Dr. Stresemann seems to have an excellent opinion of men and of the objectivity of their minds, and I congratulate him sincerely on his belief. Though the practice of politics rather spoils the freshness of our belief in man and makes us drop some of our illusions at a fairly early stage, a statesman cannot be reproached if he succeeds in retaining some of them. Men, however, are men, and, even though they are dealing with a text or a treaty embodying noble and generous aspirations, they nevertheless retain their nature. It is evident that Dr. Stresemann and we ourselves are taking up a position superior to certain contingencies. It is no less evident that we are inclined to consider the question of minorities in all its nobility, and that our minds turn towards solutions which are purely objective. If the problem depended solely on us, we should be certain of solving it in a satisfactory way.

Unfortunately, independently of us life goes on, and I shall cause no surprise when I say that, in the majority of countries, there is a certain number of people—rather large than small—who have what I should call a hateful inclination towards politics. In order to satisfy this singular but very common taste, they do not hesitate to look about them for anything which may serve their interests.[28]

Given people as they were and the world as it was, what then? Briand had an answer for that, and it was the same answer given by the League in the Aaland Islands dispute: the sovereignty of the state. It was an answer that had been worked out by states and philosophers over centuries of warfare for whatever cause—whatever good and noble cause—was thought to justify war at the time. Long experience with the many self-interested uses that could be made of principles and ideals had reinforced the idea that to prevent constant recourse to force for some end defined as good, the state's borders should be more than geographical boundaries. They should also bound an area of freedom within which a state could act without fear of interference from outside.

There were, of course, standards of behavior that had to be maintained. The minority group treaties attested to that fact. But oversight of that maintenance could not be vested in a neighboring state concerned chiefly with its own grievances and power. At the least, oversight had to be as impartial as possible in an imperfect world. To accede to Germany's request would be to destroy the system of minority protection, imperfect as it was, and make minorities the prize in the old power game that had brought the world to the disaster of World War I. The bulwark against this return to the game of push and grab was political stability, and that could be achieved by respect for the primary principle of sovereignty. In the words of Briand:

> The League of Nations, by its composition and its rules, is obliged to place above every other consideration a respect for national sovereignty. That is the principle which governs the League, though I do not propose to discuss it. Sometimes it is a good principle, because it affords a safeguard against certain improvised schemes which may be dangerous. Sometimes it is a hampering principle, because it makes it necessary to seek for compromises in an endeavour to reach peace and good understanding which must be unanimously secured. We are, however, face to face with the necessity of respecting this principle, and we must all bow to that necessity and never allow it to be ignored.[29]

Briand could see clearly the danger of allowing interested parties the right of intervention in other states' affairs. He did not foresee, and could scarcely have been expected to foresee, the abuses that took place in the next decade when whole populations were deprived of rights, freedom, and life itself by states that shielded their acts behind the barrier of sovereignty. Nor could he have foreseen the extreme assertion of sovereignty made by the states of the Pan American Union in 1933, just a year after his death. That assertion took the practical political wisdom on which the principle of state sovereignty was based and elevated it to the status of received truth, making of the principle a dogmatic creed that was not to be altered or questioned in any way.

In this form, the creed of state sovereignty passed almost unchanged into the 1948 Charter of the Organization of American States. With various minor changes, it was incorporated into dozens of other international instruments, where it provided the philosophical underpinning for many of the institutional arrangements of the post–World War II international system. The title of this assertion of sovereignty is "Convention on Rights and Duties of States." It was signed in Montevideo, Uruguay, in December 1933 and entered into force the following year.

Montevideo in December 1933 was where the chickens of United States policy in Latin America came home to roost—not just for the United States but in the long run for the whole international system as well. If the Latin American states had not been so resentful of the United States, the convention that was signed at Montevideo might well have been more moderate in its assertions: The state is inviolable. It is completely autonomous. Sovereignty inheres in the simple fact of a state's existence, an existence that gives it full and equal standing with any other state in the international system regardless of the technicality of diplomatic recognition. Existence also gives a state certain fundamental rights, but those rights do not include, and can never include, intervention. In the words of article 8: "No state has the right to intervene in the internal or external affairs of another."[30]

So far as the Latin American states were concerned, here was the crux of the matter. There were sixteen articles in the convention, and the entire discussion at Montevideo, both in the committee sessions and in the plenary session where the convention was brought to a vote, focused on one article, article 8. For the preceding thirty years the United States had intervened almost at will in Latin America, especially in the states on the rim of the Caribbean. Under Wilson alone, U.S. troops had been sent into Mexico, Haiti, and the Dominican Republic. By 1933, most of the troops were withdrawn, but bitter memories remained, fed by the fact that U.S. Marines remained in Nicaragua. Creation of the state of Panama out of Colombian territory at the beginning of the century was still a touchy subject in 1933, and Cuba still smarted under the restrictions of the Platt Amendment that, among other things, gave the United States the right to intervene in Cuban affairs when, in U.S. opinion, it was necessary to do so to preserve order.

Adding to the general sense of grievance was the memory of the Havana Conference of 1928, the inter-American conference that had preceded the one at Montevideo. At Havana, the United States had exerted its considerable power to prevent the subject of nonintervention from ever reaching the floor for a vote. And when discussion could not be avoided altogether, U.S. Secretary of State Charles Evans Hughes had made an eloquent declaration upholding the right of intervention for certain specified purposes. What this boiled down to—when eloquence and grand general principles were put to one side—was nothing more or less than the U.S. right of intervention. It was a little hard to imagine Haiti sending up troops to protect a Haitian citizen caught by a lynch mob—a fact that the Latin American states could see as well as anyone. Masters of eloquence themselves, they were also masters at penetrating to the realpolitik at the core of declaratory rhetoric.

Delegates from the Latin American states came to Montevideo with

long memories and short hopes, but the hopes increased as the conference wore on. It appeared that the new administration in Washington, that of Franklin Roosevelt, was not simply talking about good
neighborliness but was prepared to change policies, at least to a limited
extent. The last of the U.S. troops in Haiti were scheduled to leave
within a year, and the hated Platt Amendment, too, was on its way out.
Further, the new U.S. secretary of state, Cordell Hull, proved to be ap-
proachable. Not only was he, unlike Hughes, willing to talk about
nonintervention as a general rule of hemispheric behavior, he was
even willing to commit the United States to such a rule, provided that
the term was given an agreed-upon and specific meaning.[31]

For these various reasons embedded in the stormy history of Latin
American–U.S. relations and in the desire of the Roosevelt administration to clear the board of past policies, the Convention on Rights and
Duties of States signed at Montevideo embodied the strongest possible
assertion of state sovereignty. It went far beyond Briand's modest statement of the basis of the League. Nothing less than the superlative case
would satisfy the pent-up passions of the representatives of Latin
American states, where national dignity and honor had been outraged
over and over again by what was seen as an arrogant use of U.S.
power. Some indication of the depth of this passion can be seen in
statements made in the Second Committee where the convention was
discussed in detail before being brought to the floor for vote:

The Dominican Delegation will vote against any international action which
suppresses, reduces, suspends, enslaves or humbles the Sovereignty of the
State. . . . Intervention is not only the "curse of America," but, as a Cuban internationalist has said, it is the "curse of curses" of my country, the cause of all
the evils of the Cuban Republic. Full sovereignty is contrary to and does not
tolerate foreign domination. . . . [Chile supports] the principle which shall establish perfect freedom, the absolute autonomy of Nations, to rule their own
destinies in all the aspects of their activities.[32]

And, finally, Mexico, with its assertion that intervention created a
serious problem for Latin American states, a problem "derived from
the sensation of disgust, from the impression of almost constant anxiety, from the definite hindrance to progress which in our country is
intervention, which is a moral disaster at home, an insult in another's
house."[33]

In the sixteen articles of the Convention on Rights and Duties of
States, there is not one word about the reason that a state exists and
not one word about the states' responsibilities to or relations with its
own citizens. Article 10 notes that the primary interest of the states is to

conserve peace and that therefore they ought to settle their differences peacefully; beyond that, nothing except assertions of the rights of states as autonomous entities in a world of other autonomous entities—entities apparently without connection or common interests in the world in which they happen to coexist.

For the reasons that have been given, it was in this hard, assertive form that traditional ideas about the rights and duties of states first found formal expression in a multilateral international instrument. The 1933 convention was a precursor of the many later instruments in which the states set out in specific terms and in great detail the principles on which their relationships were to be founded and the rules that were to govern their behavior. In the convention were four of the nine basic principles that make up the states' code of international ethics: the sovereign equality of states, the territorial integrity and political independence of states, the peaceful settlement of disputes, and nonintervention. A fifth principle, that of no threat or use of force, was there by implication. This was the beginning of a drive by the states to put the fundamental principles of international life into an explicit, declaratory form. The only action called for in the 1933 convention was put as a duty not to recognize the acquisition of territory by force. The rest was an assertive, state-centered, philosophical disquisition upon the nation-state as it exists and acts on the international scene (see appendix 2).

The intellectual background of the tradition of rights and duties on which the American states drew for the 1933 convention will be dealt with in the next chapter. The focus here is on use and context. The examples have been chosen to demonstrate the variety of meanings that can be drawn from such seemingly obvious and simple principles as self-determination, respect for human rights, and the sovereignty of states. The uses to which the principles were put and the contexts in which they were applied made all the difference.

One final word about the subject of rights in the interwar period. In two instances the League of Nations departed from its nondeclaratory stance and tackled subjects of human rights in broad, general terms. In the mid-twenties, the Fifth Assembly adopted the Geneva Declaration of the Rights of the Child, "recognizing that mankind owes to the child the best that it has to give."[34] There followed a list of five children's rights that laid corresponding duties upon the states that signed the declaration, including "The child must be brought up in the consciousness that its talents must be devoted to the service of its fellow men."[35] The sweeping language, the use of "must," and the lack of any means of enforcement or oversight all point toward the kind of declaration by the states that became common after World War II.

The second departure was an antislavery convention signed in 1926, the culmination of more than a century of international effort to suppress the slave trade. The effort did not end with the 1926 convention but continued both in the United Nations after World War II and in the work of the International Labor Organization (I.L.O.) throughout the period.

Throughout the 1920 and 1930s, the I.L.O. continued quietly on the course it had set for itself in 1919: achieving social justice for workers and in so doing securing for them what gradually came to be seen as specific human rights. Under the dynamic leadership of Albert Thomas, the I.L.O. won the right to include agricultural as well as factory workers in its field of operations, a victory that helped to defuse much agricultural unrest in the early years of the period. Model conventions on hours of work, unemployment compensation, minimum wages, sickness insurance, forced labor, accident prevention, and the like, were hammered out by its specialists, adopted at its annual conferences, and carried back to the member states for appropriate action.

When action was slow—as it frequently was—and ratifications few—as they were at first—the I.L.O. could still take pride in the fact that it was breaking new international ground. Its split system of voting meant that primary interests were not always assumed to lie with the state. The long struggle to adopt the eight-hour workday, for example, was as apt to pit workers' delegates against delegates from their own states as it was to pit state against state in the traditional manner.[36] Further, at a time when the human rights guaranteed in the minority treaties were being squeezed out of existence by the political tensions of the day, the International Labor Organization followed a consistent course of setting international standards for the rights of workers and then keeping steady pressure on states to adopt and implement those standards. As former British Prime Minister David Lloyd George remarked in his memoirs: "There is no part of the Treaty which has functioned more smoothly or more successfully than the section which deals with international labour problems. There is no section of the Treaty which so far has brought such unmixed blessings to the lot of untold millions of the humblest workers in many lands."[37]

These, then, were some of the achievements of the interwar period. New international approaches were pioneered. Habits of consultation were established and institutions created through which international action could be taken. Methods for applying general international principles to specific international situations began to be worked out, not in the quiet confines of the study but in the contentious cut and thrust of everyday state relations. The ongoing process revealed some of the ambiguities of general principles and the sometimes unforeseen consequences of their application.

A beginning had been made, and a foundation laid. On that foundation later generations could build as they sought ways to refine and extend the ethical framework begun in Paris in 1919 and shaped by rough usage in the period between the two world wars.

4 Search for Authority

In the light of present-day experience, the League's optimism may, to many, appear excessive, its principles lacking in realism, and its faith deceptive. But would it be safe to judge . . . the value of the League's principles . . . from the point of view of to-day's lawlessness and pessimism [rather] than from that of the hopes of eighteen years ago?

Georges Kaeckenbeeck, 1942.
President of the Arbitral Tribunal
of Upper Silesia, 1922–1937

The coming of World War II gave increased importance to the ethical framework being worked out by the states, even while the conduct of the belligerents in the war sometimes made it seem as if the entire framework itself were being abandoned. The very lawlessness of which Kaeckenbeeck spoke[1] stimulated a reconsideration of the bases of an ethical system and of the relation of ethics to law in general and international law in particular. The two pillars that were to support and sustain the new international order had, in the end, proved inadequate: collective security had failed, and public opinion—which was to secure compliance with international rules of behavior—had had neither the will nor the means for enforcement.

The reappraisals in the late 1930s, when it became apparent that war was going to come, and continuing during the war added a declaratory element to the ethical framework. Implicit philosophical principles were now made explicit and appraised for their value in the ongoing struggle. It had long been customary for leaders of religious faiths to blame the ills of the world on laxity, on a falling away from accepted standards of behavior. Now the same note was sounded by political leaders overwhelmed by the enormity of the destruction taking place before their eyes. The destruction was not just of physical property or even of human lives, although that was appalling enough. The destruction seemed to be of the very standards that made human society possible.

In a declaration issued in 1942, the twenty-six states allied against the Axis powers set forth their conviction "that complete victory over their enemies is essential to defend life, liberty, independence and religious freedom, and to preserve human rights and justice in their own lands as well as in other lands." During the next three years, twenty-one other states added their formal agreement—they and the other signers being, as they said, "engaged in a common struggle against savage and brutal forces seeking to subjugate the world."[2]

Many of these states were reluctant belligerents who had, to the last, clung to the hope that the ethical framework would fend off catastrophe. For that to happen, every state had to be firmly committed to international standards of behavior. U.S. secretary of state Cordell Hull was one of those who felt keenly on this subject. It was, however, awkward for U.S. officials to call on the world's states to abide by their commitments to the principles of the League of Nations since the United States had never joined the League. For the United States to act without raising the touchy subject of League membership, a different approach was required.

In 1937, when it became clear that Japan was embarking on full-scale war in China, Hull made a determined effort to rally worldwide opinion behind what he called "Fundamental Principles of International Conduct." Here was an independent attempt to devise a comprehensive set of ethical standards for the conduct of states, and the result was a thoroughly familiar set of precepts. It included the principles of the 1933 convention discussed in the preceding chapter and added to them principles concerning international law, the international economy, and reduction of armaments.[3] There was nothing in Hull's list that was in the least antithetical to the already-existent international ethical framework based on the League of Nations system.

Hull was determined to get the states of the world to make an explicit and public commitment to this tentative code of ethics. Their commitment was to be the barrier that would protect the world from disaster, and Hull set out to make the barrier as strong as one man could. He had his official position to aid him in the task. U.S. ambassadors were instructed to call at the foreign offices of the countries to which they were accredited and ask for comments on the principles and for information on the attitudes of the respective governments "toward keeping alive and making effective the principles featured in the statement."[4]

As remarkable as Hull's determination was the fact that sixty individual states felt bound to comment on the principles. Part of the feeling of obligation was undoubtedly due to Hull's position in the government of one of the great powers and to his insistence, through U.S. diplomatic representatives, that some reply be made. But this does not completely explain the replies nor the pains taken by the states, even those engaged in expansionist activities at the time, to show that the principles set out by Hull were indeed those that had always guided their policies. The German government, for example, noted that "its basic principle is as is generally known directed toward the regulation of international relations by pacific agreement and hence coincides with the ideas developed by the Secretary of State."[5]

The Fascist government of Italy also approved, since it favored "everything which may conduce to the pacification and to the political and economic reconstruction of the world."[6] As for the Japanese, they sent a blanket endorsement that was tied firmly to their policy in East Asia: "The Japanese Government wishes to express its concurrence with the principles contained in the statement made by Secretary of State Hull on the 16th instant concerning the maintenance of world peace. It is the belief of the Japanese government that the objectives of those principles will only be attained, in their application to the Far Eastern situation, by a full recognition and practical consideration of the actual particular circumstances of that region."[7]

The Japanese reference to "actual particular circumstances" could have been a call for the kind of creative casuistry involved in the application of an international principle to the particular circumstances of the Aaland Islanders, or it could have been an assertion that in the particular circumstances faced by the Japanese army in China, the usual principles did not apply. If the latter were the case, the Japanese would not have been alone in asserting the uniqueness of a situation for the justification of an action. At one time or another almost every state had intervened in the affairs of another or had used force to gain its ends because of some compelling circumstance that, it was argued, justified an exception to the rule.

There was a difference, though, and the difference lay in the timing of the Japanese actions. What had been acceptable in 1904 was denounced in 1937 as a clear violation of commitments that Japan had made as a member of the League and as one of the original signers of the Kellogg-Briand Pact renouncing resort to war. By their bombing of Chinese cities, the Japanese further demonstrated their disregard for world opinion and for the protracted effort made by the states in the interwar years to set limits on the use of military aircraft. As the resolution adopted at the conclusion of the first phase of the disarmament conference put it in 1932, "Air attack against the civilian population shall be absolutely prohibited."[8]

In this situation, it is hard to see what the most ingenious casuistry could have done, but no opportunity was given to work out any application of international principles. Japan did not press its case through the League, from which it had withdrawn in 1933 (effective 1935), but through its military forces. It was a course of action that Italy and Germany had already shown could be effective and that Japan had used with good success in Manchuria in 1931.

Even after these examples of aggression, many states were reluctant to abandon what had been so painstakingly wrought. They could see that the expansionist states used other states' compliance with the rules to ensure that opposition to their expansion would be too little and too late. The conclusion drawn by the nonexpansionist states was not that the rules ought to be abandoned but rather that, since the rules were universal, the commitment to obey them ought to be universal, too. This basic message underlay most of the states' observations on Hull's Fundamental Principles of International Conduct. And universal commitment was exactly what Hull tried his best to get with the only means at his command: publicity. He called press conferences. He made speeches. The U.S. Department of State issued a publication setting out the principles and the many states responses. Press releases were issued, and the responses appeared in such publications as the *New York Times*. Copies were sent to the League of Nations, and the list of states, with their observations, was printed in the League's *Official Journal*.

The effort relied solely on the efficacy of rules for restraint, the rules to be backed by the force of public opinion. When that effort failed, as collective security had also failed, then reappraisals of the whole international order took on a new urgency. What had gone wrong? Why only twenty years after the end of World War I was the world again plunged into war? Now the questioners pushed their investigations beyond collective security arrangements and agreed-upon rules to ask where the deeper failure lay. Reparations and war debts, the world depression, the fact that the United States had not joined the League, all were seen as contributing causes but not as the ultimate cause.

To the question about the ultimate cause of World War II, two different answers were given. One answer concentrated on the rules themselves as the source of failure. Those who gave this answer pointed out that the rules were based not on the obvious fact of the interdependence of states but on the outmoded concept of the sovereignty of states—an error in philosophical grounding that encouraged self-centered and destructive state behavior.

The other response to the question pushed deeper yet. Here the failure was seen as more than merely an erroneous grounding of explicit rules. The real failure was a failure in morality, that bedrock of concepts of the right and the good that supports everything else and without which the structures of principles, rules, laws, and institutions are nothing but empty formalities.

Thus began a search for a way to express more clearly, accurately, and, above all, more authoritatively the needs of the international system and the behavior that these needs entailed. The period from the late 1930s through World War II and immediately after was a time of reflection on fundamentals and on their relationship to the life of the international community. It was a time of soul searching and of mental as well as physical upheavals. Much work had already been done along these lines but it had not figured largely in state reflections until the events of the period made consideration of such matters imperative, even to states whose chief concern until then had been what rights they could claim as members of the international community.

Founders of the Search

The search for a voice compelling enough to affect the behavior of states drew heavily on the work of a group of people active in public affairs since the turn of the century. Many of them had attended one or both of the Hague Peace Conferences. They had served on various arbitration panels and on the commissions of inquiry established under the Hague conventions. Many had also attended the Paris Peace Conference as delegates from their respective countries or as technical advisers to their own or other delegations. Some of them helped to draft the statute of the Permanent Court of International Justice and then saw service on that court.

They sat in the Assembly of the League of Nations, headed commissions of experts facilitating the League's activities, served as rapporteurs in League investigations of conflicts, and sat as delegates in some of the many international conferences of the interwar period: the Financial Conference at Brussels (1920); the General Conference on Communications and Transit at Barcelona (1921); the Washington Conference on the Limitation of Naval Armaments (1921–1922); the Pan American Conference in Santiago (1923); the Geneva Opium Conference (1924–1925); the International Conference on the Control of the Traffic in Arms (1925); the World Economic Conference in Geneva (1927); and so on, through the 1920s and 1930s right up to the outbreak of

World War II. Thereafter, they were involved in wartime activities and then in planning for international organization after the war (see appendix 3).

This group of people, as might be expected, varied greatly in background, temperament, age, experience, and country of origin, but they were all inhabitants of a single intellectual world that was both their vision of the future and their spiritual home: the universal commonwealth of the law. As inhabitants of this world—no matter what their differences in approach and concept—they shared a faith in the power of the law to subdue the violent forces that worked havoc in the international system—subdue them and transmute them into justiciable questions to be decided according to accepted canons of evidence, reason, and precedent.

Dag Hammarskjold, who would become the second secretary-general of the United Nations in 1953, found the words to describe the faith of this group of people. The words occur in a reflective look at his father's life. In many ways, Hjalmar Hammarskjold's career could serve as a model for the group. He had held high public office in his native country, Sweden, and he had diplomatic experience as well. He was an indefatigable worker for the primacy of law in international affairs, but not—as his son explained—because of any illusions about the perfection of that law. Hjalmar Hammarskjold knew full well how "incomplete and fluid were the rules in which the ideas of justice were reflected in international intercourse."[9] Rather, it was because of a deeply held belief that, in Hjalmar's own words, "a community of reason constitutes membership in a higher entity."[10]

This comment was the launching point for the tribute paid by Dag Hammarskjold to his father, a tribute equally apt for all these early workers in international law. Beginning with his father's idea of a community of reason, Dag want on:

Translated into terms closer to our day and age, the idea seems to be that society is welded together by that higher "reason" common to us all, which is the bearer of justice.

Against this background we can understand his faith in a "supranational" justice, through which may be created an international *Civitas Legum*. In attempting to interpret the internationalism represented by Hjalmar Hammarskjöld, this seems to me to be the key. *Civitas Dei* was a dream of the past. The present-day attempts to form an international organization with common executive organs had not yet been begun. Instead, there is a glimpse here of a world society, where national states live under the protection of an internationalism which gains its strength from the very logic of justice itself, not from dictates of power, and in which, therefore, the only international organs needed are of a judicial nature.[11]

This world society, which gained its strength from "the very logic of justice itself" was, then, the vision that sustained the members of this group of people whose views were, in the days of reappraisal and seeking, to become influential in the shaping of thought about the international system. It was a vision wide enough to contain a number of conflicting ideas about the nature and function of international law, from those of Arnold McNair with his emphasis on "hard law" to those of Albert La Pradelle with his belief in a natural law that was the source of the law of nations. The approach of James Brown Scott, who was on the staff of the Carnegie Endowment for International Peace for almost thirty years, was very different from that of James Brierly, longtime editor of the *British Yearbook of International Law*, who had many misgivings about the way Scott pushed for codification. But whether their views of law were hard or soft, whether they pushed for immediate codification or were inclined to wait for further organic growth, they shared the same vision and they used the same vocabulary. Above all, they shared a propensity to formulate their thought about law in terms of principles.

By *principles*, those in international law did not mean what Georges Kaeckenbeeck meant when he spoke of the League's principles. Kaeckenbeeck's concern was with operating principles, the beliefs on which the League acted. As he set them out, these were: optimism about "the healing virtue of organized good will," an assumption of "willingness to listen to reason in preferring compromise to hostilities," and an implicit faith in "the possibilities of international cooperation."[12]

The principles of those working in international law were different from this rather simple set of operating assumptions. They were not at all simple, and they had such deep roots in philosophical issues and controversies of the past that any attempt to set them within an intellectual context quickly becomes a tour through the history of legal thought back to the time of ancient Rome and the concept of jus gentium. Further, these legal principles were not so much operational as doctrinal, and it was in this doctrinal form that the states brought them into the debates of the late 1930s and the plans being made for the postwar world.

The confident tone of the pronouncements made by those working in international law was the logical result of their approach to the subject. It was—to use one of their favorite words—"scientific." The approach and the confidence in findings that this approach engendered were institutionalized in several of the international law societies founded in the late nineteenth and early twentieth centuries. In the words of Gustave Rolin-Jacquemyns, one of the founders of the Institut de Droit International (1873), the new organization would have as its purpose "scientific collective action" by specialists in international law in order to advance knowledge and understanding.[13] This goal found formal expression in the institute's constitutional description of itself as "an exclusively scientific organization."[14]

Exactness and effectiveness were part of what was meant by *scientific* when used by those in international law. The American Society of International Law was founded in 1905 by a group of lawyers dissatisfied with what they saw as the vagueness and sentimentality of much of the discussion about international affairs in the early part of the century. They proposed to remedy that by promoting "a correct understanding of those principles of International Law which our country is called upon to observe in its foreign relations."[15] Similarly, the American Institute of International Law, which was organized in 1912 as "an unofficial scientific association," proposed, among other purposes, "to give precision to the general principles of international law as they now exist."[16] And the Union Juridique Internationale, founded immediately after World War I to give an institutional structure for the cooperation of statesmen, jurists, and publicists, planned to secure the blessings of peace by working toward the "scientific and practical progress of international law by the study of its principles and by the spread of knowledge about them."[17]

Despite the confident tone of these statements, there was no general agreement on what those principles were. The interwar period saw a burst of activity by the international law societies and by various individuals to determine the principles and set them down in a definitive form. Study groups and committees were established by the societies, and a number of projects were undertaken. Codification was a favored vehicle for this type of inquiry, and there were codification efforts in the League of Nations, in the Inter-American Conference of States, and in several of the international law societies. Another vehicle was the listing and discussion of the "fundamental rights and duties of states." These show up again and again, and they form the intellectual background for the 1933 Convention on Rights and Duties that has been discussed. The concern for such principles was pervasive. One of the first acts of the American Institute of International Law was to compile a list of state rights and duties. The Union Juridique Internationale adopted a draft declaration of the rights and duties of nations in 1919, and the Inter-Parliamentary Union a different draft in 1928. The Institut de Droit International had committees working on a definitive listing through much of the 1920s and 1930s.

In 1925, there was a blending of the two chief vehicles of exploration in a set of proposals adopted by the governing board of the Pan American Union. The proposals were to be submitted to a special panel of international lawyers for suggestions and comments and then to the member states of the Pan American Union. The proposals, or projects, as they were called, consisted of thirty different drafts of conventions that the governing board recommended to member states for their consideration and adoption. Among the projects were several that dealt with basic issues and principles: "Fundamental Bases of International Law," "Declaration of Rights and Duties of Nations," "Fundamental Rights of American Republics."[18]

Taken altogether, the thirty projects were considered an important step toward the long-sought goal of codification of international law, at least for the Western Hemisphere. They attained contemporary importance for two reasons. They had been formulated at the request of the twenty-one American states belonging to the Pan American Union and thus had a standing with foreign ministries that the efforts of private organizations did not have. Further, U.S. Secretary of State Charles Evans Hughes had publicly endorsed them in 1925, saying that they "marked a definite step in the progress of civilization and the promotion of peace."[19]

Their importance in the present discussion lies in what they reveal about concepts of international law in this period. The various declarations of the rights and duties of states mentioned above not only differed in what those rights and duties were, they also differed in their very concepts of the international system and of the place of the states within that system. By the mid-1920s, something besides codification projects and lists of rights and duties was beginning to emerge out of the concentrated and multifaceted effort to discover and define the principles of international law. A basic conflict in philosophical grounding was taking shape, a conflict that has little to do with the split between the adherents of positive law and the adherents of a refurbished natural law usually noted in this period.

James Brierly sketched the outlines of this conflict in 1926 when he commented on the Pan American Union's thirty projects. From his position as Chichele Professor of International Law and Diplomacy at Oxford, Brierly had a commanding view of the ferment in international law during the interwar period. Within a few years of writing this critique, his command of the field would also win him the post of editor of the *British Yearbook of International Law.* There could scarcely have been a more knowledgeable observer of the American effort at codification than James Brierly. He was also, as he himself admitted, disquieted by what he saw.

It was noted earlier that the American projects blended the two main approaches to the search for the principles of international law: codification and a listing of the fundamental rights and duties of states. For Brierly, both were cause for disquiet. The codification sought in these proposals was not just of minor rules of behavior but rather of fundamentals, of the very bases of the law. Codification, of necessity, meant agreement on definitions. This, Briefly thought, was both premature and presumptuous, and reminded him of Henry VIII's attempt to draft "An Act abolishing diversity in opinions," surely a futile exercise since neither in religion nor in politics could diversity of opinion be abolished, not even—Brierly noted dryly—not even if every American state should sign and ratify a treaty based on this particular proposal.

This attempt at standardized thought was bad enough in Brierly's opinion, but he saved his most biting criticism for the emphasis in the projects on the fundamental rights and duties of states. It would, he said, be unfortunate indeed if the doctrine of natural rights and the complementary international doctrine of fundamental rights were to become entrenched in international law. No matter how useful the doctrine of natural rights had been in the past for individual human beings by raising "a barrier against the unlimited claims of the sovereign state when such a barrier was urgently needed,"[20] it was sadly out of place when shifted to the states themselves.

There was nothing in the nature of a state that entitled it to anything, Brierly argued. It was, on the contrary, an historical phenomenon, in constant process of change in a changing world. That change could be directed "wisely or foolishly by human efforts. At the present time it is being directed, and the circumstances of international life make it vitally important that it should be directed, away from the atomistic conception of international relations towards a more coherent and interdependent international society."[21]

"Interdependent" was the key word in this indictment. As Brierly and others like him saw it, the chief task before them was to turn international law away from its outmoded emphasis on state sovereignty and independence to a recognition of the interdependence of all states in an international system where anything that affected one state had repercussions for all. This was the theme of a series of lectures given by

Nicolas Politis in July 1926 at Columbia University,[22] as it had also been the focus of intense discussion at the annual meeting of the Institut de Droit International at The Hague in 1925. Institut members had systematically compared the provisions of some of the declarations of the rights and duties of states that were then being circulated. As rapporteur Albert La Pradelle pointed out, there were problems with the basic philosophy of most of these lists of principles. The declaration adopted by the American Institute of International Law in 1916, for example, was anachronistically faithful to the principles of international law that had dominated the field from the beginning to the end of the nineteenth century. It spoke not of interdependence but of independence. In like fashion, the project of the Union Juridique Internationale insisted on the independence and equality of states.

To remedy this, La Pradelle proposed, and Institut members accepted, a declaration that shifted the philosophical base of the discussion from independence to interdependence, a shift that was then reflected in an emphasis on duties rather than on rights. This shift, he said, was simply a recognition of new ideas that, since the end of the nineteenth century, had gradually been taking possession of international law. In the Institut declaration, the principles of the solidarity and interdependence of states were not attached as afterthoughts or reservations to a position of basic independence. They became the very foundation of the states' relationships: "a principle, a base, a dogma."[23]

During the 1920s, then, and on into the 1930s, there were two lines of thought running side by side in international law, lines of thought that were mutually exclusive. The older line had behind it the full weight of traditional reflections on international affairs. It had, as well, the weight of hundreds of treaties negotiated on the basis of independent sovereignties freely entering into agreements that suited their needs and interests, regardless of the effect on any other state or on the international system at large. The other line of thought—far newer, far weaker, and with little tradition to back it up—pitted the concept of interdependence against the concept of independence and tried to shift the whole base of the law onto different grounds. With so little experience to go on, it was not clear exactly how such a shift would translate into actual working arrangements, but the need was deeply felt and strongly expressed.

As the 1930s wore on and states retreated into self-protective, autarkic actions, it seemed obvious to some observers that the battle for change had been lost. The atomistic concept of international relations, of which Brierly had spoken, had triumphed. Even if a state were to follow the rules of international law—and many did not—the very tenor of the rules inclined states to individualistic actions that could be, and often were, detrimental to others.

Alejandro Alvarez used this analysis of the international system, and of international law in particular, as a starting point for his own argument in favor of a wholly new international law. Although his argument bears the stamp of his idiosyncratic emphasis on the contributions made by the "peaceful" Western hemisphere, it is still important for understanding the search for fundamentals that figures so largely in this period. His reflections on the changes occurring in international life and on the inadequacy of old institutions and concepts to deal with these changes were not his alone; they were those of his generation of workers in international law. Nothing is more striking that the acuteness of this generation's analyses of the ills of the international system, unless it is their faith that if they could only find the right expression of the principles of law, the ills could be cured.

Alvarez was one of a distinctive group of Latin American scholars and politicians active in international law at this time. They came from various South or Central American countries, but they were at home almost anywhere in the Western world. The group included such men as Ricardo Alfaro of Panama, Antonio de Bustamante of Cuba, Epitácio Pessôa of Brazil, and Francisco Urrutia of Colombia. Alvarez was from Chile, but for much of his life he lived in Paris. In between his many international commitments, he worked on a reformulation of international law to bring it from the nineteenth into the twentieth century and make it suited to the needs of modern life.

In 1938 he published a book that was in many ways a summation of the arguments discussed here and was at the same time an attempt to meld the arguments into a single, powerful restatement of the law. Recognizing that such a work would lack authority if it were only the product of individual effort, Alvarez had, in the early 1930s, succeeded in getting himself appointed by five different international law associations to draft a statement of the basic principles of modern international law. He made sure of his authoritative base through frequent consultation with association members, and he lobbied persistently for adoption of the resulting formulation. By 1938, Alvarez had managed to get the basic principles endorsed by the Académie Diplomatique Internationale, the Union Juridique Internationale, and the International Law Association; and he was still engaged in discussion with the Institut de Droit International and the American Institute of International Law when World War II demanded all their attention.

There is, then, more to be gained from examining this work than a knowledge of Alvarez's private views. As the world slid again toward a major war—the second major war for most of these workers in international law—here was an attempt by a large and important segment of the international law community to find the authoritative voice that would halt the slide. Or if it was too late for the slide to be halted by alternative perceptions of the international system and a renewed commitment to its preservation, then the principles could at least point the way to a better future. They could do so by showing how the whole base of international law as it had developed since World War I was fundamentally wrong in its emphasis on the independence of states: the emphasis should have been on the international community itself. The first article of this joint "Declaration on the Fundamental Facts and Grand Principles of Modern International Law" indicates what an emphasis on community might mean: "The interdependence of states is the foundation of their reciprocal relations, and mutual assistance is the condition for their peaceful co-existence and their material and moral development."[24]

The declaration goes on: "This interdependence is born of a general interest that is superior to the particular interests of each of the members of the community, and it creates for them common goals and, consequently, rights and duties, not only between themselves, but also in regard to the community as a whole."[25]

Talk about moral development, mutual assistance, and common goals came somewhat unexpectedly from people whose proudest boast had been that they were "scientific." It put their analysis of the world's ills and their prescriptions for the future very close to the analyses and prescriptions of those whose work they professed to scorn, the moralists. More importantly for the future of the ethical framework being developed by the states, it maintained and strengthened the strong prescriptive element that had been a part of international law from the first, even when its practitioners insisted most strongly on their purely descriptive role. It was an element that would, in the future, play an even more important part, not just in the proclamations of international law societies but in the way that states went about formulating their ideas of their own relations and the rules that ought to govern them.

Shield and Cloak

When the international system was analyzed along moral rather than legal lines, the tendency was to use the terms and points of reference that had been developed for individual human beings. This was a vocabulary hallowed by time and usage. It was familiar, and it was at hand. Moreover, it bore the imprimatur of Woodrow Wilson, whose words and conduct in the years before 1920 had a lasting influence on the thought of many who were concerned with international affairs, both then and in later years. Wilson's avoidance of moral pronouncements in the League covenant had been part of deliberate policy, not a reflection of a lack of interest. "I have not read history," he said in 1916, "without observing that the greatest forces in the world, and the only permanent forces, are moral forces."[26] And when he had gone before the U.S. Congress in 1917 to ask for a declaration of war against Germany: "We are at the beginning of an age in which it will be insisted that the same standards of conduct and of responsibility for wrong done shall be observed among nations and their governments that are observed among the individual citizens of civilized states."[27]

For moralists, the path that led to World War II began with an ancient personal vice, that of selfishness. Harold Butler, the second director of the International Labor Organization, put it this way: "A world of self-seeking nations is bound to be as unstable as a society of self-seeking individuals devoid of any generosity to each other or of any attachment to the public good. More than for any other reason the peace was lost because the policies of nations were empty of charity towards each other, dictated by nothing nobler than a close-fisted calculation of self-interest."[28]

Sir Robert Cecil summed up the assumption underlying this line of analysis, namely, that in moral terms there is no distinction to be made between the individual and the state. Both the state and the individual inhabit the same moral domain and are subject to the same moral imperatives. In his retrospective view of the League of Nations and the lessons to be learned from that experiment in which he had played such an active part, Cecil wrote: "We believe that underlying all human relationships, national not less than individual, are certain fundamental principles of right and wrong and that it is only on the acknowledgment of this truth that any tolerable international system can be built."[29]

Once it would have been thought jejeune for a political leader, even one with Cecil's high reputation, to speak of right and wrong, as if the international scene were some kind of gigantic Sunday school class. In the terror and bewilderment of the late 1930s and the early days of World War II, discussions of right and wrong seemed particularly apt. At the first meeting of the foreign ministers of the American states in 1939, the ministers reaffirmed their "faith in the principles of Christian civilization" and went on to "condemn attempts to place international relations and the conduct of warfare outside the realm of morality."[30]

A 1942 report of the Inter-American Juridical Committee moved beyond a general lament at the decline of international morality and linked that decline specifically to a change that had occurred in international law. The committee had been charged by the foreign ministers of the American states with the task of formulating recommendations for a future international organization. Committee members took the opportunity to analyze the mistakes that had brought the world to the terrible days of World War II.

The greatest mistake of all, they believed, was that the states themselves and everyone concerned with the relations between states had abrogated their duty to articulate and press the claims of morality. Traditionally, the claims of morality had found expression in international law, which in the view of committee members was not simply a set of agreed-upon rules, like a set of rules governing how a game should be played. The essential characteristic of international law, and one that had been lost, was that it was "a rule of moral conduct."[31]

Committee members pointed out that Vitoria, Grotius, and other early writers who had given careful consideration to relations between states had had "a clear conception of the moral basis of international law, however far removed from moral standards the actual conduct of nations in those times may have been." Later, however, there was a growing tendency "to adjust moral principles to the actual conduct of nations and to establish the theory that each nation was the judge of its own moral conduct."[32]

The outcome of this abandonment of "the task of formulating moral standards by which the conduct of nations might be judged" was that "the actual practice of nations, as expressed in usages and customs, came to be seen as the only valid international law. The result was that exponents of this mistaken theory came to determine the existence of rules of international law by the record of the conduct of nations, instead of judging the conduct of nations by the principles of law."[33]

An example of what was being condemned by the committee can be found in a work published in 1931 by Ellery C. Stowell, professor of international law at American University and the author of a number of works in the field. Stowell's outlook on international law was not entirely theoretical. He had served as a minor official at the second Hague Peace Conference in 1907 and at the Naval Conference in London the following year. The text on international law that he published in 1931 was subtitled, "A Restatement of Principles in Conformity with

Actual Practice." In his introduction he expanded on his subtitle by saying that he intended to present "the system of rules which actually govern international relations. No attempt has been made here to work out from predetermined principles some pretty conceit of world law."[34]

How this intention was put into practice can be illustrated by Stowell's treatment of the rules of warfare. His rejection of predetermined principles, even widely accepted ones, led him to conclusions from which he did not flinch. Regarding the use of poison gas and other modern means of warfare, he observed that a precedent had been set in World War I. The governing principles were effectiveness and military advantage, both of which were served by technological advances. Since the use of such means gave the advantage to the state "most highly developed from a scientific point of view," there was no doubt that, despite popular revulsion, in any future war, "those restrictions which are contrary to the trend of the development of civilization and of the conduct of warfare will soon be swept away. . . . Any convention which attempts to limit the use of new and effective means of warfare is without doubt a retrograde step. The claims of humanity are recognized to the extent of barring the use of means which cause suffering disproportionate to the military advantage derived from their use."[35]

As for the status of noncombatants in warfare, Stowell noted simply, "An impartial observer must recognize that the last war constitutes a precedent for directing operations against the civilian population in order to make them crave peace, and induce their government to submit."[36]

This elevation of practice into precedent, and from there into a principle of law, was what members of the Inter-American Juridical Committee explicitly condemned in 1942, citing this approach as a factor in the descent into war. One of the major conclusions of their report was that in any future international system morality would have to come first: "In the exercise of their sovereignty nations must recognize and respect the priority of the moral law and of the fundamental principles of international law derived from it."[37]

Here was the clear connection between morality and law that the early exponents of the new international order had taken for granted. So much had they taken it for granted that they had felt no need to articulate it. Indeed, they had even avoided specific references to morality—to right and wrong, good and evil—on the grounds that they were not philosophizing about an international system, they were building one. But the events of the late 1930s and the coming of World

War II had demonstrated that such basic considerations could not be taken for granted. And so, hesitantly at first, and sometimes with an air of embarrassment, people began to try to work out the moral bases for state behavior.

The promise of such an approach lay in the possibility of forging a much more binding sense of obligation to the rules of international behavior than had formerly been possible. If the states believed that such and such an action was not only prohibited by general agreement but that it was also *wrong*, intrinsically *wrong*, then they would be less likely to act in that manner. To those who were concerned with the root causes of conflict, the promise of this approach seemed evident. A collective conscience would function on the international scene as the conscience of individuals functioned on the domestic scene, and morality would be the shield to protect them all from destructive behavior.

The perils of such an approach were not so obvious. They lay in the very power of an appeal to morality, with all that that implied about ultimate values that could—simply because they *were* ultimate values—override every other consideration. If morality were simply appealed to but not defined, then the concept remained open and empty, like a bin waiting to be filled by any interested party. Elihu Root had warned against this danger in 1916. Nineteen-sixteen was far removed in time and circumstance from the late 1930s and early 1940s, but the question that Root addressed was relevant in both periods. The question was the relationship between law and morality on the international scene. Root had had long experience in international affairs. He had held many different public positions, including that of Secretary of State, and he had helped to draft the plan for the Permanent Court of International Justice. His experience had made him exceedingly wary about invoking morality as either a guide or a justification for action. It was too slippery a term, he thought, and there were too many different opinions about its nature. Moreover, as the international system was constituted, it was simply an invitation for the strongest powers to impose their own definitions. That, he said, was the reason for the ironclad international prohibition on intervention, even under claims of morality. "The rule which prohibits interference by other nations, with however good a purpose, is a rule against inevitable tyranny."[38]

The slipperiness of the term and the perils against which Root warned were made strikingly obvious in 1935 in the Baltic port of Danzig (now Gdansk), where there was an attempt to make an explicit connection between law and morality. In Danzig in 1935, those with the most power gave the term *morality* their own meaning, just as Root had predicted they would. From then until the end of World War II, morality functioned in Danzig as it was functioning in National Socialist Germany in the same period—not as a shield to protect against destructive behavior but as a cloak to give destructive behavior the look of legitimate action. The League of Nations tried to prevent this outcome in Danzig, but its power in that city had always been limited, and by 1935 its power was almost nonexistent.

Without going into the details of the League's involvement in the affairs of this port on the south coast of the Baltic Sea, it is enough to note that the involvement dated from the peace settlement of 1919 and was the result of a decision to resolve German and Polish claims to the port by giving it to neither. Instead, Danzig was made a free city with its own constitution and put under the guarantee of the League. A high commissioner appointed by the League Council lived in the city as a visible symbol of international authority that would, it was hoped, help resolve any difficulties that might arise. The stage was thus set for the League to be drawn in 1935 into the tangled question of the relationship of law and morality. Only the fact of the League guarantee made what was happening in Danzig a matter of legitimate international concern. Under the ideas of sovereignty that prevailed in the 1930s, it would otherwise have been a purely domestic matter.

The question about morality and the law came before the Council in the form of a petition from some of the citizens of Danzig. They were protesting two recent changes in the penal code of the city through which, they charged, "a fundamental and decisive change is effected in the existing practice of the penal law to make it conform with the principles prevailing in National Socialist Germany."[39]

The petition was addressed to the League high commissioner at Danzig, Sean Lester, who would later serve as secretary-general of the League during the World War II years of dispersal and exile. Very little of Lester's influence in Danzig derived from his position as League high commissioner, a post with almost no power even in the days when the League's reputation was high. Lester had to rely on his own powers of persuasion and his reputation for personal integrity. In 1935, when the National Socialist party was mounting a violent campaign for dominance in Danzig, Lester's personal integrity came under attack, and his powers of persuasion were unavailing against a determined and militant nationalism. He could do almost nothing at Danzig regarding the changes in the penal code, and he considered the matter too important to be addressed at the local level anyway. He forwarded all the relevant documentation to the League Council at Geneva and asked that the matter be put on the agenda "as soon as possible" so that "this law should be examined by the Council of the League in relation to the Constitution."[40]

Thus the issue was posed as one of constitutionality. Were the decrees passed by the Danzig senate in August 1935, effecting a change in the Danzig penal code, in conformity with the constitution of the Free City—that constitution adopted under the auspices of the League and under the guarantee of the League? In this form the question went from the League Council to the Permanent Court of International Justice, which was asked for an advisory opinion. The court held that the decrees were "not consistent with the guarantees which Part II of the Danzig Constitution provides for fundamental rights."[41]

And then the court moved beyond the narrow question of conformity with the specific provisions of the constitution into the much broader question of the philosophy on which the constitution was based. Since those defending the decrees had argued so forcefully that it was the very principle of justice that gave the new penal code force and validity, the court could scarcely avoid the issue, however much it might want to limit its finding to strict constitutionality. "Furthermore, the Court holds that the decrees violate the principles on which, as already explained, Part II of the Constitution is founded."[42]

Part II of the Danzig Constitution defined the fundamental rights of the citizens, as, for example, that the liberty of the person was inviolable (article 74); that there was freedom of movement within the city (article 75); and that people could express their opinions, within the bounds of the law, without fearing punishment or the imposition of some disadvantage because they had exercised this right (article 79). These *Grundrechte*, these fundamental rights, said the court, are "designed to fix the position of the individual in the community, and to give him the safeguards which are considered necessary for his protection against the state."[43]

It was precisely these articles of the constitution that were threatened by the changes that the Danzig senate had made in the penal code, a fact that the court noted in its advisory opinion. The threat did not come from a direct attack on the guarantees of personal liberty— the senators knew that their actions would come under the scrutiny of the League, and they were careful to avoid so obvious a move. Instead, they had tried a maneuver that would make the guarantees meaningless.

The philosophy underlying the old penal code was summed up in the Latin phrase, *Nulla poena sine lege*, which was to say, "No person could be punished except for an offense provided for and strictly defined by law."[44] The National Socialists argued that that philosophy was wholly inadequate. There had been a steady evolution of the law since the eighteenth century when the principle of *Nulla poena sine lege* had found expression in the French Declaration of the Rights of Man and the Citizen. Society had changed, and the law had changed accordingly. It now reflected a truer sense of justice than was possible under the old individualistic principle. The law was now clearly and directly based on morality, a fact that was expressed in the principle on which the Danzig senate had acted: *Nullum crimen sine poena;* under the new philosophy of the Danzig penal code, there was to be no crime without punishment.

And if a crime could take place without there being a specific statute that defined an act as criminal, how was the definition to be determined? That was the very point of the changes that the Danzig senate had made. Under the new penal code, if an act were "deserving of penalty according to the fundamental conceptions of a penal law and healthy national consciousness," then the person committing that act was liable to punishment, whether or not any specific law defined the act as criminal. The sound moral sense of the people and the fundamental principles on which positive law was based were enough to condemn the act, and the person could be brought to trial under any analogous law. In the words of the decree, "Should no particular penal law be directly applicable to the act, the act shall be subject to penalty under the law the fundamental conception of which is most closely applicable to it."[45]

The changes in the Danzig penal code copied changes that had recently been made by the National Socialists in Germany. In their defense of what they had done, the Danzig contingent of the party relied heavily on arguments being made in the late summer and fall of 1935 by the German minister of justice, Franz Gürtner. Gürtner's speeches and writings offer a clear exposition of the case that can be made for an explicit link between morality and law—just the link that the worried political leaders of the late 1930s and early 1940s were hoping to make on the international scene. Abstracted from the violence with which the National Socialists pursued their goals, the case can be a strong one, and Gürtner set out to show that it was so.

"Opposed to the principle of *Nulla poena sine lege* is another principle, *Nullum crimen sine poena,*" he wrote in September 1935. "National socialism imposes a new, higher mission on penal law: the realization of true justice." A law based on the old principle of *Nulla poena sine lege* has a purely formal notion of illegality, whereas, "National socialism replaces that concept with that of real illegality; it considers any attack

on the interests of the community, any attack on the necessities of social life, as being contrary to law. . . . True law cannot exist solely on
the basis of formal legislation. It must also rely on the fundamental
idea from which the formal law springs, an idea which perhaps has not
found perfect expression in the formal law itself."[46]

Gürtner's arguments were echoed by Dr. Graf Gleisbach, agent of
Danzig, who presented the Free City's case before the Permanent
Court. He ridiculed the notion that a crime and its punishment must be
specified in law before anyone could be charged with that crime. "Can
we seriously pretend that the security of law demands that an individual be able to calculate in an absolutely precise manner just how far
he can go in doing wrong and still escape punishment?"[47]

And Arthur Greiser, president of the Danzig senate, painstakingly
spelled out the link between morality and law. Under the old philosophy, he noted, the penal code of Danzig was "dominated by the
conception of a *formal* offense." Under the new philosophy, this purely
formal conception "is replaced by the living conception of a *material*
offense. The result of this change can be formulated as follows: Every
act deserving of punishment shall be expiated. There can be no doubt
that this new conception of the duty of the State to inflict punishment
represents a highly moral conception of penal law and in practice constitutes an advance in the development of penal law."[48]

The opinion of the Permanent Court of International Justice made
little difference to events in Danzig, where every gain for the National
Socialists in Germany undermined what little respect the National Socialists in Danzig still had for the League. "Sound popular feeling" or
"healthy national consciousness" meant just what the National Socialists said it did, for it was an article of party dogma that the people
and the party were one. It did little good for League high commissioner
Lester to point out that more than forty percent of the voters in Danzig
had expressed their opposition to the National Socialists in an election
held in the spring of 1935. The fact had no weight at all, either in the
arguments advanced in the cause of morality and true law or in the
behavior of the Danzig National Socialists. They continued to mimic
the party faithful in Germany. They closed opposition newspapers, denied access to radio broadcasting, imprisoned opposition leaders
under the new "highly moral" penal code, and began to move openly
against socialist political parties, labor unions, and Jews.

All of this was, of course, far from what was in the minds of the
American foreign ministers and the jurists who called for "the priority
of the moral law." But the assumption underlying the call of the jurists
and ministers, the reflections of Sir Robert Cecil and Harold Butler, and

the pronouncements of Woodrow Wilson was that there was one moral law, one morality on which people agreed. All that was necessary was for people to abide by it. The events in Danzig and in National Socialist Germany showed how fallacious this assumption could be, and how dangerous as well, given an international system committed to noninterference and an organized group determined to define morality on its own terms and then to enforce it over mere rules of positive law.

For those who analyzed the failure of the international system as a failure in morality, the international situation of the late 1930s and early 1940s posed a dilemma. They were convinced that there had to be standards by which to judge the behavior of states, and they were equally convinced that the actual behavior of states was not an adequate source from which to derive those standards. If warring states were to use poison gas against civilian populations, for example, was there no standard by which to judge that use except that of military effectiveness? There was, of course, the 1925 Geneva Convention, in which many states had agreed to prohibit the use of asphyxiating, poisonous, or other gases, and of bacteriological methods of warfare. But was a formal international instrument an adequate response to this or any other international problem? International instruments were being broken right and left. How could a formal agreement be made so binding on the consciences of states that a prohibition, or any other course of action, would become effective?

There was only one answer to that in this line of analysis, and that answer was morality. Yet calls for states to comply with "the principles of Christian civilization" or to recognize "the priority of the moral law" seemed, in practice, only to license the powerful to behave according to their own concepts of morality, freed from the restraints of the rules of statute law.

Into this gap in the ethical thought of the time stepped Nicolas Politis, Greek delegate to the League of Nations, who has appeared several times in this account. When he set down his reflections on the morality suitable for international relationships, he was within a few months of his death at age seventy in Cannes on the south coast of France. Cannes was his place of refuge after he had fled Paris before the advancing German army. He died in March 1942, before German control was extended over the whole of France.

La morale internationale was Politis's intellectual last will and testament. It was a summary of his lifelong reflections on international affairs. It was his legacy to the world, a legacy directed especially to those who would be making plans after the war for a time of peace that he knew he would not live to see. Despite the conditions under which he wrote, in which all that he had lived and worked for was apparently being destroyed before his eyes, he did not despair. His concern was not with the violent present of the early 1940s. His concern was with the future when the reconstruction of Europe and the international system would take place.

Even then, he warned, one must not expect too much. After discussing the kind of organization that would enable the states to move quickly and effectively against aggression, he added, "We would sadly deceive ourselves if we set our hopes on the states rushing eagerly in the near future to create such a barrier against war."[49] Progress would come more slowly, with many preliminary steps and only after some successes on a smaller, regional scale.

This was the man, the situation, and the mood behind what was the most comprehensive attempt by anyone in this period to set out a system of international morality with terms so closely defined that they would not be subject to abuse by the powerful. What distinguishes Politis's work from that of Alvarez or others who took a legal approach is his embrace of ethical standards. Prescriptive norms were smuggled into much of the work in international law, under the guise of an objective description of reality. Politis took an open stand with the moralists to say: thus and such is the way that the world *ought* to be, the way that states *ought* to behave. What distinguishes his work from that of other moralists of the period is his sense that international morality might be different from private morality. He used the moral vocabulary that had been developed for individuals—that being what was available to him—but his use shows a sensitivity to the changes that occur when private morality is writ large for different kinds of actors in an environment very unlike that of the living room or the city street.

And yet, there were connections, a fact that Politis was careful to point out. In all these separate spheres, morality consisted of certain rules of conduct that arose from the requirements of a life lived in society. There were, of course, other rules of conduct—courtesy, custom, law—each with a different degree of obligatory quality. What was important about morality was that, while it did not have the obligatory force of law, it was as indispensable as law "for the good order, peace, and prosperity of the international community."[50] And the difficulty of making a list of such rules or principles was that they were always in the process of change, some being incorporated wholly or in part into formal legal instruments and others remaining outside the law, where they functioned as standards by which such instruments and the actions of the states might be judged.

Having drawn boundaries within which morality might be defined and related to law, Politis then set out and discussed six principles of international morality that, in his experience, were a necessary part of the international system. Even if all that the states wanted to do was to serve their own interests—their "essential, long-term interests," as Politis put it—these principles were necessary: loyalty, moderation, mutual assistance, mutual respect, the spirit of justice, solidarity.[51] In each case, the point of reference for the principle and its application was the system of which the state was a part, a system that would become a true society through the states' responses to the demands made on them as actors in continuing relationship with each other. In his discussion, Politis wove a tight net of reciprocal and reinforcing obligations arising from the six principles. For example, the claim of justice could not justify an act if it transgressed any of the other five principles. This close net of obligations constituted for the states the unwritten laws of their existence.

The importance of this set of unwritten laws behind the formal laws negotiated by the states lies in Politis's ability to base them not in the domain of natural law, on which moralists tended to rely, but rather in a social domain, that of the relationships of the states in an emerging international society. Here his thought touches the same ground on which the Danzig National Socialists took their stand, that of social necessity. But Politis passes quickly on to the task of adapting private virtues, such as moderation and respect, to the demands of a world of contentious states. In such a setting, social necessity wears a different face and has a different meaning.

In the foreword to his intellectual testament, Politis set out the theme of the book in a paragraph that is also the conclusion he had come to after a lifetime of effort in negotiating many of the specific agreements that were the body of positive international law. As he wrote, the world was again plunged in war, against all the rules and restraints that many of the states through leaders such as Politis, Cecil, Alvarez, Hull, and others like them had tried to raise against just such an eventuality. Politis wrote: "When the positive rules of law in society become inoperative or arbitrary as a result either of a deficiency or an excess of power, people are prompted by their unfailing sense of justice to look higher, to put their hope of salvation in those superior and permanent precepts that the ancient Greeks called 'unwritten laws.'"[52]

Much of the history of this period in the development of international ethics consists of a search for those "superior and permanent precepts." When World War II was nearing its end in the spring of 1945 and many of the searchers gathered at San Francisco to lay plans for a new world organization, they brought with them the urgencies that had driven the search, as well as the profusion of approaches that made a clear path difficult to discern. Politis's approach by way of moderation and respect within a modest institutional framework—perhaps, as he suggested, limited at first to Europe alone—had to await a quieter day.

The Halfway House

The United Nations organization that emerged from the conference at San Francisco in 1945 was a kind of halfway house for those who had been engaged in the search for "superior and permanent precepts." They were convinced that those precepts offered the only hope for the future and that, to be useful as guides for international behavior, the precepts had to be set out explicitly as so many fundamental principles on which this second attempt to create an international order of peace and security could be built. Two months of negotiations produced a charter that did pay more attention to abstract statements of principle than the covenant of the League had done. It did not, however, fulfill the desires of either the legalists or the moralists in regard to specific statements of the rights and duties of states, nor did it address the general concern about deteriorating human rights standards by including a list of specific human rights and fundamental freedoms. Advocates of declaratory statements of principles along these lines had to be content with the understanding that these matters would be taken up in more detail when the new international organization began to function.

They could take some comfort from the fact that it was only through their efforts that certain principles were included in the charter at all. The original form of the new international organization, as laid out in the Dumbarton Oaks proposals, had been short on references to such matters as justice or respect for international law. The four states who were the authors and sponsors of the proposals—China, the United Kingdom, the Soviet Union, and the United States—had either felt that such references were not necessary or that others would be sure to add them anyway while the Big Four concerned themselves with matters such as the requirement for great power unanimity before the UN Security Council could take action on a threat to world peace.

The requirement of great power agreement is the feature of the UN Charter that most clearly distinguishes it from the Covenant of the

League of Nations. The difference was a deliberate one. In the planning for a new international organization, which began well before the end of World War II, the League of Nations served as a constant point of reference. Sometimes it was a model to emulate, sometimes an example of what not to do; but always it was there, the backdrop for all the plans and activities taking place on stage. Nothing more sharply differentiates the 1945 San Francisco Conference on International Organization from the Paris Peace Conference of 1919 than this unchanging backdrop of an effort that had failed to prevent another world war. If this gave added determination to the efforts of the delegates, it also cast a kind of pall over the proceedings. At San Francisco no one spoke of creating a new international order, and the emotional setting was neither springtime nor dawn. Indeed, like the beseiged at dusk preparing for a night attack, the delegates spoke of raising an even stronger bulwark against destruction. They spoke also in muted tones of apprehension of what might happen if they, too, should fail to halt aggression. So dominant was this theme that Jan Masaryk, who chaired the Czechoslovakian delegation, begged at one point, "Let us please stop talking of the next world war."[53]

As drama, as a set of events and people that could catch and hold the popular imagination, the San Francisco conference was a failure. There was extensive public coverage, not just of the plenary sessions but also of the meetings of the several commissions charged with working out the details of the new international organization. Despite this, the proceedings were, and still are, unmemorable. Of the thousands of words spoken, few exist outside the pages of official records. The journalists who were accredited to the conference—more than twenty-six hundred of them—did what they could to dramatize procedural battles over the admission of Argentina and Poland and efforts to limit the institutional preponderance of the great powers, but this was thin fare. As food for the hopes of the millions still locked in combat, it was thin to the point of starvation. There was more sustenance in the world outside, where the war in Europe was drawing to a close, than in the apparently endless haggling in San Francisco over phraseology and voting procedures.

The trouble was that, although the shooting war was still going on, the companion war for peoples' hearts and minds had already been won. No one disputed the need for an international organization. In many ways, the League of Nations had succeeded despite its failure to prevent World War II. The ideas of collective security and international cooperation that had been embodied in the structure of the League were carried over for embodiment in the new structure of the United

Nations. The hope was to give those ideas a better vehicle, not to replace them with something else. The delegates at San Francisco were,
in a sense, doomed to the parliamentary maneuvering that seems in
retrospect petty and dull, although the long-term consequences of
such maneuvering may well be momentous. Unlike their counterparts
in Paris some twenty-six years before, they had not gathered to write
terms of peace, parcel out territories and peoples, draw the boundaries
of new states, or battle the forces of reaction to create an organization
to lead the way to a new international order.

The organization that the delegates at San Francisco were laboring
to bring into being was simply supposed to carry on where the League
had left off and to succeed in the one particular area where the League
had failed. The delegates were not starting with a slate that was even
relatively clean. Months before, their governments had been handed
the Dumbarton Oaks proposals, the preliminary plans for the organization. This set of proposals provided a starting point for discussion and
for the criticisms and suggestions that constituted the bulk of the proceedings at San Francisco. It provided an ending point as well, for there
was no question of jettisoning the proposals for some other plan. There
was thorough discussion, and modifications were made; but the discussion and the modifications took place within the limits set by the
great powers.

This was a practical recognition of the part played by the great
powers in the prosecution of the war against the Axis and of the part
that they would have to play if peace were to be kept in the future. One
consequence of this recognition was, however, that the conference
took on the air of a charade, played out for the benefit of the public and
the smaller powers. The consultations and procedures to assure great
power agreement—an agreement that everyone acknowledged was
essential to success—had the unlooked-for effect of draining the proceedings of substance. They did not seem so much a vehicle for the
hopes of a suffering world, as a platform for tired oratory.

The death of Franklin Roosevelt only a few days before the conference opened in late April 1945 occasioned one of the few authentic
notes at the conference. Even that sting of sadness was, however,
quickly blunted by the repetition of public utterance. Delegate after
delegate lamented a loss that affected not only the people of the United
States but, as they tirelessly reminded each other, the peoples of the
free world as well. The delegates had perhaps lost more than they
knew. Roosevelt, like Wilson before him and like his contemporary
Winston Churchill, had had the power to evoke a vision and cast it
about the grubby business of political compromise in such a way that

short-term means were bathed in the glow of long-term ends. It was a vision lacking at San Francisco.

Without a Wilson or a Roosevelt, and with Churchill still absorbed in the war effort, the bones of political practicality showed starkly through the Dumbarton Oaks proposals and its companion piece, the great power voting agreement worked out in the Crimean conference at Yalta. They showed too starkly for the comfort of some of the delegates at San Francisco, who insisted that ultimate values and goals ought to have a more prominent place in the charter than the great powers had given them.

The case for including a detailed statement of the rights and duties of states and of essential human rights was pressed most strongly by several Latin American states. Chile, Cuba, Mexico, and Panama pointed out the inadequacy of the Dumbarton Oaks proposals in this respect. The government of the Netherlands had a similar complaint, noting that peace and security without justice and morality could be a poor bargain indeed: "The maintenance of international peace and security is a most desirable goal. But if, speaking *ex hypothesi,* a case arose of peace being bought at the price of what would be widely felt as injustice, that price might well seem unreasonable to many."[54]

Justice. Morality. Law. These were the touchstones of validity for some of the states represented at the conference, whatever the great powers might say. There were six principles listed in the Dumbarton Oaks proposals, which were to provide the standards for action by the organization and its members: (1) the sovereign equality of peace-loving states, (2) fulfillment by the members of charter obligations, (3) peaceful settlement of the members' disputes, (4) no threat or use of force in a manner inconsistent with the purposes of the organization, (5) assistance to the organization in actions undertaken in accordance with the charter, and (6) no assistance to states against which the organization was taking preventive or enforcement action.[55]

These principles were all very well, the Mexican foreign office observed. Undoubtedly they were recognized as fundamental principles of international law. "Nevertheless, the enumeration made therein is incomplete with respect to the Rights and Duties of States and contains a serious hiatus in regard to the International Rights and Duties of Man, respect for which constitutes one of the essential objectives of the present war."[56]

Panama, too, pressed for inclusion of these rights and suggested that the purposes of the proposed organization be expanded by adding after the words "to maintain peace and security" the following: "to maintain and observe the standards set forth in the 'Declaration of the Rights and Duties of Nations' and the 'Declaration of Essential Human Rights' which are appended to the present Charter, and which are made an integral part thereof."[57]

A strong strain of American exceptionalism ran through some of the suggestions of the Latin American states. They frankly felt that they had handled their continental relations better than Europe had done and that they had much to teach the Old World. They had recently brought a hemispheric conference at Chapultepec, Mexico, to a successful conclusion with a ringing restatement of principles that, they said, "the American states have been incorporating in their international law, since 1890, by means of conventions, resolutions and declarations."[58] As Alberto Camargo, chairman of the Colombian delegation to the San Francisco conference, observed with unconscious arrogance, the United Nations system "is a compromise between the realities of 1945 and the aspirations of humanity. No American state can think otherwise because the inter-American system, functioning, of course, in a less complex continent, is unquestionably more perfect."[59]

In conference after conference, especially throughout the 1930s, the American states had discussed, expanded on, refined, and restated fundamental principles that were to govern their relations with each other and provide standards by which to judge their own conduct. The principles owed much to the codification efforts that have been discussed, for there was a constant interchange of ideas and personnel between the governments of the American states, the League of Nations, and the international law societies. What was important about these activities in the Western Hemisphere was not that the inter-American system was "more perfect" but that here was a functioning system that had long been concerned with such matters. Moreover, that concern was expressed at the state level where decisions could be made and actions taken when the time was right.

The time was not quite right at San Francisco in the spring of 1945, but it clearly was near. Pressure for explicit statements of the fundamentals of international life—whether expressed as principles of international law, as rights and duties of states, as essential human rights, or as some combination of these—was building to the point where it could not be denied. In response to that pressure, references to justice and international law, equal rights and self-determination, and respect for human rights and fundamental freedoms were added to the purposes and principles of the United Nations as originally set out in the Dumbarton Oaks proposals. These were concepts that would be developed much more fully in the years to come. Here they stood as signs of the states' intentions to articulate international standards.

The task would have been difficult even if the intellectual heritage on which the states would draw had been systematically composed and their own intentions had been directed toward consistent ends. This account has suggested the complex and contradictory nature of that heritage. As for intentions and consistency, it is only necessary to note that at San Francisco the states also insisted on adding, besides the principles noted above, a principle forbidding intervention "in matters which are essentially within the domestic jurisdiction of any state."[60]

There is no doubt that some of the states were more serious than ever before about setting down a detailed code of international behavior. There is no doubt also that, despite the interwar efforts to shift the base of state relationships from independence to interdependence, many, if not most, of the states were determined that a basic principle of that code would be an affirmation of their own sovereignty.

5 States and Peoples

The Organization is based on the principle of the sovereign equality of all its Members.

Article 2(1), United Nations Charter, 1945

All States enjoy sovereign equality. They have equal rights and duties and are equal members of the international community, notwithstanding differences of an economic, social, political or other nature.

Declaration on Principles of International Law, UN General Assembly, 1970

A triple legacy from the period of reflection upon fundamentals helped to shape the explicit code of international ethics created by the states after World War II. The oldest and strongest line of thought concerned the independence of states and what that entailed, both for the individual state and for the international community of which it was, perforce, a part. The outcome of the states' reflections upon independence was strongly expressed in the UN Charter itself through the membership requirements, the emphasis on sovereign equality and the right of self-determination, and the arrangements that looked toward the eventual independence of territories held in trust. The political independence, territorial integrity, and sovereign equality of states was the bedrock of the states' reflections upon their own relationships and behavior. It had been that way before the second World War, when the international system was still dominated by the West, and it was that way after the war when the system became truly global.

The second part of the legacy was derived from interwar reflections upon interdependence. The reflections had tended more toward exhortations to respect the principle than toward specific arrangements through which it might be either respected or expressed. This changed after World War II, when the new states in the system seized on the principle of interdependence as an appropriate vehicle through which to make their demands for economic equity. The New International Economic Order, in its many forms, drew legitimacy from this principle, which was hallowed by years of exhortation. The exhortation had

113

overtones of meaning that reached well back into the nineteenth century, when "the solidarity of states" was a staple of those who wanted to reach beyond what they saw as a sterile insistence on autonomy and independence. In the context of post World War II, *solidarity, interdependence,* and *cooperation* were transformed from general ideas, suitable for oratory, to specific warrants for calls for action in the redistribution of capital and resources.

Reflections on morality furnished the third part of the legacy on which the states drew in creating an explicit code of international ethics. The reflections had emphasized the accountability of states to standards derived from some other source than their own agreements or behavior. Whatever the source of those standards, they were presumed to stand outside the tug and push of everyday—to be, if not eternal, at least so long-lasting that they stood like mountains above the passing, restless scene below and, if not unalterable, at least so resistant to the tinkering hand that they could be counted the same from generation to generation.

Concern with objective moral standards carried over into the postwar period where it combined with revulsion at the excesses of World War II to stimulate a burst of activity in regard to human rights. The rights included entitlement rights that depended on the state for fulfillment and inherent rights that could be asserted against the state. So important was this development in the code of international ethics, where the primary focus shifted from states to people, that it will be treated separately in the next chapter. Here it will only be noted that sustained postwar attention on the part of the states to universal standards that could be urged against them had unforeseen results. It introduced into the code a dynamic element not wholly within the control of the states. The ramifications of this development are still being worked out by people in countries around the world.

Another development in the postwar period deserves mention because it has expanded the vocabulary of international affairs to include a rich and varied rhetoric of revolution and moral purity. It is not unusual for those who have achieved independent statehood through armed struggle to ascribe their success, at least in part, to virtuous character, but never before had so many of the virtuous and successful entered the international system in so short a period as in the thirty years following the end of World War II. And never before had the center of the international stage been so easily accessible and declamations there so widely disseminated.

Various gatherings of newly independent states and those new to the international system—at Bandung in 1955, Belgrade in 1961,

Lusaka in 1970—produced declarations filled with self-confident analyses of the ills of the system, and predictions of good health if the other, older states would only follow the paths of African or Asian or nonaligned purity. The drama of the several occasions and the richness of the rhetoric have obscured the fact that the new states have almost without exception endorsed the principles they at first denounced as "Western"—a fact that will be examined in more detail later in this chapter. Throughout much of this period, the rhetoric of particularity and virtue held center stage, but the production as a whole was given definitive form by the international system itself, a system of independent, competitive, sovereign states.

Mention has been made several times thus far in this chapter of the states' creation of an explicit code of international ethics in the period after World War II. The statement has been made as an assertion of fact, but it is, rather, an argument that certain actions and international instruments do in fact constitute a state-sponsored code of ethics. The code, like any ethical code, serves a double purpose. It offers guidance to the states for their behavior, chiefly but not exclusively in the international environment. It also provides universal standards by which that behavior can be judged. As an argument, the statement requires amplification, and its terms need to be defined.

Until this chapter, the term *ethical framework* has been used to describe the states' efforts to articulate and give substance to the principles underlying their life together in the international system. *Framework* rather than *code* was used to suggest that formal articulation of the principles was the less important part of the enterprise, which until World War II tended more toward the structural than the doctrinal. The founding, elaboration, and testing of international institutions, and the attempt to establish certain habits of thought and action received the primary emphasis in the early period of this study. This plus the few formal expositions made by the states constituted—it is argued—an ethical framework within which action could be directed toward the stated goal of peace.

Like much else, this approach changed after World War II. For reasons that have been suggested here, the states moved rapidly to set out formal statements of the basic principles of international life. A flood of pacts, charters, covenants, conventions, protocols, declarations, and resolutions suddenly appeared upon the international scene. The argument made here rests on the contention that consistency of purpose and content tie these various international instruments together and justify calling the body of such works a code.

Code is used in the broadest sense of the term as a set of authoritative principles and rules of conduct. It is not a code in the sense of a body of law collected and rationalized at the instance of a central authority, as was the Code of Justinian or the Napoleonic Code. Nor is it a code in the sense of a collection of ethical statements and precepts formulated by the members of a profession and then formally adopted as an expression of the profession's goals and ideals.

Yet this state-sponsored code shares some characteristics with both these examples. Much of it, but not all, is concerned with law. In this instance, the concern is with international law, and that concern is expressed in repeated attempts to determine the principles on which are based the more routine formulations of that law, such as fishing quotas and standard aircraft landing procedures. If international law is seen as the set of courtesies, customs, and agreements by which states regulate their relations, then the emphasis on principles that is the subject of this discussion can be seen as an attempt by the states to extract and codify the fundamentals of the relationships that tie them together in an international system.

There are even more similarities to a code of professional ethics. First is the fact that the code has been voted on and adopted by those it is supposed to affect. The various conventions, declarations, and so on, that make up the code have been formally adopted by the states either in the United Nations or in various regional groupings such as the Organization of American States or the Council of Europe. The fact that the votes took place at different times and locations over a period of years does not negate the significance of the votes. As might be expected in either the international system or a professional association, not every member voted in favor of every component of the code, some out of disagreement and some because—for one reason or another, depending on the instance—they were not eligible. Then too, the membership of the system has been constantly growing since World War II, and latecomers have not had a chance to vote on the earlier components. However, as will be shown, they have thoroughly examined an important part of what was done before their arrival and have given it their approval. Further, they have added components to the code even more rapidly than did their predecessors.

A second similarity to a code of professional ethics is in subject matter, both what that matter is and what it is intended to accomplish. Although much of the code is cast in terms of legal obligation such as, "the States shall" do such and such, many of the stipulations would not be enforceable even if a strong, central international authority existed. As an example, this from the 1989 Convention on the Rights of the Child, in which the signatory states "agree that the education of the child shall be directed to . . . [t]he preparation of the child for responsible life in a free society, in the spirit of understanding, peace, tolerance, equality of sexes, and friendship among all peoples, ethnic, national and religious groups and persons of indigenous origin."[1]

Bringing up a child in a spirit of understanding, peace, tolerance, and so on, is an ideal, a goal to be sought, not an enforceable legal obligation. The statement—which is far more detailed and lengthy than the quotation given here—reflects the states' collective vision of the way the world ought to be. This vision of an ideal world runs throughout the code, sometimes in the form of a standard to follow, sometimes as a legal obligation, sometimes as an inherent or entitlement right, sometimes as a factual assertion of a certain state of affairs, but always expressing the states' conceptions of the way things ought to be as shown by these extracts from four separate international instruments:

All peoples always have the right, in full freedom, to determine, when and as they wish, their internal and external political status, without external interference, and to pursue as they wish their political, economic, social and cultural development.[2]

States shall make every effort to build their international relations on the basis of mutual understanding, trust, respect and co-operation in all areas.[3]

The participating States will refrain in their mutual relations, as well as in their international relations in general, from the threat or use of force against the territorial integrity or political independence of any State, or in any other manner inconsistent with the purposes of the United Nations and with the present Declaration. No consideration may be invoked to serve to warrant resort to the threat or use of force in contravention of this principle.[4]

All States are juridically equal and, as equal members of the international community, have the right to participate fully and effectively in the international decision-making process in the solution of world economic, financial and monetary problems, *inter alia,* through the appropriate international organizations in accordance with their existing and evolving rules, and to share equitably in the benefits resulting therefrom.[5]

Full freedom for self-determination, mutual trust and understanding, no threat or use of force, equitable shares in economic benefits—these are only a few features of the ideal world that has been painted in detail by the states. And since the code depicts the ideal, the way that the states think the world and their relationships ought to be, the argument is made here that the code is, in fact, a code of international ethics. No matter the language in which it is cast, no matter that the states persistently confuse *is* and *ought;* the code sets out standards for guidance, emulation, and judgment, and that puts it squarely within the realm of ethics.

In some instances, only part of an international instrument addresses basic international issues, as in the 1948 Charter of the Organization of American States that in chapter 2, sets out fundamental principles and in chapter 3, the states' rights and duties derived from those principles, while the balance of the charter is devoted to other matters. In contrast, the entire 1948 Universal Declaration of Human Rights is concerned with specific applications derived from the basic principle, "All human beings are born free and equal in dignity and rights."[6] Given the states' well-known and obvious pursuit of power and advantage, what is surprising about all of this is the number and frequency of the states' attempts to deal with the fundamentals of international life and to set them out as components of a code of behavior.

The emphasis in this and the following chapter, then, is on the articulation and development of that explicit code, but a word needs to be said about the related activities that have been dealt with in previous chapters. They did not stop at the end of World War II. There is a strong continuity in many activities between the interwar period and the period after World War II. Work that was begun before the war went forward, with only a change in scope or organizational form and sometimes a change in name. The International Court of Justice took the place of the Permanent Court of International Justice and continued its work. Matters of health, nutrition, intellectual cooperation, economic organization and financial stability, which had been the province of various organs and committees of the League of Nations, were divided up among new organizations that were part of or associated with the United Nations, and the work went on. The International Labor Organization survived the war intact and continued to press for health, safety, and welfare standards.

These were continuations of approaches that had already shown their value in the international system. They were institutional expressions of the ethical heritage described in an earlier chapter. The institutions had been pioneered in the days of the League. They had functioned right up to and in some cases right through the second world war. In their new forms and with expanded scope, they continue today, so much a part of the international system that it is hard to imagine the system without them. In the development by the states of ideas of international ethics, these institutions of international cooperation had already made their contribution. They had made it so well that the habits of thought and action they had struggled to implant in the interwar period were accepted without question when the time came to rebuild the international order after World War II.

A focus on the states' efforts at articulation of the principles of international life might be seen as a shift from the field to the academy, from actions to words, except that these efforts by the states are not insulated from the everyday turbulence of international affairs. The drive to discover and then to articulate the philosophical underpinnings and ultimate goals of the states' existence and activities is not being conducted by philosophers, remote from the scene of action. It is being conducted by political and military leaders and professional diplomats who are very much on stage. In such as setting, context and change retain their crucial importance for understanding the development of this code of international ethics by the states of the international system.

Rhetoric and Structure

At the Paris Peace Conference in 1919, the Ethiopians there for the proceedings were a matter for curiosity and comment. Thirty-six years later at an international conference in Bandung, Indonesia, there was so little comment about the Ethiopians who attended that it is easy to forget they were there. Striking dress and bearing and conscious national pride were the norm at Bandung, where representatives of twenty-nine Asian and African states met in mid-April 1955. They met for a number of reasons, but a major motivation was to assert their claims as independent actors on the international scene. No longer were they to be acted upon, as in the days of European empire. They would no longer serve as a kind of exotic background to events in which they had little part—ranks of human palm trees, as it were, before which the main action took place. Now they were to act, themselves, and thus to influence the outcome of events.

Evaluation of this conference has depended largely on the context in which it is placed. To someone such as Dag Hammarskjold, whose concern was with the international system as a whole, the conference was both a threat and a promise. At the time the conference was held, he had been secretary-general of the United Nations for two years, and he was learning to press conferences as platforms for his views. When the subject of the Bandung Conference came up, he was able to shape an answer that emphasized the potential promise of such a meeting. "Have you any thoughts on this Asian Conference going on in Bandung?" he was asked. "Do you think it is going to strengthen the United Nations or weaken it?"

Hammarskjold easily turned this bid for a headline into an opportunity to make the point he wanted to make: "I feel that the

manifestation of the Asian world in positive terms, just as any manifestation of a great region with a great contribution to make, tends to
strengthen the United Nations. I am not in any way a believer that
there is a conflict between a regional approach and a universal one. On
the contrary, a strong and sound constructive development in a region
certainly helps also the universal effort."[7]

The "universal effort" was that of the international community as a
whole to realize the goals set out in the UN Charter. For Hammarskjold
and others like him, that was the context within which evaluation
took place, and his words were, perhaps, a subtle effort on his part to
influence the outcome at Bandung. At the time that he spoke, the conference had not yet ended—as he himself pointed out in his reply—
and the reports coming out of Bandung were too preliminary for predictions on where the conferees were likely to come down. Twelve of
the states represented there, including the People's Republic of China,
were not members of the United Nations, and the candidacy of each of
these nonmembers was a potential storm center in the political climate
of the times.

A second context, and a more common one, in which to evaluate
and comment on the Bandung Conference was that of the cold war.
Evaluation here was much simpler than in a context of joint international endeavor. Points could be allotted and scores kept as in some
elaborate and deadly serious game. If the conference should denounce
military alliances, such as the North Atlantic Treaty Organization
(NATO), the Southeast Asia Treaty Organization (SEATO), or the
Baghdad Pact in the Middle East, it would be counted a major setback
for the West—the United States and its allies in the cold war. In such
case, points might be allotted either to Prime Minister Jawaharlal
Nehru of India and Prime Minister U Nu of Burma and the neutralist
position they championed, or to Premier Chou En-lai (Zhou Enlai) of
China and through him to the entire Soviet bloc.

The leaders at Bandung had to thread their way cautiously through
the world as it was before they could even speak to the subject of the
way they thought the world ought to be. They were determined to prevent their historic meeting from being either presented as or turned
into yet another sideshow of the ongoing cold war. And so, despite
their pride in the fact that they represented Asian and African states,
acting on an Asian initiative, meeting in an Asian city, to discuss matters of interest to Asians and Africans, they protected themselves by
exclusionary tactics. They deliberately refrained from inviting either
North or South Korea, because a Korean presence would have brought
with it a whole train of grievances arising out of the recent Korean War

that would have set the East-West confrontation squarely in their midst.

This cautious line was not extended to European powers as symbols of empire, however. When it came to colonialism, the leaders at Bandung did not mind bearding the great and powerful. They expressed open support for liberation movements in European colonies because that, in their view, was a different matter entirely. Liberation movements in Asia, the Middle East, and Africa were very much their business. The movements were part of the drive of the people of that part of the world to take a full, active, and independent part in the international system. As Indonesian president Sukarno put it in his address of welcome to the delegates: "For many generations our peoples have been the voiceless ones in the world. We have been the un-regarded, the peoples for whom decisions were made by others whose interests were paramount, the peoples who lived in poverty and humiliation."[8]

Now all of that was to change. No matter what differences divided the Asian and African states at Bandung—and there were many—they shared a common determination that this was to be *their* conference and the conclusions were to be *their* conclusions. The words they spoke were to be their own, not those of the former imperial powers, nor were they to be yet another outpouring of cold war rhetoric.

Without this background, it would be difficult to understand much of what was said and done at Bandung in 1955. And since Bandung is being used in this account to illustrate the changing context of the international system as it expanded in the postwar period, it would be difficult to understand the passion and the rhetoric of the newcomers to the system without an understanding of Bandung. The emotional load carried by the leaders of these Asian and African states was immense. Many of them had struggled through years of imprisonment, exile, armed conflict, betrayal, and scorn to arrive where they were. They knew what it was to be voiceless and disregarded. They knew also the bitterness of struggle with those in their own camp. They knew the factional battles, the ceaseless maneuvering for resources and control. Out of all this they had emerged to find the world locked in the hostile confrontation of the cold war, with an international organization that was already functioning and the high ground already occupied by states that had achieved their independence years before.

The African and Asian leaders were in a double bind at Bandung. The states that they represented were subject to all the pressures of a competitive system in which power was paramount. There were numerous points of conflict between them, and every word at every meeting had to be examined for a hidden meaning that might in the future affect their states' claims or policies. Underneath the smooth, rolling tide of oratorical unity was the Indian-Pakistani dispute over the Kashmir, the Sino-Indian border dispute, Indonesian alarm over the dual-nationality claims of the Chinese in their multiethnic state, Chinese resentment over refuge granted by neighboring states to fleeing and defeated Nationalists, Thai fears of large groups of armed Chinese near their borders, and Burmese suspicions that the Communist government of China was arming and supporting the insurgents that the Burmese government was fighting.

And yet, while keeping all this in mind, the leaders at Bandung kept also in mind that they were leaders of a movement that was greater than the sum of their individual states and that transcended the conflicts between them. There is a genuine wave-of-the-future ring about the oratory at Bandung. It was a fervent and hope-filled outpouring, an international populist paean that had not yet become stale through repetition and that was not yet the cliché of revolutionary hacks maneuvering for personal advantage. Putting China and India to one side, the rest of the states represented at Bandung were weak in the ways that power was usually calculated in the international system, and they attempted to make weakness an advantage by showing that there were different ways to reckon power—non-European ways, Asian ways, which recognized the force of spiritual strength.

Out of this mix of newfound pride and long-standing resentment, of short-term calculations of national advantage and long-term perceptions of a great historical movement, came the rhetoric of Bandung. It is a rhetoric repeated endlessly in the years after 1955 as more and more states achieved independence and as the Eastern bloc socialist states, for reasons of their own, adopted it as a standard form of international political discourse. Little was standard at Bandung. The combination of new states and new leaders made for a heady sense that a new day could dawn. Their struggles were behind them, and their triumphs were sweet. At Bandung the rhetoric was still fresh.

First, they did not want to follow the European way. Prime Minister Nehru of India: "Europe has been in the past a continent full of conflict, full of trouble, full of hatred; and their conflicts continue and we have been dragged in their wars because we were tied to their chariot wheels."[9]

There was a better way, an Asian way. Nehru again: "If there is something that may be called an approach to the minds and spirit of

Asia, it is one of toleration and friendship and cooperation, not one of aggressiveness."[10]

And John Kotelawala, prime minister of Ceylon (Sri Lanka): "I say then, in all seriousness and in all humility that the peoples of this region have it in their power to apply to the problems of the present day world, and for the first time in history, that traditional respect for the spiritual values of life and for the dignity of the human personality, which is the distinguishing feature of all their great religions."[11]

What, then, did it mean to be independent and an Asian state or an African state? It was not simply the trappings of statehood. The right to raise an army and issue postage stamps was not the real issue. Not even the right to be accepted as an equal at the United Nations was the point of the struggle, although that might be part of it. There was more than that, and those who had been the outcasts of the world were peculiarly fitted to define what that "more" might be.

President Sukarno on the meaning of the Indonesian revolution: "We knew how to oppose and destroy. Then we were suddenly confronted with the necessity of giving content and meaning to our independence. Not material content and meaning only, but also ethical and moral content, for independence without ethics and without morality would be indeed a poor imitation of what we sought."[12]

And, finally, Nehru again, speaking of the Final Communiqué issued by the conference: "It represents the ideals of Asia, it represents the new dynamism of Asia, because if it does not represent that, what are we then? Are we copies of Europeans or Americans or Russians? What are we? We are Asians or Africans. We are none else."[13]

These statements place the conference at Bandung in yet a different context: that in which the delegates to the conference saw themselves as potential saviors of the international system through the introduction of the ideals, morality, and ethics peculiar to their part of the world. The concept is striking enough in itself. It is even more striking when the background of these seasoned fighters is considered, a background that was an important part of their credentials for leadership. In their own view, they had started from a position of moral superiority, they had been tested and purified in revolutionary struggle, and they were thus fit to lead the world to better days.

If even half the Bandung rhetoric contained statements of true belief, then the conclusions arrived at by the leaders at Bandung should have been of exceptional interest, not just to Asians and Africans but to every member of the international system. The ten principles they included in their Final Communiqué's Declaration on the Promotion of

World Peace and Cooperation should have broken new ground and offered hope to the world. For those expecting something different, however—something particularly moral and specifically non-Western—the principles are all but inexplicable. What is Asian or African about "respect for the sovereignty and territorial integrity of all nations" (principle 2), or "abstention from intervention or interference in the internal affairs of another country" (principle 3)?[14] So far as distinctiveness goes, they might as well have been written by Léon Bourgeois or Cordell Hull.

Why this gap between rhetoric and performance? There is nothing to indicate that these leaders did not sincerely desire to introduce a new element into international affairs. Where was the slip between desire and outcome? It is a question that goes beyond the leaders at Bandung and addresses the broader issue of the relationship between structure and ethics in the international system. How does the system itself affect what the states do and what they try to do? Light can be shed on that question by looking more closely at the ten principles in the Bandung Final Communiqué. If they do not reflect much that is peculiarly Asian or African, what is it that they do reflect?

There was a great deal of talk about principles at Bandung. The members of the political committee, which framed the Declaration on the Promotion of World Peace and Cooperation, had a repertoire from which to choose. The content of the repertoire was purely political, although an important portion was given a religious gloss by calling it *Panscheel* (or *Panch Shila*), a term out of Theraveda Buddhism. On a personal level, Panscheel was a ceremonial commitment to a set of five moral precepts. At the state level, it became a treaty commitment to a set of agreed-upon principles, in this case to a set called the Five Principles of Peaceful Co-existence. They had been included a year earlier in a treaty between India and China, and they stipulated respect for each other's territorial integrity and sovereignty, nonaggression, nonintervention, equality and mutual benefit, and peaceful coexistence.

The specific occasion for agreement on these principles was a dispute between India and China over trading privileges in Tibet and over the delineation of their common border. The religious terminology was, perhaps, intended to suggest a source and validity that transcended this merely local quarrel and, consequently, that imposed a more binding obligation. However that might be, and however that might affect the Chinese Communists who made a point at Bandung of saying that they were atheists, the Five Principles of Peaceful Coexistence had, by the time of the Bandung Conference, begun to take on an almost mystical significance. This significance had less to do with the stipulated actions and more to do with the position of the Asian and African states in a divided world. For the communist states, *peaceful coexistence* was at the time the official language of approach to the outside world. For the noncommunist states, *peaceful coexistence* was the hope of existing at all and getting on with their own affairs without being attached to the two power blocs.

All of this made it certain that the Five Principles of Peaceful Co-existence would receive serious consideration as the leaders at Bandung tried to agree on principles to promote world peace and cooperation, but their repertoire was larger than that. Prime Minister Gamal Abdel Nasser of Egypt and Prime Minister Mohammed Ali of Pakistan each offered seven principles, Ali's under the title of "Seven Pillars of Peace," one of which was the collective right of self-defense. Chou En-lai reaffirmed China's adherence to the Five Principles of Peaceful Co-existence and in a later statement suggested that they be expanded to include "respect for the people of all countries who choose freely a way of life as well as political and economic systems," and "recognition of equality of races."[15]

These various suggestions, arising from the various and particular interests of the states involved, help to explain the ten principles that were finally made a part of the Bandung Final Communiqué. They help to explain also why there is so little that is distinctive about them. No less than seven of the ten principles address the problems of sovereign states existing in a world of other sovereign states where each defines its national interest on its own terms. The seven: peaceful settlement of disputes, nonintervention, the equality of states, no threat or use of force, respect for sovereignty and territorial integrity, cooperation with other states, and respect for international obligations.[16] In the final analysis, it made little difference whether a state was new or old, African, Asian, or European. The problems for the state as a state were the same, and the principles invoked to help solve the problems were the same as well.

If Bandung were an isolated instance, there would be little point in discussing in such detail the gap between rhetoric and outcome. The pattern of passionate revolutionary proclamation and subsequent affirmation of traditional international principles was, however, a common one in the years after 1955 as new states entered the system and found platforms for their views in the UN and in various regional organizations. At Belgrade in 1961, at Addis Ababa in 1963, at Cairo in 1964, and in later meetings elsewhere, the old system of colonialism and domination was repeatedly condemned, and a new system of freedom, equality, and social justice was repeatedly invoked. The new age was to arrive under the banner of *peaceful coexistence,* a term that by the late 1960s carried as much emotional and symbolic weight as any national flag. Important as this might have been for the self-esteem of states trying to find a place for themselves in a bipolar world, it made very little difference in the structure of that world. The variations on the principles of peaceful coexistence that surfaced in the declarations, programs, and charters produced in such abundance in this period were variations on the familiar themes of equality, nonintervention, territorial integrity, and the like. With one important exception that will be dealt with in the next section of this chapter, the new and non-Western states did not want to change the basic structure of the international system. They wanted to enter it as full and equal members.

The effect on the ethical endeavor in which the older states had been self-consciously engaged since the end of World War I was threefold. The first was to reinforce the demands that the principles of the international system be set out in more detail than they were in the UN Charter. The second was to divert this demand from the old prewar vehicle of the rights and duties of states. The Latin American states and the United States had incorporated a list of state rights and duties in the 1948 charter of their Organization of American States, but an effort to extend this method of articulation to encompass the whole international system brought little response from other states. The need for explicitness and detail was still strongly felt, but a new vehicle of expression was wanted.

After extended debate in UN committees and in the General Assembly, there gradually emerged a focus on the UN Charter itself and a determination to examine the principles listed there and set them out in greater detail as the agreed-upon standards for state behavior and for judgment of that behavior. For the newer states in the system, the most important aspect of the project could be summed up in the words "agreed-upon." Since many of them had not even existed as states in 1945 when the UN Charter was written, this project of examination and expansion gave them a voice in setting out the rules by which they were to be governed. This role was far more satisfying than simply accepting the charter as given, which they had done on becoming members, and they took full advantage of the role. With their strong emphasis on principles, the project was particularly congenial to them.

The third effect of the new states' entry into the international system was—with the single exception that will be dealt with later—to reinforce the traditional elements of the system. Not surprisingly, since they had just achieved statehood, they were concerned with their existence as states. The seven charter principles chosen for consider-

ation by the expanded membership of the UN had the same significance for them as for the older states because the principles were
derived from the same underlying, necessary condition of their existence: independence. Briefly, the principles were: (1) no threat or use
of force, (2) peaceful settlement of international disputes, (3) nonintervention, (4) cooperation, (5) equal rights and self-determination
of peoples, (6) sovereign equality of states, and (7) fulfillment in good
faith of international obligations. The difference from the past was that
the newer and predominantly non-Western states would now be involved in the explication of the principles.

They were not just involved. They were heavily involved. Of the
thirty-one states represented on the special committee that worked
through the principles and put them into final form, more than half
were from the group that by the mid-1960s was identifying itself as
the Group of 77. The group shared several characteristics that tied
it loosely together and sometimes gave it common interests in the
international system. Many of the states were new, most were non-
Western, they were rhetorically nonaligned in the ongoing cold war,
and they were economically less developed than the older states.
Membership of the special UN committee was thus—and was
intended to be—a microcosm of the whole international system. Five
socialist states were represented, nine Western and developed states
(including Japan), and seventeen states from the Group of 77 (see appendix 4).

Debates within the committee reflected the tensions of the cold war
and tensions between the older and newer states, but they reflected
also the seriousness with which the states approached their task.
Since committee members sat as representatives of their governments,
national honor had to be guarded through every exchange, a requirement that lengthened the proceedings considerably. Still, there was
extensive committee discussion of the principles and extensive input
from states that were not members. The committee met in 1964, 1966,
1967, 1968, 1969, and 1970 before it put its recommendations into final form for presentation to the General Assembly on the twenty-
fifth anniversary of the founding of the United Nations. The final form
was entitled, "Declaration on Principles of International Law Concerning Friendly Relations and Co-operation among States in accordance
with the Charter of the United Nations."[17]

The cumbersome title and document scarcely hint at the importance of what had been accomplished. At the beginning of the project
of examination and reformulation, the newer states had made it clear
that they were not comfortable with rules they had had no hand in

formulating. Before the special committee was even formed, and before the decision was made to concentrate on the charter principles, the new states were speaking eloquently of Bandung and of the principles of Panscheel and coexistence, as well as of the eclipse of the idea of a purely Western family of nations with a purely Western code of behavior. The family of nations was now truly universal, and there was a need for a truly universal code.[18] With the declaration that was offered to the General Assembly in the fall of 1970, that need had been met, as speaker after speaker pointed out in the statements of support. The socialist bloc, the bloc of Western and developed states, the Asian, African, and Latin American blocs, all had been involved in the formulation of the principles, and all expressed their support before the declaration was adopted by acclamation.

"Its significance is tremendous," said Paul Engo of Cameroon, who had presented the declaration to the General Assembly. "It represents a monumental advancement for international law, reducing to an absolute minimum the divergencies of view on the scope of the norms and principles enshrined in the Charter. Perhaps more significant, however, is the fact that it represents a symphony of ideas, commanding a consensus in an international community that has undergone substantial change in structure and nature since 1945."[19]

There was indeed unanimous agreement on principles that had essentially been designed by independent states for their own protection in an environment created by their own pursuit of independent goals. Still, this step toward universalization was an important one, and one that was necessary if the code of conduct that the states were developing were not to be seen as an imposition by a small number of states upon the rest of the world. And as it turned out, the code could be made responsive to the changing needs and concerns of an international system that continued to evolve in new and sometimes unexpected ways. That happened in regard to human rights, a subject that will be dealt with in the next chapter. And it happened in regard to the general term *cooperation,* which the new states appropriated and to which they gave a specific and narrowly restricted meaning.

Rhetoric and Content

In its comments on the Dumbarton Oaks proposals for an international organization, the Panamanian government had sounded a note at San Francisco that would be heard more and more frequently in the years after World War II until it became a major theme of the period. The theme was the international economy and what should be done to make it more equitable.

The organization and maintenance of peace, said the Panamanian government, "is identified with the problem of the establishment of a world economic system based on the understanding that the world is a unit of interdependent parts whose equilibrium and progress depend upon an equitable participation by all countries in the productive resources of all of the earth. Economic stability and political security are, consequently, different aspects of the same problem."[20]

Out of their experience with Europe and the United States, the Latin American states could speak for all the less-developed states. From the mid-nineteenth century on, the Latin American states had sought economic development through the importation of capital and technical and managerial skills. Many of the governments had granted exploration and exploitation rights, leases, and franchises on terms that subsequent generations found highly disadvantageous to the state but which they were powerless to change. They also found themselves saddled with debts that the export of commodities and primary products, on which many of the states depended, would not even service, much less reduce. Defaults on development bonds issued and sold on the world market complicated the situation and invited the intervention of foreign governments. Since the full faith and credit of the bond-issuing government was sometimes as shaky as the government itself, the bonds were frequently guaranteed by the banks of the countries where the bonds were being sold to private investors. A default could start a chain reaction from investors to banks to governments and from there to various forms of intervention from gunboats (in the early part of the century) to customs receiverships to interstate commissions that worked out the allocation of what resources were left.

It was a situation in which everyone felt aggrieved, from the private investor in the developed country looking for a steady income to the peasant in the Latin American hinterland looking for a stable market for coffee beans or jute. Governments in the lending countries were pressured by banks, the business community, and individual citizens. Governments in the receiving countries were pressured by nationalist sentiments while they struggled with debts they had not themselves contracted and leases they would not themselves have granted. Relations at the state level were not only complicated by this situation of economic imbalance, they were frequently made tense and antagonistic. Unilateral actions taken by the developed states for debt recovery or by the less-developed states to gain control over their own

economic resources could embitter relations for years, as relations between the United States and Mexico were embittered by the Mexican
government's attempts from 1916 on to gain control of its resources
of oil.

While analyses of the problem were abundant and acute, agreed-
upon solutions were in short supply, and the unsolved problem became part of the general economic disarray of the 1930s. The point
here is that when the new states began to enter the international
system in significant numbers after World War II, their level of development and their status in the economic system were an extension
and a magnification of a situation that had existed before the war. In
their expression of grievances and their struggle to change the system,
they found natural allies in the Latin American states, who knew what
it was to be latecomers to the feast and who had evolved a comprehensive vocabulary of economic disadvantage. When that vocabulary was
joined to the Bandung rhetoric of national pride and particularity, the
result was an outpouring of populist prose on a scale not seen before in
the international system. This prose had a specific purpose. The disadvantaged states wanted to change the structure of the international
economy to one that was more equitable, and they had concrete ideas
as to what constituted the equity they were demanding.

This demand for economic equity is, perhaps, the best known of
the effects of the postwar influx of new states into the system, and it
would be redundant to go into much detail here. The context of their
calls for a New International Economic Order was different from that
in which the Latin American states, by themselves, had called for
economic equity. The few international economic institutions of the
prewar period, such as the Bank for International Settlements, had
been joined by many new institutions, different in scope and purpose,
such as the Bank for Reconstruction and Development (the World
Bank) and the International Monetary Fund, which were not only
involved in the international economic system but which, by their
presence and activities, helped to make that system truly international.

Throughout its existence, the League of Nations had been involved
in studying the international economy and had held a highly successful tariff-reduction conference in 1927 (the effects of which were
nullified by the Depression), but the League's activities cannot compare
with the initiatives undertaken by the United Nations in response to
the new states' demands for economic equity. The special sessions of
the General Assembly, the UN Development Decades, the special international conferences of the UN Industrial Development Organization

(UNIDO), and the institutionalization of the United Nations Conference on Trade and Development (UNCTAD) into a body meeting at regular intervals, all attest to the impact that the new states had on activities in the international system.

Here was an instance in which the new states' rhetoric did not bow to the structure of the system. Instead, the rhetoric was designed to reshape that system in particular ways and recast it in a form that could more adequately meet their passionately felt needs. "The economic gap between the developed and developing countries is increasingly widening—the rich growing richer and the poor remaining poor." So declared the heads of state and government of fifty-three nonaligned countries at their 1970 meeting in Lusaka, Zambia. "World solidarity is not only a just appeal but an overriding necessity; it is intolerable today for some to enjoy an untroubled and comfortable existence in exchange for the poverty and misfortune of others."[21]

The reference to solidarity suggests the ways that the new states' demands interacted with established ideas. The tradition of thought that was part of the states' ethical enterprise offered the new states a language that could be turned to their own use and still seem a familiar part of the ongoing effort. The concept of *interdependence,* for example, was used by the Panamanian government in its comments on the Dumbarton Oaks proposals to justify its call for a world economic system in which there would be "an equitable participation by all countries in the productive resources of all of the earth."[22]

Interdependence was a staple of thought about the international system and, as noted earlier, was at the heart of the dispute over the proper grounding of the principles of the system. Should they be based on the concept of *independence* or of *interdependence?* Those, such as Albert La Pradelle and James Brierly, who had argued that *interdependence* was the only proper base and was, furthermore, nothing more than a recognition of a condition that already existed, had argued in the abstract terms that were usual in such discussions. They might well have been taken aback to find their concept removed from the realm of unthreatening abstractions and given the concrete meaning of a specific kind of world economic order. It was to happen frequently in the years after World War II as the new and disadvantaged states seized on certain abstract and venerable elements in thought about international affairs and turned them to their own immediate and concrete purposes.

The *solidarity* invoked at Lusaka is another example. As originally conceived in the socialist thought of some one such as Léon Bourgeois, who wrote an entire book on the subject, *solidarity* evoked powerful images of the unity and strength of the working classes in their struggle against exploitation.[23] The ideas of unity and of strength through unity remained with the term when it was taken over by the American states in the 1930s and used to denote their determination to present a united front in the face of Fascist aggression. The 1936 Declaration of Principles of Inter-American Solidarity and Co-operation and the 1938 Declaration of the Principles of the Solidarity of America (the Declaration of Lima) set out the terms of "a moral union of all of the American Republics" and recorded the American states' determination to make their solidarity effective through appropriate action "in case the peace, security or territorial integrity of an American Republic is thus threatened by acts of any nature that may impair them."[24]

When the new states came on the scene, the meaning of the term changed again. Still trailing its connotations of a shared status and a unified response, the term became part of the debates over the international economy and took on new color and meaning from that different setting. "World solidarity is not only a just appeal but an overriding necessity," said the heads of state and government at Lusaka, meaning that capital and technology should be transferred immediately from the developed to the less-developed states, with no conditions attached. And to reinforce the point, this from the address of Mexican president Luis Echeverría at the third UNCTAD meeting in Lima in 1972: "We must reinforce the precarious legal foundation of the international economy. It is impossible to have a just order and a stable world until such time as rights and duties are created to protect weak states. Let us remove economic cooperation from the realm of good will and root it in the field of law. Let us transfer the consecrated principle of solidarity among men to the sphere of relations among nations."[25]

Interdependence. Solidarity. Cooperation. All of these terms, which had been used over and over again in international discourse, came to have a specific meaning in the context of demands for a New International Economic Order. Of the three, *cooperation* came to be the preferred term, and *economic cooperation,* when used in this context, meant assistance in the economic development of the less-developed states. The assistance that was asked for—or more usually, demanded, in the rhetoric of the time—varied in nature from the stabilization of commodity prices through international regulation of world markets to the wholesale transfer of technology. Whatever the form and whatever the venue in which the demands were made, the message of the disadvantaged states was clear: assistance was required.

The turmoil and anger of the times when the new states discovered the economic limitations on their newly won political independence were reflected in the stridency of their demands—couched, nonetheless, in the traditional terms of the international system. It is a case where the form was preserved and the meaning was changed. And when the turmoil and anger of the times coalesced into a specific international instrument, the 1974 Charter of the Economic Rights and Duties of States, the form chosen was also a traditional one. Indeed, it could hardly have been more traditional. To cast the entitlements and obligations of states in terms of their rights and duties as members of the international system was to evoke the whole centuries-long effort on the part of philosophers and of the states themselves to bring order and predictability into their anarchic relationships. In this case, the evocation of the past was deliberate. The form had been rejected for the new states' more general concerns, but here they were depending on the favorable connotations of traditional terms to provide legitimacy for the expression of their pressing, present-day economic concerns.

That their concerns were pressing, there was no doubt and very little argument. The argument was over how their concerns were to be answered and their needs met. To set out the response of the international community would require a book in itself; what is needed here is an indication of how the pressing concerns of the economically disadvantaged states and the demands arising from them affected the ethical code that the states were developing.

In the first place, they created a different category in the code, a secondary or auxiliary principle. Not every state was willing to commit itself fully to the principle of the creation of an equitable international economic order, at least not in the terms in which it was set out in the Charter of Economic Rights and Duties of States. When that charter was adopted by the UN General Assembly, six of the developed states, including the United Kingdom and the United States, voted against it. They could subscribe to the general principle of economic equity, but the detailed provisions of the charter intended to facilitate "the encouragement of co-operation on the basis of mutual advantage and equitable benefits for all peace-loving States"[26] could, in their opinion, be seen as of "mutual advantage" only if a wholly novel definition were given to the term *mutual*.

The creation of an equitable international economic order thus became a secondary principle of the code, endorsed as of primary importance by those members of the system who expected the greatest immediate benefit but not by those members whose money and expertise were essential for the undertaking. Since, however, their lack of endorsement was a response to the form in which the principle was given concrete expression, and not a rejection of the principle itself, the principle remained in the code, at a secondary level. The continuing needs of the disadvantaged states, along with the recognition by the international community that at some level of generality the states were indeed interdependent and that cooperation was necessary to solve common problems, insured that the principle would remain a vital one.

The most important contribution made by the new states to the international community's ongoing ethical endeavor was thus the introduction of a singularly dynamic element into the somewhat static, traditional concepts of nonintervention, territorial integrity, and the like. The dynamic element is that of social justice, not for individuals in the area of human rights (as will be dealt with in the next chapter), but social justice for states as embodiments of the collective will and aspirations of their peoples. *Social justice* here is given a particular content: What is meant is *distributive justice,* a concept that opens a world of speculation and discussion on just what is truly a just portioning-out of the world's economic resources and opportunities, and under what circumstances. The needs from which the concept of distributive justice arises and the questions that immediately follow as to what benefits may be involved, and how much, and to whom and by whom provided, insure that the principle of international economic equity will continue to exert pressures for change in the international system as a whole.

The Permanent Presence

In the days of support for new international initiatives immediately following World War I, there was hope that war could finally be banished from the world. Therefore, in their early code-making efforts, the states turned their attention toward creating what the Mexican government called a "Code of Peace"[27]—that is, those international instruments setting out the standards that were to govern state relationships in times of peace. Nineteenth-century writers had divided the subject of international law into two categories: rights and duties of nations in time of peace, and rights and duties of nations in time of war. Now, since there would be no need for principles and rules to govern the conduct of warfare, all that was to change.

Vespasian V. Pella, Romanian subdelegate to the League of Nations, expressed these general hopes in 1927: "This scheme should aim, as has been said, at determining the fundamental conditions of the re-

gime of peace. The irrational division of international law into the law
of peace and the law of war must thus give way to the only law which
can henceforth be conceived: the law of peace."[28]

The "law of peace" is exactly what the states have been striving for,
both in the interwar period and in the period since World War II. This
study would not be complete, however, without at least a mention of
what the states have done to try to regulate the conduct of war. Their
attempts at regulation have drawn on a long and complex tradition of
thought about the subject. The thought derives, ultimately, from a concept of war that relies on just cause for legitimacy, and that stipulates
that war is to be carried out in a humane manner, using no more force
than necessary to achieve the war's limited purpose. The just-war concept has received extensive treatment elsewhere. In fact, most of the
work that deals with the states' efforts to regulate their own behavior
has dealt with this concept and with the states' approach to war. What
will be done here is to relate that approach to what the states have seen
as their basic tasks since World War I: working out and giving meaning
to the principles of peace.

Considering how frequently the states resort to force, the statement
that they have seen peace as their basic objective may seem anoma-
lous. There are many reasons for this apparent contradiction. Sincerity
of intent has often been overbalanced by sincerity of national interest
and even more often by sincerity of grievance. Basically, for whatever
reason, the states have never succeeded in creating an environment in
which they felt safe enough to live together without arms and the resort to arms.

Jonkheer van Blokland, Dutch delegate to the League at the same
time as Pella, neatly summed up the dilemma in one of the League's
perennial discussions of disarmament. He warned that in the world as
it was, no state could possibly disarm without risking its very survival.
If disarmament were not general, it was nothing. And if it were nothing, then each state would have to look to its own defenses: "No State
can act alone. Unless other States support it, it may eventually have to
decide whether it will not be obliged to take measures dictated by its
national interests and to conform, much against its wishes, with the
exigencies of a policy which it considers to be disastrous and which has
been condemned by the League."[29]

Out of this fear, the states arm; and out of the multitude of reasons
they find to justify force, they resort to war. It is the most obvious fact
about their relationship. And yet, speaking in general terms, they no
longer see war as just another instrument of policy. And they do not
view war as the normal state of their relationship in the international

system but rather as a divergence from the norm that must be justified before the eyes of the world in some acceptable way. This point of view helps to explain why, in their code-making efforts, they have devoted so much more attention to matters of peace than to matters of war. Their approach to the regulation of war has at times been a reluctant one because they have feared, by their consideration of the subject, to give the appearance of accepting the very condition they were trying to eliminate.

This point of view also helps to explain why so little was done in the interwar period to update the rules of warfare that had last received thorough consideration at the Hague conference of 1907. From a post–World War II perspective, it would seem that the experiences of World War I, with its submarine warfare, its extended blockades, its use of poison gas on the battlefields and aircraft to bomb cities, would have stimulated a great upsurge in attempts to frame rules to cover these developments. It had had the opposite effect. It stimulated efforts to outlaw war entirely and made states reluctant to admit that rules would be needed for what they were trying to define as a criminal act. From the point of view of these efforts, making such rules would be like setting up rules for the orderly commission of murder.

This is not to say that nothing was done in the interwar period. As noted before, the Geneva Protocol of 1925 banned the use of gases and bacteriological warfare. Two 1929 Geneva Conventions dealt with the treatment of prisoners of war and the treatment of the wounded and sick in the field. The most comprehensive consideration of warfare took place in the various committees preparing for the League-sponsored disarmament conference that opened in 1932. When the conference failed, the work of the committees dropped into the limbo of the failed and forgotten, and the world moved toward war without benefit of a major review of the rules of warfare.

This failure is hard to understand unless it is remembered that even in 1934, when the disarmament conference met for the last time, many of the states in the international system were still hoping that war would not come. There were problems to be dealt with, but the League and the states outside the League had dealt with problems before, and there was still hope that they could so deal again. The legislative bodies of countries in the grip of the Depression were reluctant to spend any money on defense, despite clear indications that Japan, Italy, and Germany were building formidable war machines. This disinclination to spend money on defense was reinforced by powerful public sentiment in favor of peace and an inchoate but strongly expressed feeling that to prepare for war was somehow to legitimize war.

The mood of the interwar period and the confidence with which rules of warfare were excluded from serious consideration by the states can be seen in the thirty projects, mentioned earlier, adopted by the governing board of the Pan American Union in 1925. The first of the projects is a preambular statement that sets the tone for what follows. According to the preamble, "the American Republics are more interested in regulations concerning the peaceful relations of the Nations and neutrality than in those concerning war, in the hope that the latter has happily and forever vanished from the American Continent."[30]

This very fact commended the undertaking to Charles Evans Hughes who, as U.S. secretary of state, was chair of the governing board. His ties with the list of projects were those of organization as well as sympathy. He was a member of the American Institute of International Law that had framed the projects at the request of the Pan American Union, in order that they might be considered by the states at their next inter-American conference. When Hughes presented the projects to the governing board, he praised the fact that considerations of the conduct of war were wholly excluded: "It is significant that the executive committee of the American Institute of International Law has stated that their projects relate to the international law of peace. Their members were a unit in believing that the law of war should find no place in the relations of the American republics."[31]

Very noble, commented Jesús María Yepes, a Colombian member of the International Commission of Jurists, which considered the proposals and modified them for submission to the American states at their conference in Havana in 1928. The commission concurred in the decision to exclude any reference to the laws of war, and Yepes noted, in an observation that could scarcely have made him popular with his fellows on the commission, "This is undoubtedly a very noble and humanitarian point of view, but it does, perhaps, sin against long-standing relationships in international politics."[32]

And then, in a move that must have made him unpopular indeed, Yepes set out some of the realities of those long-standing relationships as they had manifested themselves in the Western Hemisphere: national rivalries, opposing political interests, commercial competition. These had left wounds that appeared to be healed but that needed only a touch to start them bleeding again. When an impartial observer surveys the scene "from the boundaries of Canada to the regions of Tierra del Fuego, he has to conclude that all is not cordiality and good harmony in the relations of those states."[33]

A year after Yepes wrote, a border skirmish between Bolivian and Paraguayan troops lent point to his observation. Four years later, the point was underlined in blood as Bolivia and Paraguay embarked on a full-scale war over the Chaco territory that lay between their two states. To the fullest extent that their resources allowed, they reenacted World War I, with trench warfare and aerial bombardment as essential elements of combat. Meanwhile, Colombia and Peru were exchanging shots and recriminations over the district of Leticia, important to both states because of its direct access to the Amazon.

The point is not that the relationships of Latin American states were any worse than those of the rest of the world. The point is, they were exactly the same. In the interwar period, war was a permanent presence on the international scene, as it continued to be after World War II. Its presence was so prominent and its forms so diverse after World War II that the old definition of war as a state of legally declared hostilities between states had to be modified to the more general and inclusive term of "armed international conflict."

The two Latin American conflicts were eventually settled—the Leticia conflict much more rapidly than the Chaco War, which dragged on until 1935—but international order continued to be shaken by the better-known conflicts of the 1930s, until it was shattered entirely by the onslaught of World War II. The war was fought along lines that disregarded many of the oldest rules of warfare: the use of means proportionate to the ends to be achieved, humane treatment of prisoners of war, combat immunity of religious and hospital personnel, the rights of inhabitants of occupied territories, the protection of noncombatants.

If the states *had* been willing to undertake a comprehensive review of the rules of warfare during the interwar period, that would not, of course, have guaranteed observance by the belligerent states. By not doing so, however, they lost what chance there was for compliance. More importantly, they lost the opportunity to try to frame the rules in such a way as to make them workable in conditions of modern warfare.

In World War II these were conditions of total war. The French chamber of deputies and the French senate had foreseen as early as 1928 that a future war between the great powers would take the shape of total war, and they had tried to prepare for it by drawing up a plan for the mobilization of the nation. When the rapporteur for the bill presented it to the senate, he set out in vivid terms what it was that the states feared: "The conception of *la guerre totale,* which is the formula that we have to envisage in the future . . . this conception condemns the peoples who tomorrow may find themselves engaged in a fresh conflict to find that their efforts can no longer be limited to the action of armed masses, but that they must be ready to throw into the battle, in order to snatch victory out of it, the totality of their forces and resources."[34]

Such a conception of war blurs at the outset any distinction between combatants and noncombatants and military and nonmilitary targets, a distinction that in World War II was not only blurred but often lost altogether. In revulsion at what happened, the states began an extended effort after World War II to expand and reaffirm the rules for the protection of noncombatants and the care of those no longer able to fight, and to put some actions completely outside the bounds of the permissible by making those who committed such acts criminally liable. Thus we have the Charter of the International Military Tribunal (1945) and the 1950 affirmation by the UN General Assembly of the principles of the charter of the Tribunal and of its judgment at Nuremberg. There is also a 1948 convention against genocide and four 1949 conventions, known as the Geneva Conventions, designed to strengthen the protection of victims of war. Two 1977 protocols attempt to extend protection to victims of new types of warfare and weapons.

This list is not comprehensive. It is intended to do no more than suggest the degree of attention that the states have paid since World War II to working out limits and restraints on their own use of force. While almost all states in the international system have agreed to the four Geneva Conventions, the 1977 protocols have not found nearly that level of agreement. They are legally in force, but in practical terms they cannot function as the universal standards intended until agreement is more nearly universal.

The problem the protocols present is at once specific and general. Specifically, many of the newer states have insisted on defining as international armed conflicts those situations in which "peoples are fighting against colonial domination and alien occupation and against racist regimes in the exercise of their right of self-determination."[35] Many of the older states have argued that the terms of this bit of Bandung rhetoric are so ill-defined that they could as easily cover acts of terrorism as popular movements for liberation, and who would be the judge?

In general terms, the problem goes much deeper than this controversy over the terms of 1977 Protocol I. The problem lies in the conflicting purposes that the states bring to the task of setting restraints on the use of force. They want to have it both ways: justification of their own use, condemnation of others'. Given this basic desire to retain as much freedom of action as possible while restraining others as much as possible, it is remarkable how much the states have accomplished since World War II in setting out principles and rules, regulations and restraints to cover the ever-present use of force in the international system. Year by year, despite the changing numbers in the system and the constant shifting of policies and priorities, the ground of common agreement has grown. It is considerably larger and better defined than it was before World War II, and this despite the states' repeated insistence that the basic purpose of their code-making efforts is to discover and set out the principles and rules, not for war, but for peace.

It is, in fact, in their consideration of the conditions of peace that the states have made their greatest contribution to the evolving code of international ethics. Their treatment of war has been more conventional, being chiefly directed, as noted above, to restraints on the methods of warfare. They have also given the old concept of just war three specifically modern meanings: the right of a state to self-defense, the duty of states to participate in collective action against aggression, and the right of peoples to struggle against oppression to achieve self-determination.

These considerations on the just uses of force are relatively simple. By contrast, the states' reflections on the conditions for what might be termed a "just peace" are complex and extraordinarily detailed. Much of their thought about a world where a just peace prevails can be found in that part of the code that shifts the focus from states to people. The underlying principle has been repeated so often that it has a banal quality, but this last principle to be discussed, "respect for human rights and fundamental freedoms," has an unpredictable, dynamic quality that can rise above banality and repetition—as the states have frequently discovered. The principle poses the basic question of the relationship of people to the states of which they are a part, and that, in turn, poses the even more basic question of the significance, if any, of this whole effort by the states to set out standards of international behavior.

6 Peoples and States

A people of 70,000,000 suffers but does not die.
German declaration upon signing the Armistice, 1918

Publicity alone will enable the League of Nations to extend a moral sanction to the contractual obligations of its Members.
Memorandum, Council of the League of Nations, 1920

We the peoples of the United Nations . . .
Preamble, United Nations Charter, 1945

The participating States recognize the universal significance of human rights and fundamental freedoms . . .
Principle 7(5), Final Act, Conference on Security and Cooperation in Europe, 1975

Throughout their efforts to create the code of international ethics that is the subject of this study, the states have paid close attention to self-definition. As the chief actors on the international scene, the question of who or what constitutes the collective entities that will be acting there is naturally of vital interest to them. On the subjects of legitimacy, recognition, successor governments, membership in international bodies, and the like, volumes have been written and numerous discussions held in order to come to at least a rough general agreement. The continuing emergence of groups that claim state status insures that the question of state definition will remain a vital one as the states continue to work out standards for their relationships.

What, then, of the people on whose behalf the states are presumed to be acting? Here definitions are fuzzy or nonexistent. Much state attention has been given to citizenship and residency requirements, but answers to the larger question of the states' views on who or what these people are, taken collectively, must be inferred, since definitions are rarely given. "People," "the public," "peoples"—the references found or implied in the first three quotations at the head of this chapter each has a different meaning and each implies a different relationship to the states of which they are part. As a further complication, the several meanings also imply different relationships to the international system itself, a question that states did not have to deal with in the past but that is now very much to the fore. The fourth quotation above, dealing with the status of human rights, is an attempt by the states to deal with this question while hewing firmly to "stateness" as the essential characteristic of the international system.

One way of untangling these conceptual complications is to trace the development of thought about people from the German declaration of 1918 to the Conference on Security and Cooperation in Europe (CSCE) Final Act of 1975. That development is not a straight line progression; rather, it is a cumulative process, with later ideas being added, willy-nilly, onto earlier conceptions or forced into institutions designed to express entirely different approaches. Sometimes the earlier conceptions drop temporarily from sight, only to surface again when circumstances are propitious or it is to someone's advantage to revive them. It has been that way, for example, with the conception of the people as identical with the state, an idea that has never completely disappeared and that continues to find international expression. Analytically speaking, the result is a muddle, and yet it is possible to pick out some major themes from this tangle of conflicting and overlapping concepts. Those themes are the focus of this chapter.

In the 1920s, while the states were engaged in working out new international approaches and habits of cooperation, human beings collectively in relation to this cooperative endeavor were seen as "the public." It was public opinion that was to be both the guiding and legitimating force for international action by the states. Thus the relationship was one of collective supervision by the public and, when necessary, admonition. Like the gods of old, the public was to keep a watchful eye, administer reproofs if needed, and, by approval, give sanction to international proceedings. The states' central position was assured by the assumption that the members of the public would make their views known and bring pressure to bear on the states of which they were a part.

The turbulence of the 1930s was reflected in a confusion of thought about human beings and their relationships to states and to the international system. On the one hand, the idea of the people as the watchful public continued throughout the decade and found concrete expression in mass demonstrations for peace, in isolationist legislation, in the British peace ballot of the mid-1930s, and in official fear of public outcry if defense budgets were raised. On the other hand, there was a revival of an idea that had not received much attention during the 1920s, namely, that the people were coexistent with and, collectively, identical to the state. When the German signers of the 1918 Armistice observed that "A people of 70,000,000 suffers but does not die," they were talking about the German state. Along with the resurgence of power of some states in the 1930s came a resurgence of the idea of state-people identification and a renewed and aggressive interest in the rights that a state could claim on the people's behalf.

Reaction against this trend by other states in the system was slow in coming before World War II. There was plenty of criticism by nonstate actors of the trend of ideas and events, but the states themselves stayed for the most part within the restraints imposed by the knowledge that today's enemy may be tomorrow's friend. They were muted in criticism even when it became clear that some governments were, through discriminatory laws and outright persecution, bent on defining "people" in their own narrowly conceived terms and consigning the rest to a kind of civil nonexistence—if they were allowed to exist at all.

This behavior focused renewed attention on the relationships of human beings to the states in which they lived. As the persecutions of the late 1930s mounted, the states themselves began to join the anguished reexamination of relationships, even though doing so might mean trespassing on the sacred ground of sovereign prerogatives. No state was anxious to tread anyway but softly there, or even to tread there at all, since comments on the internal affairs of another state invited retaliatory examination and comment. By 1938, however, the situation, especially in Germany, was such that traditional diplomatic restraint and the preservation of formal civilities were not felt to be adequate. These two conflicting impulses, the desire to speak out and the circumspection of habit, can both be seen in the proceedings of the Eighth Conference of American States, meeting in Lima, Peru, in 1938. Through their delegates, the states declared: "In accordance with the fundamental principle of equality before the Law, any persecution on account of racial or religious motives, which makes it impossible for a group of human beings to live decently, is contrary to the political and juridical systems of America."[1] And by implication such persecution *ought* to be contrary to the political and juridical system of any other region of the world as well, or why bring the subject up? No one was accusing the *American* states of making it impossible for any group of human beings to live decently.

The experiences of World War II entirely breached traditional walls of caution, and after the war there was a flood of state-sponsored reflections on the proper relationship between human beings and the state, beginning with two 1948 declarations, the American Declaration of the Rights and Duties of Man and the Universal Declaration of Human Rights. This change of attitude was signaled at the San Francisco conference by the drive already mentioned, a drive to include in the UN Charter a specific listing of universal human rights. It was signaled in another fashion by the adoption of a preamble to the charter that differed in a particularly significant way from the preamble that had been proposed.

The Dumbarton Oaks proposals for an international organization had not included a preamble. Since the larger purposes and principles of an international agreement are usually set out in a preambular statement, many states, especially those in the British Commonwealth, felt it important to include such a statement in the charter of the international organization being planned at San Francisco. They turned to Jan Christian Smuts for suggestions, and he proposed a text that would, he hoped, stir the hearts as well as the minds of those who had suffered, and were still suffering, in yet another world war.

For Smuts there was a strong sense of "once more into the breach." In 1945, as Prime Minister of South Africa, he was head of the South African delegation to the San Francisco conference. In 1919 he had been a member of the British delegation to the Paris Peace Conference, after having served throughout the war as a member of the British Imperial War Cabinet. For the second time in his lifetime the European continent was devastated, and the rules for state behavior painstakingly wrought through centuries of experience and reflection had been shattered or cast aside. And this time the devastation was not confined to Europe but was widespread in Asia as well.

In 1945, South Africa did not have the tarnished international reputation it was later to acquire, and Smuts could feel he was speaking on behalf of the whole world when, in his proposed preamble, he spoke of renewed international determination "to prevent a recurrence of the fratricidal strife which twice in our generation has brought untold sorrow and loss upon mankind, and to reestablish faith in fundamental human rights, in the sanctity and ultimate value of human personality, in the equal rights of men and women and of nations large and small."[2]

For those with any sense of the efforts made by the people of Smuts's generation to avoid the very situation that had brought them all to San Francisco, there was a special poignancy in his confidence that such a faith could be reestablished. Smuts had signed the 1919 peace treaty with great reluctance because of its punitive provisions and had issued a public statement widely reproduced and quoted by people who shared his doubts. The saving feature of the treaty for Smuts, and for the many who felt as he did, had been the covenant with its provisions for the establishment of the League of Nations. At the time, he had warned that the League was only a form. "It still requires the quickening life, which can only come from the active interest and the vitalizing contact of the peoples themselves"[3]—an interest and a contact that had not been forthcoming.

Now, at age 75, Smuts was ready to try again. In his proposed preamble to the charter, however, he said nothing about people or peoples, either because they had failed the first time around or because he held to the traditional view that sovereignty was derived from and inherent in the very existence of the state and that only a state could make international commitments of this nature. His eloquently expressed determination to prevent a recurrence of war and to reestablish faith in fundamental human rights was set out in the preamble as the determination, not of the peoples of the world, but rather of "the high contracting parties" to the charter agreement.[4]

In the preamble as finally adopted, much of Smuts's wording was retained, but the phrase "the high contracting parties" was changed to the now-familiar "We the peoples of the United Nations." The change was an extraordinary departure from the traditional form of international instruments. It reflected, in part, the desire of the United States delegation to echo the opening words of the U.S. Constitution, but the support of other states cannot be wholly explained as being a courtesy to the United States. There also was a feeling that the people who had fought and were fighting the war should at least be acknowledged in the charter of the organization that was to keep future peace. The change from "high contracting parties" to "we the peoples" advocated by the United States was also supported by the Soviet Union, China, and a number of Latin American states.

The change was, however, too much for some states to stomach. They objected strongly to the vagueness of the phrasing and to its lack of standing in international law. And backed by the legal advisers at the conference, they managed to return the charter to an emphasis on states. At the end of the preamble, following a list of a number of aims of "the peoples of the United Nations," they inserted a qualifying statement: "Accordingly, our respective governments, through representatives assembled in the City of San Francisco, who have exhibited their full powers found to be in good and due form, have agreed to the present Charter of the United Nations and do hereby establish an international organization to be known as the United Nations."[5]

This was an aesthetically awkward but politically realistic compromise between those who pointed out that states were the primary actors in the international system and those who responded that states were only the vehicles for the will of the people, from whom political legitimacy was derived. That people were included at all in such a document was a testament to yet another concept of the relationship between human beings and the state. Here human beings, taken collectively as *peoples,* were linked in two different ways and in two different directions. They were linked to each other across state lines through their joint resolve to combine their efforts in order to achieve certain aims. They were linked to their own state governments through the need for suitable political instruments to accomplish these aims.

The inclusion of *peoples* as initiators and parties to an international agreement may have been regarded by some states as a mere rhetorical flourish, born of the high emotion of the moment and not to be taken seriously. In the late 1960s and on into the 1970s and 1980s, however, some people began to take seriously indeed the notion that the governments of their states were to be serviceable instruments through which collective international goals might be accomplished. Here at last was a sign of that "active interest and vitalizing contact of the peoples themselves" for which Smuts had vainly called in 1919. It was an interest and a contact that many states were not pleased to see shifted out of the realm of rhetoric into the arena of international life.

The old idea of people as identical with the state persisted after the second world war, as it had after the first. In a hypothetical and plural form it was written into the UN Charter in the stipulation of "respect for the principle of equal rights and self-determination of peoples"[6]— the assumption being that any people, given free choice, would choose to be a state. The powerful appeal of the identification of people and state can be seen in the whole decolonization movement of the post–World War II period and in the resolutions and declarations that continue to pour out of the UN General Assembly and other international forums. Most of these statements are couched in very general terms, such as this caveat from a 1987 General Assembly declaration that "nothing in the present Declaration could in any way prejudice the right to self-determination, freedom and independence, as derived from the Charter, of peoples forcibly deprived of that right."[7]

There is no denying the emotional resonance of such a statement, nor its hold on the states. They have affirmed it on every possible occasion. There is also no way of knowing exactly what is meant by the statement until circumstances demand that decisions be made and action taken. It is through specific choices that the fluid concepts of peoples, states, rights, self-determination, and the like are given definite shape and more precise definition. For now it is enough to point out the persistence and strength of the idea that the state is the people writ large and then to note the effect of that idea on other ideas about people, states, the international system as a whole, and the relationships of one to the others.

Warders at Large

At a meeting of the commission writing the Covenant of the League of Nations, Ferdinand Larnaude raised what he thought was a routine question regarding treaty interpretation. One of the provisions of the covenant was that member states, by accepting the covenant, thereby abrogated all other treaty obligations inconsistent with those of the covenant. There was, however, no covenant provision that addressed the question of how this was to be determined. Larnaude's question was a simple one: Who was going to decide whether or not a treaty was inconsistent with the covenant?

Woodrow Wilson was chairing the meeting, and his answer came with the calm assurance of one who has seen the future. "That decision," he said, "will lie with the court of public opinion."[8]

Dropping his voice, Larnaude turned to Léon Bourgeois, the other French delegate, who was seated beside him. "Tell me, my friend, am I at the Peace Conference or in a madhouse?"[9]

Larnaude was dean of the law faculty at the University of Paris. To someone with his background, Wilson's answer must indeed have suggested a certain remoteness from reality. It was more than a little remote from the international system with which Larnaude was familiar, in which the interpretation of a treaty was a technical matter to be investigated and decided by experts such as himself. From Larnaude's point of view, what did the public have to do with the question?

From Wilson's point of view, the public had everything to do with this and every other question that might arise, since the public was central to what the commission was attempting to do. Nor was Wilson alone in this view. It would be hard to overstate the importance of the role that the public was supposed to play in the new international order being planned at Paris in 1919. Peace and justice were the goals of the new order. The League of Nations was the vehicle through which these goals were to be achieved. Public opinion was to keep the goals steadily in view and bring its full pressure to bear on the states of the international system if they should stray from or falter in the path.

As this summary suggests, the public's involvement in the new international order was to be indirect. It was to make itself felt through expressions of approbation or displeasure and through an indication of its desires and the policies it was prepared to support. When the Covenant of the League was being drafted, the question of direct involvement of the public through elections to a special organ of the League was considered and discussed at some length before being discarded as impracticable. Wilson noted the problem when he presented the draft of the completed covenant to a plenary session of the peace conference in February 1919: "It was impossible to conceive a method or an assembly so large and various as to be really representative of the great body of the peoples of the world, because, as I roughly reckon it, we represent as we sit around this table more than twelve hundred million people."[10]

The framers of the covenant were aware, however, of what Wilson called "the practically universal opinion" of people around the world that, in the new international organization being planned at Paris, there should be "a door left open to a variety of representation instead of being confined to a single official body with which they might or might not find themselves in sympathy."[11]

Two provisions of the League covenant were designed to address this "practically universal" desire of the people for some control of and involvement in the new system of international relationships. The first was the method of representation in the Assembly, the deliberative body of the League. Each state was to have only one vote in the Assembly but was allowed to have three delegates. These delegates could be chosen in any way that the state desired, and the hope was that public pressure for representation would force the states to select some delegates from outside the usual official and diplomatic pool.

The determination of most foreign offices to keep international affairs firmly in professional hands frustrated this idea from the start. In many countries there was already a competition between the cabinet ministers who were presumably in charge of foreign affairs and members of the permanent foreign office staff with their entrenched positions and their almost total confidence in their understanding of the international scene. Whatever their other disagreements, the ministerial side and the professional side could unite in refusing to add members of the public at large to this already-complicated foreign policy mix.

The second provision for involvement in the activities of the League cast the public in the indirect role mentioned above. This provision took the form of a requirement that all treaties concluded by members of the League, whether with each other or with non-League members, should be registered with the League Secretariat. No treaty would be considered binding until it had been so registered. Further, the registered treaties were to be published under League auspices as soon as possible.

Far from being the dry procedural requirement that it might appear, this provision of the League covenant embodied part of the framers' deepest hopes for the future. Collective security was only the backup tactic on the way to a new international order; it was to be used rarely, and then in cases where the need was extreme and everything else had been tried. In contrast, public opinion was to be the constant companion and guide on this journey to peace and justice. To be effective as a guide, however, that opinion had to be informed—hence the requirement for treaty registration and publication. Secret deals between states, secret combinations against other states, quiet provisional agreements for territorial appropriations and divisions, all were to be things of the past.

Some idea of the hopes that were invested in public knowledge can be gained from the Council memorandum quoted at the head of this chapter. The memorandum was issued by the League Secretariat as one of its first official acts and reads in part:

Publicity has for a long time been considered as a source of moral strength in the administration of National Law. It should equally strengthen the laws and engagements which exist *between nations.* It will promote public control. It will awaken public interest. It will remove causes for distrust and conflict. Publicity alone will enable the League of Nations to extend a moral sanction to the contractual obligations of its Members. It will, moreover, contribute to the formation of a clear and indisputable system of International Law.[12]

If the public were to play the key role allotted to it, full and accurate information was a necessity. After some initial hesitation about Council proceedings, League practice moved steadily toward a policy of the fullest possible disclosure. In a retrospective view of the first ten years of League activity, the Secretariat stated the philosophy underlying this policy: "Broadly speaking, interest and support will depend upon the League's accomplishments, and, at a moment of crisis, upon the equity of its decisions. The League's main force is publicity, in the sense of public discussion and public documents by which world opinion may judge the results. The League recognizes this. It opens its doors and makes information available."[13]

The Assembly, and the six basic committees through which the Assembly conducted its affairs, met in public. Most of the Council meetings were open to the public, as were most of the meetings of the Council's standing and advisory committees. The many conferences sponsored by the League were public. The reports and minutes of the meetings of those bodies such as the Mandates Commission, which met in private, were all published. As more and more members of the press were assigned to Geneva, the Secretariat created a special section, the Information Section, to facilitate the work of journalists through the translation, duplication, and distribution of League documents and press releases, and through arrangements for the on-site transmission of news stories to the journalists' home offices.

The League's efforts at gathering information and conveying it to the public were complemented by the work of new voluntary associations and specialized publications started after the war to fill what was widely perceived as a pressing need. In the United States, this was the impetus for the founding of the Council on Foreign Relations and the Foreign Policy Association. Toward the latter part of the 1920s, the Catholic Association for International Peace was founded as a research organization to prepare reports for dissemination and discussion, "to help American public opinion, and particularly Catholics, in the task of ascertaining more fully the facts of international life and of deciding more accurately what ought to be done that the relations between nations may become just, charitable and peaceful."[14]

In Great Britain, immediately after World War I, the Institute of International Affairs was formed to take up the task of studying "the relation between national policies and the interests of society as a whole" and with these findings to educate the public, since "the passions which embroil nations against each other and wreck civilization all have their roots in the ignorance born of isolation."[15]

The conveying of information was only part of what these organizations and publications had in mind. They were also trying to help create a new way of looking at international affairs. As the founding statement of the Institute of International Affairs noted, "Until recent years it was usual to assume that in foreign affairs each government must think mainly, if not entirely, of the interests of its own people. In founding the League of Nations, the Allied Powers have now recognized that national policies ought to be framed with an eye to the welfare of society at large."[16]

Such a change in the formation of national policies would require a change in the attitude of the national publics that would be called on to support the policies. This change of public attitude was the goal of many official and unofficial groups during the interwar period, particularly during the 1920s. It was the impulse behind the founding in 1927 of the quarterly *L'Esprit International,* published by the European Center of the Carnegie Foundation for International Peace. The very title, "The International Mind," epitomized this approach to the public.

The journal epitomized something else as well, and that was the realization on the part of some that access to the public was not a monopoly of those trying to create an informed public opinion and a new way of looking at international affairs. *L'Esprit International* had as its specific purpose counteracting government efforts at influencing public opinion. The editorial committee of the journal noted that governments had learned that they could not ignore public opinion, and so they attempted to shape and direct it to their own ends. Often, governments tried to inflame their own citizens against the peoples of other states. This, said the committee, was dangerous to everyone. Public opinion ought to be, rather than a divisive force, "the grand moral force that sustains the work of peace."[17]

A "grand moral force," or an easily manipulated chauvinism? This question hung over all attempts to give the public watch and ward over the future of the new international order. Ferdinand Larnaude's inquiry about treaty interpretation had raised the question in a particularly pointed form in the meeting of the League of Nations commission. Would even the English or the Americans, he asked Wilson with polite incredulity, want to give public opinion the power to decide technical questions regarding their *statute* law?

The reply to Larnaude's question was a lecture by Wilson on the superiority of the public over the courts on an issue such as treaty interpretation. In this instance, interpretation was not so much technical as moral, being simply a case of deciding on the validity of already-existing treaties in light of the new relationships established by the League covenant. Wilson observed, "Matters which relate to the good faith of nations are extremely delicate; in such a case the only sanction is that of public opinion. The Courts of Justice make their decisions according to the rules of law, and in such a matter as this the moral judgment of peoples is more accurate than proceedings before a tribunal."[18]

To which Milenko Vesnitch, the Yugoslav delegate, replied with a restrained delicacy of his own that public opinion was often shaped by powerful outside forces toward unpredictable ends: "Public opinion is pliable and fluid and of such a nature that propaganda can mould it."[19]

In these conflicting views of public opinion, the power of that opinion was taken for granted. The need to take public opinion into account when planning the new international order was also taken for granted. The conflict turned on whether the public occupied the high moral ground that Wilson and other framers of the covenant assumed that it did, or whether its residence was a considerably lower abode, vulnerable to attack and annexation by forces inimical to peace. In either case, the response that seemed to be demanded was a continuing flow of full and accurate information so that the public, first, might have the facts necessary to make informed judgments and, second, might begin to relate differently to international affairs and thus begin to think in ways that were different from the past.

By 1930 this change in thinking still had not happened, to the regret of those who were most attentive to such matters, since the success or failure of their undertakings depended to a large extent on public support. "There is a rough stratum of universal opinion," the League Secretariat noted, "but the moment has not arrived when international questions can in practice be dealt with on a foundation of international thought."[20]

Beyond the problems of agreeing on just what public opinion was and deciding on its nature and proper role was the problem suggested by the Secretariat's reference to "international thought." Exactly what was *international thought?*—not in the general terms of awareness of a community that transcended the boundaries of the nation-state but, rather, as regards the specific problems with which the League had to deal year after year. What was the international view of the location of the boundary between Albania and Yugoslavia? Did the international mind sympathize with Poland or with Lithuania in their conflicting claims to the city of Vilna? Where did international thought come down in the matter of enlargement of the membership of the League Council, and who—internationally speaking—should get the extra seats?

It was easy enough to see such matters in traditional terms. National affinity provided ready orientation and a guide for public opinion. What, though, did it mean to have an international orientation? Was it, as the League's enemies charged, nothing more than an attachment to the status quo and an expression of the fervent wish that everyone would just be quiet and not disturb the peace?

In a pair of lectures given in Lisbon shortly before his death, Nicolas Politis reflected upon such questions. The relationship of the League to the governments of the member states and to the public at large was a matter of great concern to him. Looking back on his long service with the League, he concluded that there were two chief reasons for the League's demise: the attachment of the states and of the people within those states to the idea of sovereignty—which they interpreted as freedom of action—and the failure on the part of League officials and advocates to understand the strength of that attachment. There was no such thing as the public at large, he concluded. There were only many separate national publics. In Geneva, agreements were worked out that were thought best for the international community as a whole. These agreements were sent to the member states, where they promptly foundered in the seas of national politics.

You could, said Politis, make two charts that would illustrate the downward path of the international system from 1919 to 1941. On one chart would be the "principal steps in the decline of the Treaty of Versailles and the League of Nations system." On the other chart, and matching each of these steps in decline, would be "a political event in one of the Great Powers—an election, or the eve of an election; a ministerial crisis, or the threat of a crisis; the formation of a cabinet or the reshuffling of a cabinet; etc., etc."[21]

And so, at the last, in the opinion of one of the most experienced and sympathetic participants in the experiment of the League, it was the public who had undermined this first systematic attempt at international cooperation and organization—that public on whom the framers of the League covenant had relied to balance and restrain the selfish inclinations of states. Afraid always of public displeasure, the governments of the states had insisted for twenty years that they could not make this or that concession, that they could not disown this or that violent act, because if they did they would surely be swept from office by an outraged public whose moral judgment seemed, for the most part, to have found its outlet in strong national feeling.

The question of what constituted *international thought* remained an open one, to be taken up again after World War II and taken in directions not imagined by those of Politis's generation and convictions. By that time, the concept of the *public,* with its connotation of watchful spectatorship, had been largely replaced by the concept of the *people* or *peoples,* a very different idea.

There was authority in the word *people,* an authority that derived from sovereignty itself. Through the years, sovereignty had devolved from the Divine, to the Church Universal, to a single head of state, and, finally, to the populace. When, after World War II, some of the people began to involve themselves directly in shaping the second system of international cooperation and organization, they shaped it in new ways. Unlike the internationalists of the interwar period, they were not chiefly concerned with preserving peace between squabbling states. Instead, they devoted their efforts, and sometimes gave their lives, to asserting the universality of certain values for the people within those states. In word and action they said that there are problems that transcend state boundaries and that people everywhere have a stake in those problems. *International thought,* in the context that these people created, took on a precise and vital meaning it had never attained during the days of the League.

Rhetoric and Action

In October 1929 the Institut de Droit International adopted a Declaration of the International Rights of Mankind in which were set out certain minimum standards to be guaranteed to every person in every state. These included such civil and political rights as life and liberty, the ownership of property, equal protection under the law, and freedom of conscience. According to the preamble, the declaration was a response "to the conscience of the civilized world which demands the recognition of the rights of individuals, rights that are beyond the reach of the state."[22] To this end, the declaration laid duties on the states to recognize and protect these rights and to see that they were enjoyed by everyone in the territory of the state's jurisdiction. As one commentator remarked with satisfaction, the Institut's declaration had made the states' duty to guarantee certain human rights a duty that was owed not just to their citizens but to the whole international community.[23]

It would be nineteen years before the Universal Declaration of Human Rights brought the states close to this thinking with its assertion that the declaration was "a common standard of achievement for all peoples and all nations."[24] It would be forty-one years more before even a portion of the states admitted that their human rights responsibilities were to a wider community, extending beyond their borders. The fact that this position was first articulated by a private group (in modern terms, a nongovernmental organization) is typical of the development of the human rights component of this code of international ethics. No other portion of the code owes so much to the interaction between private individuals, nongovernmental organizations, and the states themselves.

This portion of the code is also the best known, and it has been the subject of a number of comprehensive studies that set it within a philosophic context. Human rights, as philosophic constructs, are not the focus of this discussion. Rather, the focus is on the relationship of such rights to the rest of the code and the effect of their inclusion on the concepts of peoples and states noted earlier in this chapter.

What is frequently overlooked in discussions of this subject is that the various civil, political, social, economic, and cultural rights for human beings articulated by the states, especially since 1945, were not set down upon a blank page. They were inserted into a thickly textured mesh of already-existing state rights and duties to which the states were bound by the strongest possible tie, that of survival. As has been shown in this study, there was precedent for the welfare of human beings to be a part of this interlocking mesh of articulated rights, but historically that part had been small. After World War II, this relationship changed drastically as human rights began to be set out in unprecedented abundance and detail in international instruments of every conceivable form.

A glance at the list of some of the components of the code of international ethics (appendix 1) will show the predominance of the human rights dimension since 1945. Of the fifty-three international instruments and declarations listed for the period 1945 through 1989, a little more than ninety percent deal in some fashion with the rights of human beings, either as individuals or as members of groups. In seventeen cases this is a general reference, as in the first principle of the 1955 Bandung Final Communiqué, "Respect for fundamental human rights and for the purposes and principles of the Charter of the United Nations."[25] In thirty-one other instances, as in the 1950 (European) Convention for the Protection of Human Rights and Fundamental Freedoms or the 1981 African Charter on Human and Peoples' Rights, the specification of the rights of human beings, as the titles indicate, is the whole purpose of the instrument.

Even statements that focus on other international concerns almost always, since World War II, include a reference to human rights. Thus, participants in the first meeting of nonaligned states in 1961, chiefly concerned with their own precarious position between the power blocs of East and West, took time to affirm their "absolute respect" for the rights of ethnic or religious minorities to be protected against any violation of their fundamental human rights.[26] And when it adopted a declaration in 1987 to enhance the effectiveness of the principle prohibiting the threat or use of force in international relations, the UN General Assembly felt compelled to note that even though it was talking about force, it was also bearing in mind "the universal significance of human rights and fundamental freedoms as essential factors for international peace and security."[27]

There are two major reasons for this post–1945 outpouring of instruments reflecting human rights concerns. First, the experiences of World War II and of the years immediately preceding the war made clear the terrible vulnerability of human beings in unequal contest with the state. Revelations of brutal conduct as a part of official state policy were all the more shocking because they undercut the assumption of progress that had provided unconscious assurance that such brutalities were in the past. Reaction was strong, and it was prolonged. Individuals and private groups, as well as many of the states, sought ways to buttress the position of human beings vis-à-vis the state.

Second, many of the ongoing concerns for social justice and for the protection of human rights that have been mentioned in this study were taken up with renewed vigor after World War II. They became part of the drive to, on the one hand, bind the states of the international system to observance of clearly articulated human rights and, on the other hand, stimulate action by the states to provide opportunities and services to which human beings were entitled. The International Labor Organization, which survived the war, was joined in its active pursuit of social justice and human rights by a host of organizations with related concerns, many of them with ties to the United Nations, particularly to its Economic and Social Council.

The human rights project of the post–World War II period was thus a joint project in which individuals and private organizations, as well as states, were deeply involved. How this worked out in practice can be seen by looking briefly at the long-term effort to establish as a universal standard the civil, political, and legal equality of women with men. This was not a major theme of the states' efforts at standard setting in the interwar years, but they could not ignore it completely. The subject was kept alive as an international issue by private advocates who made repeated demands on international bodies, beginning right at the beginning with the commission to draft the Covenant of the League of Nations. Early in April 1919 a delegation from the International Council of Women presented a memorial to the commission and spoke strongly in favor of the equal suffrage for which they had been battling in their respective states for many years. They also urged the appointment of women both as delegates to and officials of the League. The response of the commission was bland and noncommittal. The delegates were told that these were excellent ideas and that equal suffrage was a principle of the plebiscites being held under provisions of the various peace treaties.[28]

In a pattern that was to become fairly common during the interwar period, advocates of legal equality for women then began a drive through the international conferences of American states, a drive that, in turn, stimulated and merged with efforts through the League and, finally, became part of the groundswell of human rights activity following World War II. This private initiative brought pressure through international organizations (first, the Pan American Union, then the League of Nations, and, finally, the United Nations) for states to take action in establishing universal standards for the treatment of human beings. In this instance, the people whose interests were in theory being represented by the states set out to make it so in practice. They took the initiative and prodded the states to address their areas of concern.

It is instructive to look at the list of private groups that were involved, in one way or another, with the Women's Consultative Committee established by the League in 1931. The list includes: the Inter-American Commission of Women, the International Council of Women, the International Alliance of Women for Suffrage and Equal Citizenship, the Women's International League for Peace and Freedom, Equal Rights International, World Union of Women for International Concord, the All-Asian Conference of Women, and the International Federation of University Women. In addition, there were the Acción Feminista Dominicana, the Six Point Group (England), the Ligue des Droits de Femmes (France), the Open Door Council (Germany), the Alianza Nacional Feminista (Cuba), the National Woman's Party (United States), the Subcommittee of Brazilian Women, the Brazilian Federation for the Advancement of Women, and the International Federation of Business and Professional Women.[29]

The list has been given at length to show how, even in the interwar period, many private individuals and groups from many different countries were pressing for the articulation of certain international human rights standards. In this period in particular, and in this area of action, the states were more responders than initiators. Some segments of the public, whatever their attitude toward the bulk of the League's activities and the problems with which it had to deal, perceived the possibility for the advancement of their own concerns through an international organization, and they acted accordingly.

After World War II this attitude became much more widespread, and such activities multiplied. Individuals and groups concerned about educational opportunities, racial discrimination, religious intolerance, the rights of children, social policies, welfare benefits, cultural freedom, and a whole range of other matters, pressed for international action and were involved every step of the way from initial demand to final international declaration or agreement. It was in this way, for example, that protection of the environment was added as an auxiliary principle to the code of international ethics.

Concerned that the states were lagging behind in addressing environmental problems, some groups in the private sector brought enough pressure that the states felt compelled to take action. One response was the convening of a special conference on the subject, the

United Nations Conference on the Human Environment, held in Stockholm in 1972. Even at Stockholm, however, where the environment was the focus, environmental concerns were put in terms of the rights of human beings. As the first principle of the Stockholm Declaration put it, "Man has the fundamental right to freedom, equality and adequate conditions of life, in an environment of a quality that permits a life of dignity and well-being."[30]

In the atmosphere of openness to human rights concerns that prevailed after World War II, those who had worked for women's legal equality finally got the international action they had been demanding. The Universal Declaration of Human Rights and other general rights statements had, of course, included women as possessors of those rights and entitlements, but supporters felt that something more was needed. Beginning in the 1950s, the UN General Assembly turned its attention to the special problems faced by women, addressing the problems with a Convention on the Political Rights of Women (1953), a Convention on the Nationality of Married Women (1957), a Declaration on the Elimination of Discrimination against Women (1967), and a convention on the same subject (1979). The International Labor Organization was also involved, with a Convention Concerning Equal Remuneration for Men and Women Workers for Work of Equal Value (1951).

For its significance to be seen, this abundance of standard setting needs to be set against the early 1930s, when advocates of women's equality labored, usually in vain, for one simple change in the prevailing norms. They wanted a woman to have the right to retain her own nationality after marriage to a nonnational, if she chose to do so, and to transfer her nationality, equally with her husband's, to their children. The right to nationality was a major issue for women of that period. The reasons are suggested by a provision of one of the 1919 peace treaties regarding a choice of nationality: "Option by a husband will cover his wife, and option by parents will cover their children under eighteen years of age."[31] German, Austrian, Hungarian, and Russian residents of Poland were, by the provisions of this treaty, to be allowed to decide whether to accept Polish nationality or to choose any other nationality open to them—a statement that has to be immediately qualified by the proviso, adult *male* residents were to be allowed to decide.

Resentment at this kind of discrimination provided emotional fuel for the long battle for international recognition of the rights of women, as for recognition of the rights of dozens of other disadvantaged groups and for the rights of human beings in general. And the rage that this kind of discrimination engendered was a force that had to be reckoned with—as the states were to discover, especially after World War II. When, in 1933, Margarita R. de Mendoza of Mexico told the gathering of official delegates at the Seventh International Conference of American States, *"We demand our rights because they are ours,* and you must give them to us if you hope to maintain your principles of justice and honor,"[32] she may have been one of a lonely few. She was, however, a forerunner of those who made similar demands on states in the 1970s and 1980s, especially following the signing of the Helsinki Accord.

The Final Act of the Conference on Security and Cooperation in Europe, signed in Helsinki, Finland, in 1975 and better known as the Helsinki Accord, provides an outstanding illustration of the changing relationship of peoples to states in light of the code of international ethics that the states themselves have developed over the years. Much of the language of the Final Act reads like any other international instrument in which national interest asserts itself through qualifiers and ambiguous phraseology. Much of the substance of the accord differs from the usual state agreement, however, and that difference is important. The opening section, Declaration on Principles Guiding Relations between Participating States, is a short and effective summary of the code of behavior that is the subject of this study.

Here are the state rights that are, in the words of the declaration, "inherent in sovereignty," but here also—and on the same level of importance—are "respect for human rights and fundamental freedoms, including the freedom of thought, conscience, religion or belief."[33] The *respect* that is stipulated for human rights is not left at that high level of generality. Later in the document it is given specific content through provisions for the reunification of families across cold war borders, marriage between citizens of different states, regular meetings of families divided by state lines, freedom of travel for personal or professional reasons, greater access to and exchange of information, improved conditions for tourists and for journalists, increased cultural exchanges, etc. Finally, and as it turned out, most importantly, there were provisions for a continuation of the work of the conference through meetings at which progress would be reviewed. This provision, too, was made specific, with the date and place of the first meeting stipulated as part of the accord.

There were thirty-five signatories to the Helsinki Accord: all the states of Europe except Albania, plus Canada and the United States. At the time the Accord was signed, there was a slight thaw in the ongoing cold war between the Western and Eastern blocs, and the states purpose of the conference was "to make détente both a continuing and an increasingly viable and comprehensive process, universal in scope."[34] A continuing and increasingly viable and comprehensive process did develop in the years after 1975, but it was not the process envisioned by the signers. For what became "universal in scope," so far as Europe was concerned, was not détente, which faded quickly in the late 1970s, but demand for the human rights that had, in this agreement, been elevated to the same status as state rights.

The CSCE reviews of progress developed along two lines, institutionally connected but conceptually distinct. Gradually they evolved into a flexible means by which negotiations could be carried on by members of separate and competing groups such as the North Atlantic Treaty Organization and the Warsaw Pact. At the same time they became increasingly prominent forums for discussion of human rights concerns across state boundaries. This development was a direct result of the fact that people in both the Eastern and Western blocs seized on the human rights provisions of the Helsinki Accord and demanded that the signatory states live up to their commitments. Helsinki Watch groups sprang up in the Soviet Union, Czechoslovakia, Poland, and other eastern European states. In the United States, the U.S. Commission on Security and Cooperation in Europe, with members from both the executive and legislative branches, was formed specifically to monitor compliance with the human rights provisions of the accord.

This public reaction caught the foreign offices of most of the states concerned by surprise. The United States had been a reluctant participant from the start, the policy makers of that period being more concerned with containment of Soviet expansion and influence than with cooperation. Since the Western allies insisted, however, the United States was willing to go along, limiting the damage as far as possible and regarding the ten guiding principles as just another instance of the ethical rhetoric that was so popular a feature of the postwar period. The states of Western Europe saw the CSCE conference from the point of view of those on the potential front line. They placed great emphasis on the security measures outlined in the accord since, should détente finally and completely break down, they would be the battlefields in any war between East and West. As for the Eastern bloc states and their rulers of 1975, what they wanted was agreement on the third principle, the inviolability of frontiers. That would set the seal of international approval on the status quo in Eastern Europe, a status quo that had depended on Soviet military dominance and, until Helsinki, had been legitimated only by agreement among the Big Three wartime allies at Yalta in 1945.

The fact that the Eastern bloc rulers wanted international approval of a situation that they had maintained for thirty years without that approval was, in itself, a sign that times were changing. So was the fact that they sent representatives to the subsequent review conferences at Belgrade and Madrid, despite their knowledge that human rights violations would be brought to the fore. The violations were brought forward by the Western states because by the time of the review meetings the Western states had realized that the Eastern bloc's commitment to the human rights provisions of the Helsinki Accord gave them an effective weapon to use in the public forum of a review.

This realization came, however, only after groups of private citizens in both the East and the West had made it clear that they took these commitments seriously and expected the governments of their respective states to take them seriously, too. In this respect, the Helsinki Watch groups of the 1970s and 1980s had an advantage over Margarita R. de Mendoza who, in 1933, could only demand rights for women on the basis of justice and honor. The grounds for the Helsinki Watch demands were state commitments, publicly made. The Watch groups were not impressed with the argument that the Helsinki Accord was not formally a treaty and was, therefore, not legally binding. Legality was not the point. Human rights were. Neither confiscation of property, police harassment, imprisonment, nor the death of some of their members could convince these groups to give up their struggle.

When this struggle was at length picked up at the state level in the West, that, too, was partly in response to public pressure, often from professional groups that had maintained ties with their counterparts in the Eastern bloc countries. It was a case where the people led and the states followed. The rhetoric of human rights, often paraded since World War II, had proved to be a stimulus for action, and that action could not be ignored. At the 1989 Vienna review conference, the states of the CSCE reaffirmed the principle of the "universal significance of human rights and fundamental freedoms"[35] that they had all approved in the 1975 Helsinki Accord, and the changed context gave the words new meaning.

In 1989 the governments of the whole Eastern bloc were being shaken by the winds of change as the reality of human rights in that area was forced closer to the rhetoric of human rights. Because people had acted to see that the states were indeed the instruments of the general will that they claimed to be, human rights had become a communitywide concern. As U.S. secretary of state George Schultz noted regarding the Vienna review conference, it "has created a mechanism permitting any country to raise any human rights issue with any other country at any time."[36]

It had been a long road from the 1929 Institut declaration to the concluding document of the Vienna review conference, but the states of the CSCE finally arrived at the conclusion that Institut members had come to sixty years earlier: a state's duty to guarantee to its citizens certain basic human rights was a duty not just to those citizens but to the international community of which the state was a part. That being so, the cry of intervention could not legitimately be raised against international comment and pressure.

Under the League covenant, any state had had the right to direct the attention of the international community to any situation that threatened international peace and security. Under the Vienna Concluding Document, any of the thirty-five states of the CSCE could call attention to any situation that threatened human rights in any of the CSCE countries. Action by people and then by states had succeeded in putting concern for the welfare of individual human beings on the same level of importance as traditional concerns about international peace and security. Whether such a move would become a general rule of the whole international system, a standard for that system to aspire to, or a subsystem rule of the CSCE alone remained to be seen.

What was clear was that people, especially in the Eastern bloc states, had seized on the rules that the states had said should apply and demanded that the states apply them. The states of the West had joined the campaign, using state-level tools of diplomatic pressure and then, at the review conferences, public disclosures of human rights violations—a move that threw the initiative back to the people again. The Helsinki Accord provided the framework for an intricate interplay of actions by people and actions by states. The actions were sometimes adversarial, sometimes cooperative, but they were always mutually dependent. Year by year, through this complex set of interactions, new relationships were created between peoples and states. Because the people had acted, the states had been obliged to act. Because the states had acted, the principles and rules they had devised with such care became something more than mere rhetoric. If only in this limited time and place, they became the guides for action and the standards for judgment that they were supposed to be.

The Continuing Process

The American columnist and political philosopher Walter Lippmann once remarked that, in politics, there can be no concluding chapter because in politics there is always more future out in front than recorded history behind. At no point is there a pause where all mysteries are solved and every idea finds its proper place.[37]

If this is true of politics taken by itself, it has particular force when the subject is the effort to bring politics and ethics into a working relationship. Ideally, politics keeps ethics from becoming so abstract that it is of no use in the real world, and ethics keeps politics from becoming nothing more than an amoral contest of force and guile. This ideal situation is easier to imagine than to achieve, and there will be no attempt here to tidy up and tie off what is essentially a messy and continuing process. What *will* be attempted is a temporary stance outside the process. From that position the argument of this book can be summarized and suggestions made as to its place in the ongoing global conversation about international affairs.

The argument began with three questions:
—Are there ethical standards that apply to relations between states in the international system?
—If there are such standards, are they or can they be universal, given the diversity of cultural traditions represented in the international system today?
—If such standards exist and they are universal, what difference does it make, since the most obvious rule of behavior followed by the states is that of self-interest?

This study has been devoted to answering these questions. If that effort has succeeded, then it should be clear that there *are* ethical standards that apply to relations between states. The standards are not a set of theoretical propositions but are, rather, the outcome of the states' own reflections on their own behavior. Since these standards have been considered and confirmed by states from the several major cultural traditions represented in the present international system, they are truly universal. And, finally, the standards matter because without them the whole question of judging the behavior of states would become a matter of individual preference. The standards provide a common ground for evaluation, and in the particular case of the Helsinki Accord, they provided a common ground for action.

Before proceeding, it may be useful to list again the nine basic and two auxiliary principles that were set out in the Introduction. The nine fundamental principles on which the states are agreed:
1. Sovereign equality of states
2. Territorial integrity and political independence of states
3. Equal rights and self-determination of peoples
4. Nonintervention in the internal affairs of states

5. Peaceful settlement of disputes between states
6. Abstention from the threat or use of force
7. Fulfillment in good faith of international obligations
8. Cooperation with other states
9. Respect for human rights and fundamental freedoms

The two auxiliary principles on which there is broad, but not universal agreement:

—Creation of an equitable international economic order

—Protection of the environment

What is interesting about the first nine of these principles is not that the states follow all of them all of the time, or even some of the time, but that they exist at all and that the states reconsider and reaffirm them time after time. Governments come and go. New states make new demands upon the system. Weapons and strategies change their forms, if not their functions, and technology continues its headlong rush to make interdependence less of a rhetorical flourish and more of a daily fact. Through it all, these nine principles remain at the core of state reflections, a solid and enduring base for the states' code of international ethics.

The term *code* is accurate in one sense and misleading in some other senses. *Code* conveys the necessary quality of stability and agreement—these are the principles on which the states can agree—but it misses the inherent dynamic quality. That quality has been noted several times in this study, but it is so important that it will be pointed out again. Neither the code nor the states are exempt from the pressure of events. As the code was formed under pressure, so it changes under pressure. Now one and now another principle is emphasized. Different contexts give different meanings, which in turn give rise to different actions and results, as, for example, with the principle of self-determination that had one outcome for the Aaland Islanders in 1920 and a different outcome for the inhabitants of the Saar in 1935.

A principle such as the sovereign equality of states remains more or less unchanged through the years as it is steadily asserted as a balance to the obvious role that power plays in the international system. On the other hand, a principle such as the cooperation of states, while it looks the same from year to year, may have many different meanings. In the UN Charter, *cooperation* is the principle under which respect for human rights and fundamental freedoms is subsumed. For the new states coming into the system after 1960, the principle of *cooperation*, as this study has shown, took on quite a different, specifically economic, meaning.

There is another way in which the word *code* is misleading. It is a shorthand term for a large and complex body of thought, and while it may provide a way into that thought, it in no way encompasses it, any more than the Ten Commandments encompasses Judaism. One way of suggesting that larger context is to say that here is an international culture in the making. It rests on the ground of agreement that is necessary for any culture to sustain itself, an agreement on fundamental values. The goals of this culture are as clear as the principles and rules on which it relies to attain its aims. Those goals are peace, security, and justice. At the head of this international trinity is the goal of peace. "What does peace require of us?" is the basic question that the states have been asking, and the ethical code that has been studied here is the shorthand response to their sustained effort over the past seventy years to answer that question.

In the process of working out this response, the states have also created a complete imaginary world. It is a mythical world of extraordinary richness. In dozens of international instruments the features of this world have been portrayed right down to the smallest detail. Little has been overlooked in this figuring forth of the perfect lives and the perfect international system that will result when everyone abides by every ethical stipulation.

Children born into that world will have nothing to fear. They and their mothers will enjoy special protection, and means will be provided for the children to develop along physical, mental, spiritual, moral, and social lines. All of this will take place within an atmosphere of love and understanding, and moral and material security.[38]

Education for the children will be widely available, and in the primary grades it will be free. Further, this schooling will be available to everyone; there will be no discrimination on the basis of race, sex, language, religion, national origin, or political opinion. Education will have a double purpose. The children's natural abilities will be developed and strengthened so that they may lead full and satisfying lives. They will also be taught to be fully responsible members of society and of the international community at large. To this end they will be taught tolerance and understanding so that they may live in a spirit of friendship with all nations.[39]

As the children reach adulthood, they will be free to marry whomever they please, with no limitations because of race, nationality, or religion. The marriage will be with the free and full consent of both parties. The rights, privileges, and responsibilities of the marriage will be shared equally between the man and the woman, making it a true partnership of equals. The married couple will be free to found a family, and since the family is recognized as the natural unit and basis of society, it will be protected by the state. The family's role as the custodian of morals and of the community's traditional values entitles it to such protection.[40]

This world of the states' imagining is filled with entitlements: civil, political, religious, economic, cultural, social. Supported by these rights, which cannot be alienated or abridged, the citizens of this world live out their abundant and satisfying lives. They work at fulfilling jobs in safe and pleasant surroundings, where they are free to express their opinions and to join fellow workers, if they wish, in associations for their mutual benefit. They can worship or not, just as they please. They need never be hungry, nor out of work, nor without a home. When they are sick, they will be cared for. When they are old, they will be sheltered and protected so that they may live out their lives in dignity and comfort.[41]

When this world comes to be, there will be no inequity between rich and poor, whether individuals or states. The fruits of technology will be available to all. The wide distribution of capital and resources will insure that the equality of the states is an actual fact, not just a juridical fiction. There will be no discrimination in this world, no torture, and no genocide. No state will threaten any other state nor intervene in its affairs. Disputes will be resolved peacefully through conciliation, arbitration, or adjudication, and the disputants will abide by the judgments that are given. When problems occur, the states will cooperate to find and implement a solution.[42]

Above all, there will be peace. That is the center of the mythical world, its reason for being. And peace is also the justification given by the states for most of the principles and rules of their code of international ethics. As if in recoil from the force and bloodshed that have characterized their relations through the centuries, they have dwelt at length and lovingly on peace: the conditions for peace, the nature of peace, the desirability of peace. They have put their reflections into the code that has been the subject of this study and have said that the code is to guide their behavior and to serve as a standard of judgment.

In the short term, the states' efforts may seem to make no difference at all, but in the long perspective of history, this code of international ethics stands as a possible bridge between the world the warlords have made and the world the warlords have dreamed. Whether or not the bridge is crossed will depend entirely on what states and peoples decide to do in the future being shaped even as these words are being written and read.

Appendix 1

Major International Instruments from Which the Principles of the States' Ethical Code Are Drawn

		Source*
1. Covenant of the League of Nations	1919	16a
2. Polish minority treaty (as an example of the type)	1919	16c
3. Constitution, International Labor Organization (ILO)	1919	16b
4. Treaty to avoid or prevent conflicts between the American states (Gondra Treaty)	1923	14a
5. Declaration of the rights of the child	1925	15a
6. Antislavery convention	1926	14b
7. General treaty for renunciation of war	1928	14d
8. Pacific settlement of international disputes	1928	14e
9. General Convention of inter-American conciliation	1929	14f
10. General treaty of inter-American arbitration	1929	14g
11. Convention concerning forced or compulsory labor	1930	19a
12. Convention on rights and duties of states	1933	14h
13. Convention on the nationality of women	1933	2a
14. Antiwar treaty of nonaggression and conciliation	1933	14i
15. Additional protocol relative to nonintervention	1936	14k
16. Declaration of principles of inter-American solidarity and cooperation	1936	11a
17. Convention for the maintenance, preservation, and reestablishment of peace	1936	14j
18. Fundamental principles of international policy	1937	23a
19. Declaration in favor of women's rights	1938	11e
20. Declaration against persecution for racial or religious motives	1938	11d
21. Declaration of American principles	1938	11b
22. Declaration of the principles of the solidarity of America	1938	11c
23. Atlantic Charter	1941	2b
24. Declaration by the United Nations	1942	2c

(*continued*)

*See pp. 170–72 for key to sources.

Source

25. Dumbarton Oaks Proposals	1944	7a
26. Declaration concerning the aims and purposes of the International Labor Organization	1944	4a
27. Pact of the League of Arab states	1945	8a
28. Declaration on reciprocal assistance and American solidarity	1945	6a
29. Charter of the United Nations	1945	2d
30. Convention on the prevention and punishment of the crime of genocide	1948	19c
31. Convention on freedom of association and protection of the right to organize	1948	19d
32. Charter of the Organization of American States (OAS)	1948	22a
33. American declaration of the rights and duties of man	1948	3a
34. Inter-American charter of social guarantees	1948	10a
35. Universal Declaration of Human Rights	1948	19b
36. Convention on the right to organize and collective bargaining	1949	19e
37. UN affirmation of the charter and judgment of the International Military Tribunal at Nuremberg	1950	20a
38. European human rights convention	1950	4b
39. Convention concerning equal remuneration for men and women workers for work of equal value	1951	3b
40. Protocol amending the slavery convention	1953	22b
41. Convention on the political rights of women	1953	22c
42. Affirmation of the American declaration of the rights and duties of man	1954	5a
43. Five principles of peaceful coexistence	1954	1a
44. Final communiqué of Asian-African conference	1955	1b
45. Supplementary convention on abolition of slavery	1956	22d
46. Convention on the abolition of forced labor	1957	19f
47. Treaty establishing the European Economic Community	1957	18a
48. Employment and occupation discrimination convention	1958	19g
49. Declaration of the rights of the child	1959	19h
50. Convention against discrimination in education	1960	19j
51. Declaration on the granting of independence to colonial countries and peoples	1960	19i
52. Declaration of the heads of state or government of nonaligned countries	1961	13a
53. Declaration of Punta del Este	1961	3d

(*continued*)

		Source
54. European Social Charter	1961	3c
55. Convention on equality of treatment in Social Security	1962	3e
56. Social policy convention	1962	3f
57. Charter of the Organization of African Unity	1963	4c
58. Declaration on the elimination of all forms of racial discrimination	1963	19k
59. Final act, United Nations Conference on Trade and Development (UNCTAD I)	1964	21a
60. Program for peace and international cooperation	1964	21b
61. Employment policy convention	1964	19l
62. International convention on the elimination of all forms of racial discrimination	1965	19m
63. Declaration on the inadmissability of intervention in the domestic affairs of states	1965	20b
64. International covenant on economic, social and cultural rights	1966	19n
65. International covenant on civil and political rights	1966	19o
66. Optional protocol to the international covenant on civil and political rights	1966	19p
67. Declaration of the Association of Southeast Asian Nations	1967	12a
68. Proclamation of Teheran	1968	19q
69. Vienna convention on the law of treaties	1969	4d
70. American convention on human rights	1969	3g
71. Declaration on principles of international law concerning friendly relations and cooperation among states	1970	4e
72. Declaration of the United Nations conference on the human environment	1972	9a
73. Charter of economic rights and duties of states	1974	4f
74. Final act, Conference on Security and Cooperation in Europe (Helsinki Accord)	1975	3h
75. African Charter on Human and Peoples' Rights	1981	17a
76. Single European Act	1986	18b
77. Declaration on the enhancement of the effectiveness of the no-force principle	1987	12b
78. Additional protocol to the American convention on human rights	1988	12c
79. Concluding document, Vienna meeting, Conference on Security and Cooperation in Europe (CSCE)	1989	12d

Sources for International Instruments

1. *Asian-African States: Texts of International Declarations.*
   New Delhi: Scindia House for the Indian Society of International Law,
   1965.
   1a   Five principles (1954), 1.
   1b   Final communiqué (1955), 2–10.
2. Bevans, Charles I., comp.*Treaties and Other International Agreements of the
   United States of America, 1776–1949.* 12 vols. Washington, D.C.: G.P.O.,
   1968–.
   2a   Nationality of women (1933), 3:141–44.
   2b   Atlantic Charter (1941), 3:686–87.
   2c   United Nations Declaration (1942–45), 3:697–98.
   2d   UN Charter (1945), 3:1153–95.
3. Brownlie, Ian, ed. *Basic Documents on Human Rights.* 2d. ed. Oxford:
   Clarendon Press, 1981.
   3a   American Declaration of the Rights and Duties of Man (1948),
         381–87.
   3b   Equal remuneration (1951), 200–203.
   3c   European Social Charter (1961), 301–19.
   3d   Punta del Este (1961), 388–90.
   3e   Social security (1962), 212–18.
   3f   Social policy (1962), 219–27.
   3g   American Convention on Human Rights (1969), 391–416.
   3h   Helsinki Accord (1975), 320–77.
4. *Brownlie, Ian, ed. Basic Documents in International Law.*
   Oxford: Clarendon Press, 1983.
   4a   Aims and purposes of the ILO (1944), 71–74.
   4b   European human rights convention (1950), 320–38.
   4c   Organization of African Unity (1963), 76–84.
   4d   Law of treaties (1969), 349–86.
   4e   Friendly relations (1970), 35–44.
   4f   Economic rights and duties (1974), 235–49.
5. *Foreign Policy Bulletin* 33 (1 May 1954).
   5a   Affirmation of the American Declaration of the Rights and Duties
         of Man (1954), 8.
6. *Foreign Policy Reports* 21 (1 May 1945).
   6a   Declaration on reciprocal assistance (1945), 49–50.
7. Goodrich, Leland M., et al. *Charter of the United Nations: Commentary and
   Documents.* New York: Columbia University Press, 1969.
   7a   Dumbarton Oaks Proposals (1944), 665–74.
8. Hassouna, H. A. *The League of Arab States and Regional Disputes.* Dobbs
   Ferry, N.Y.: Oceana Publications, 1975.
   8a   Pact of the Arab League (1945), pp. 403–10.
9. Henkin, Louis, et al. *Basic Documents Supplement to International Law,
   Cases and Materials.* 2d ed. St. Paul, Minn.: West Publishing, 1987.
   9a   Declaration on the Human Environment (1972), 633–39.

10. International Conference of American States. *Final Act of the Ninth International Conference of American States, Bogota, Columbia, 30 March–2 May 1948.* Washington, D.C.: Pan American Union, 1948.
  10a   Social guarantees (1948), 29–38.
11. *The International Conferences of American States, First Supplement, 1933–1940.* Washington: Carnegie Endowment for International Peace, 1940.
  11a   Inter-American solidarity (1936), 160–61.
  11b   American principles (1938), 309–10.
  11c   Solidarity of America (1938), 308–9.
  11d   Racial and religious persecution (1938), 260.
  11e   Women's rights (1938), 250–51.
12. *International Legal Materials.*
  12a   Association of Southeast Asian Nations declaration (1967), 6:1233–35.
  12b   Enhancement of the no-force principle (1987) 27:1672–79.
  12c   Additional protocol, American Convention on Human Rights (1988) 28.156–89.
  12d   Concluding document, Vienna meeting, CSCE (1989), 28:527–66.
13. Jankowitsch, Odette, and Karl P. Sauvant, comps. *The Third World without Superpowers: The Collected Documents of the Non-Aligned Countries.* 4 vols. Dobbs Ferry, N.Y.: Oceana Publications, 1978.
  13a   Non-aligned declaration (1961), 1:3–7.
14. League of Nations. *Treaty Series.* 205 vols. London: Harrison, 1920–46.
  14a   Gondra Treaty (1923), 33;25–45.
  14b   Antislavery convention (1926), 60:253–70.
  14c   Civil strife (1928), 134:45–63.
  14d   General treaty for the renunciation of war (1928), 94:57–64.
  14e   Pacific settlement of international disputes (1928), 93:343–63.
  14f   Inter-American conciliation (1929), 100:401–15.
  14g   Inter-American arbitration (1929), 130:135–60.
  14h   Rights and duties of states (1933), 165:19–43.
  14i   Antiwar treaty (1933), 163:395–413.
  14j   Maintenance of peace (1936), 188:9–29.
  14k   Nonintervention protocol (1936), 188:31–51.
15. League of Nations. *Official Journal,* spec. supp. 23. Records of the Fifth Assembly, Plenary Meetings, *Text of the Debates.* Geneva: 1926.
  15a   Declaration of the rights of the child (1925), 177.
16. Parry, Clive, and *Consolidated Treaty Series.* 231 vols. Dobbs Ferry, N.Y.: Oceana Publications, 1969–81.
  16a   League Covenant (1919), 225:195–206.
  16b   ILO (1919), 225:373–86.
  16c   Polish minority treaty (1919), 225:412–24.
17. Sieghart, Paul. *The Lawful Rights of Mankind.* Oxford: Oxford University Press, 1985.
  17a   African Charter on Human and Peoples' Rights (1981), 231–37.

18. *Treaties Establishing the European Communities.* Luxembourg: Office for Official Publications of the European Communities, 1987.

18a   Treaty establishing the European Economic Community (1957), 119–323.

18b   Single European Act (1986), 527–76.

19. United Nations. *Human Rights: A Compilation of International Instruments.* New York: United Nations, 1983. UN Publ. ST/HR/1/Rev. 2.

19a   Forced labor (1930), 65–69.

19b   Universal Declaration of Human Rights (1948), 1–3.

19c   Genocide convention (1948), 56–59.

19d   Freedom of association (1948), 114–16.

19e   Right to organize (1949), 116–18.

19f   Forced labor (1957), 70–71.

19g   Employment discrimination (1958), 32–33.

19h   Rights of the child (1959), 129–30.

19i   Colonial independence (1960), 20.

19j   Discrimination in education (1960), 33–36.

19k   Racial discrimination (1963), 22–23.

19l   Employment policy (1964), 123–24.

19m   Racial discrimination (1965), 23–29.

19n   Covenant: Economic rights (1966), 3–8.

19o   Covenant: Civil rights (1966), 8–15.

19p   Optional protocol (1966), 16–17.

19q   Proclamation of Teheran (1968), 18–19.

20. United Nations. *Official Records of the General Assembly.*

20a   Affirmation of Nuremberg principles and judgment (1950), resolution 488 (V), suppl. 20:77

20b   Inadmissibility of intervention (1965), resolution 2131 (XX), suppl. 14:11.

21. United Nations. *Proceedings of the United Nations Conference on Trade and Development, Geneva, 23 March–16 June 1964.* 8 vols. New York: United Nations, 1964.

21a   Final act, UNCTAD I (1964), 1:3–65.

21b   Peace and international cooperation (1964), 1:66–68.

22. United Nations. *Treaty Series.* New York: United Nations, 1947–.

22a   OAS Charter (1948), 119:3–97.

22b   Amending the slavery convention (1953), 182:51–72.

22c   Women's political rights (1953), 193:135–73.

22d   Supplemental slavery convention (1956), 266:3–87.

23. United States Department of State. *Foreign Relations of the United States, 1937.* 5 vols. Washington, D.C.: Department of State, 1954.

23a   Fundamental principles (1937), 1:699–700.

Appendix 2

1933 Convention on Rights and Duties of States

Article 1. The state as a person of international law should possess the following qualifications: a) a permanent population; b) a defined territory; c) government; and d) capacity to enter into relations with the other states.

Article 2. The federal state shall constitute a sole person in the eyes of international law.

Article 3.The political existence of the state is independent of recognition by the other states. Even before recognition the state has the right to defends its integrity and independence, to provide for its conservation and prosperity, and consequently to organize itself as it sees fit, to legislate upon its interests, administer its services, and to define the jurisdiction and competence of its courts.

The exercise of these rights has no other limitation than the exercise of the rights of other states according to international law.

Article 4. States are juridically equal, enjoy the same rights, and have equal capacity in their exercise. The rights of each one do not depend upon the power which it possesses to assure their exercise, but upon the simple fact of its existence as a person under international law.

Article 5. The fundamental rights of states are not susceptible of being affected in any manner whatsoever.

Article 6. The recognition of a state merely signifies that the state which recognizes it accepts the personality of the other with all the rights and duties determined by international law. Recognition is unconditional and irrevocable.

Article 7. The recognition of a state may be express or tacit. The latter results from any act which implies the intention of recognizing the new state.

Article 8. No state has the right to intervene in the internal or external affairs of another.

Article 9. The jurisdiction of states within the limits of national territory applies to all the inhabitants.

Nationals and foreigners are under the same protection of the law and the national authorities and the foreigners may not claim rights other or more extensive than those of the nationals.

Article 10. The primary interest of states is the conservation of peace. Differences of any nature which arise between them should be settled by recognized pacific methods.

Article 11. The contracting states definitely establish as the rule of their conduct the precise obligation not to recognize territorial acquisitions or special advantages which have been obtained by force whether this consists in the employment of arms, in threatening diplomatic representations, or in any other effective coercive measure. The territory of a state is inviolable and may not be the object of military occupation nor of other measures of force imposed by another state directly or indirectly or for any motive whatever even temporarily.

[Articles 12 through 16 are concerned with ratification and denunciation procedures, and with the relationship of this treaty to other international obligations.]

Signed, 26 December 1933 at Montevideo, Uruguay, by the delegates of Argentina, Brazil, Chile, Colombia, Cuba, the Dominican Republic, Ecuador, El Salvador, Guatemala, Haiti, Honduras, Mexico, Nicaragua, Panama, Paraguay, Peru, the United States, Uruguay, and Venezuela. It entered into force a year later, and remains in force.

League of Nations Treaty Series 165:19–31

Appendix 3

Career Characteristics of International Lawyers, 1918–1983: A Select List of 66 Lawyers from 24 Countries

	A	B	C	D	E	F	G	H	I	J	K	L	M	N	O	P	Q	R	S
Adachi Mineichira 1869–1934, Japan					x	x		x	x	x									
Alfaro, Ricardo 1882–1971, Panama		x	x	x	x								x				x	x	
Alvarez, Alejandro 1868–1960, Chile		x	x	x			x				x	x	x	x				x	x
Azevedo, José 1894–1951, Brazil			x															x	x
Badawi, Abd al-Hamid 1887–1965, Egypt			x	x										x				x	x
Barbosa, Ruy 1849–1923, Brazil	x			x	x	x	x	x											
Basdevant, Jules 1877–1968, France			x		x		x	x						x				x	x
Baxter, Richard 1921–1980, United States		x																x	x
Borchard, Edwin 1884–1951, United States			x	x							x	x	x						x
Brierly, James 1881–1955, England														x		x			x
Bustamante, Antonio de 1865–1951, Cuba	x	x		x	x	x	x	x			x								x
Chamberlain, Joseph 1873–1951, United States								x	x										x
Cheng T'ien-hsi 1884–1970, China		x		x	x		x		x										
De Visscher, Charles 1884–1973, Belgium		x		x		x		x		x	x			x	x	x		x	x
Dickinson, Edwin 1887–1961, United States		x											x						x
Drago, Luis 1859–1921, Argentina	x		x	x	x														
Eagleton, Clyde 1891–1958, United States														x		x			x
Fabela Alafaro, Isidro 1881–1964, Mexico	x	x	x	x			x	x	x								x	x	

(*continued*)

176　*Appendix 3*

	A	B	C	D	E	F	G	H	I	J	K	L	M	N	O	P	Q	R	S
Fenwick, Charles 1880–1973, United States												x	x						x
Fernandes, Raul 1879–1968, Brazil	x		x	x	x	x		x		x	x				x				
Finch, George 1884–1957, United States				x		x					x			x					x
Fromageot, Henri-Auguste 1864–1949, France			x	x				x	x					x					
Guerrero, José 1876–1958, El Salvador			x	x	x			x	x		x	x						x	
Hackworth, Green 1883–1973, United States		x	x	x							x			x	x		x	x	
Hambro, Carl 1885–1964, Norway				x				x	x						x	x			
Hambro, Edvard 1911–77, Norway		x	x	x	x				x						x	x		x	x
Hershey, Amos 1867–1933, United States				x		x													x
Hill, David Jayne 1850–1932, United States	x			x	x														x
Hsu Mo 1892–1956, China				x	x										x			x	x
Huber, Max 1874–1960, Switzerland	x	x		x				x											x
Hudson, Manley O. 1886–1960, United States						x		x		x	x						x		x
Hughes, Charles Evans 1862–1948, United States		x	x	x	x			x					x						x
Hurst, Cecil 1870–1963, England		x		x		x		x	x										
Jenks, Clarence 1909–73, England										x	x				x				
Kellogg, Frank 1856–1937, United States				x	x			x											
Kelsen, Hans 1881–1973, Austria				x															x
Lammasch, Heinrich 1853–1920, Austria	x	x	x	x															x
Lansing, Robert 1864–1928, United States				x	x		x												
Lauterpacht, Hersch 1897–1960, Austria		x															x	x	x
Loder, Bernard 1849–1935, The Netherlands		x		x	x		x	x		x									
McNair, Arnold 1885–1975, England		x		x														x	x

(*continued*)

	A	B	C	D	E	F	G	H	I	J	K	L	M	N	O	P	Q	R	S
Mello-Franco, Afranio de 1870–1943, Brazil				x	x				x			x	x						
Miller, David Hunter 1875–1961, United States				x		x						x		x					
Moore, John Bassett 1860–1947, United States		x		x				x				x	x						x
Peaslee, Amos 1887–1969, United States					x	x									x				
Pessôa, Epitácio 1865–1942, Brazil				x		x	x						x						x
Politis, Nicholas 1872–1942, Greece				x	x	x		x		x									x
Redlich, Joseph 1869–1936, Austria				x			x												x
Reinsch, Paul 1869–1923, United States					x						x								x
Rolin, Henri 1891–1973, Belgium		x		x		x	x	x								x	x		x
Rolin-Jaequemyns, Edouard 1863–1936, Belgium	x	x	x	x		x		x	x										x
Root, Elihu 1845–1937, United States		x	x	x	x		x				x	x							
Rostworowski, Michal 1864–1940, Germany		x					x							x					x
Schücking, Walther 1875–1935, Germany				x		x	x												x
Schurman, Jacob 1854–1942, Canada				x	x														x
Scialoja, Vittorio 1856–1933, Italy				x		x	x		x										x
Scott, James Brown 1866–1943, United States	x			x		x	x												x
Taft, William Howard 1857–1930, United States				x	x														x
Thomas, Elbert 1883–1953, United States				x					x										x
Urrutia, Francisco José 1870–1950, Colombia				x	x			x	x		x			x					
Wang Ch'ung-hui 1881–1958, Hong Kong	x			x			x				x			x	x				x
Wehberg, Hans 1885–1962, Germany				x															x
Winiarski, Bohdan 1884–1969, Poland						x		x	x	x							x		x
Wold, Emma 1871–1950, United States												x	x						x

(continued)

	A	B	C	D	E	F	G	H	I	J	K	L	M	N	O	P	Q	R	S
Wright, Quincy 1890–1970, United States				x															x
Yepes, Jesús Maria 1892–1962, Colombia				x	x			x			x	x		x	x				x

A. Delegate or adviser, one or both Hague Peace Conferences (1899, 1907)
B. Member of Permanent Court of Arbitration
C. Service on an arbitration commission
D. Public office or government service in home country
E. Diplomatic service
F. Delegate or adviser, Paris Peace Conference (1919)
G. Member of committee to frame statute of Permanent Court of International Justice
H. Service on Permanent Court of International Justice
I. Delegate to League of Nations Assembly
J. Service in League Secretariat, on League special committee, or in the International Labor Organization
K. Delegate or adviser, one or more international conferences, interwar period
L. Delegate to one or more Inter-American conferences
M. Member one or more Inter-American commissions
N. Delegate or adviser, Hague Conference on Codification of International Law (1930), and/or member of one of League preparatory committees
O. Delegate or adviser, San Francisco Conference (to frame United Nations Charter, 1945)
P. Delegate to UN General Assembly
Q. Member or adviser, (UN) International Law Commission
R. Service on International Court of Justice
S. Teacher of international law

Source: "Types of Internationalists: International Law and Legalists," in Warren F. Kuehl, ed., *Biographical Dictionary of Internationalists* (Westport, CT: Greenwood Press, 1983), 846–47. Career characteristics are drawn from the biographical sketches.

Appendix 4

Membership of the United Nations Special Committee to Consider the Principles of International Law

(Unless otherwise noted, representation on the committee was for the full term, 1964–70.)

Group of 77
1. Algeria (1966–70)
2. Argentina
3. Burma
4. Cameroon (1966–70)
5. Chile (1966–70)
6. Dahomey (Benin)
7. Ghana
8. Guatemala
9. India
10. Kenya (1966–70)
11. Lebanon
12. Madagascar
13. Mexico
14. Nigeria
15. Syria (1966–70)
16. United Arab Republic
17. Venezuela

Socialist states
18. Czechoslovakia
19. Poland
20. Romania
21. Union of Soviet Socialist Republics
22. Yugoslavia

Developed states
23. Australia
24. Canada
25. France
26. Italy
27. Japan
28. Netherlands
29. Sweden
30. United States
31. United Kingdom

Sources: UN Special Committee Reports, 1964–1970: UN General Assembly, *Official Records*, 19th sess. (1964), A/5746; 21st sess. (1966), A/6230; 22d sess. (1967), A/6799; 23d sess. (1968), A/7326; 24th sess. (1969), A/7619; 25th sess. (1970), A/8018.

Notes

Introduction

1. George Kennan, "Morality and Foreign Policy," *Foreign Affairs* 64 (Winter 1985/86): 205–18.
2. United Nations Charter (26 June 1945), chap. 4, art. 13a.

1. The World the Warlords Made

1. Theodore Roosevelt, *Applied Ethics* (Cambridge, Mass.: Harvard University Press, 1911), 46.
2. Ibid., 45.
3. Alfred Thayer Mahan, "The Peace Conference and the Moral Aspect of War," in *Lessons of the War with Spain* (Boston: Little, Brown, 1899), 233.
4. Theodore Roosevelt, Fourth Annual Message, 6 Dec. 1904, in *The Works of Theodore Roosevelt* (New York: Charles Scribners' Sons, 1926) 15:254.
5. Ibid., 256.
6. Mahan, *Lessons of the War,* 163–64.
7. Edward Bruce Hamley, *The Operations of War Explained and Illustrated,* 5th ed. (Edinburgh: William Blackwood and Sons, 1889), xi, xiv, 127–30, 207–14.
8. Léon Bourgeois, *Les conditions de la paix,* speech to the Sixth National Peace Conference, 31 May 1909, Rheims, in *Pour la Société des Nations* (Paris: Eugène Fasquelle, 1910), 13, 14–15.
9. Thomas Hardy, "Then and Now," in *A Treasury of War Poetry,* ed. George Herbert Clarke (Boston: Houghton Mifflin, 1917), 119.
10. William E. Hall, preface to the 3d ed., in *A Treatise on International Law,* ed. J. B. Atlay, 6th ed. (Oxford: Clarendon Press, 1909), ix–x.
11. Ibid., x.
12. Woodrow Wilson, speech before Congress, 11 February 1918, in *The Papers of Woodrow Wilson,* ed. Arthur S. Link et al. (Princeton: Princeton University Press, 1984), 46:320.

2. The Ethical Heritage

1. Stephen Bonsal, *Suitors and Suppliants* (New York: Prentice-Hall, 1946), 279.
2. Gilbert Seldes, *Tell the Truth and Run* (New York: Greenberg, 1953), 54.

3. David Hunter Miller, *The Drafting of the Covenant* (New York: G. P. Putnam's Sons, 1928), 1:261.

4. Ibid., 262.

5. Ibid.

6. The Hague Permanent Court of Arbitration, *The Hague Court Reports,* ed. James Brown Scott (New York: Oxford University Press, 1916), 404–10.

7. Ibid., 403.

8. Samuel Gompers, *Seventy Years of Life and Labor* (New York: E. P. Dutton, 1925), 2:485.

9. Ibid., 485–86.

10. National Child Labor Committee, *The Child Labor Bulletin* 4 (February 1916):171.

11. Richard K. Conant, "The Eight Hour Day for Children in Massachusetts Factories," *The Child Labor Bulletin* 3 (May 1914):94.

12. Jérome Blanqui, *Cours d'economie industrielle,* 2d ed. (1838–1839); quoted in James T. Shotwell, ed., *Origins of the International Labor Organization* (New York: Columbia University Press, 1934), 1:4.

13. Treaty of Peace between the Allied and Associated Powers and Germany (28 June 1919), pt. 13, sec. 1, preamble.

14. Ibid., sec. 2.

15. Ibid., sec. 1, preamble; annex, agenda (1); sec. 2, 4th principle.

16. Ibid., sec. 1, chap. 1, art. 405, para. 5.

17. Pope Leo XIII, *Rerum novarum* (15 May 1891), para. 1.

18. *Bulletin of the International Labour Office* 1 (1906):275; ibid., vol. 2 (1907):VIII.

19. Ibid., 1(1906):XXXVI–XXXVII.

20. Ibid., 275; also 3 (1908):373; 4 (1909):18, 68; 5 (1910):XVIII, XIX, LII, LXXIV, LXXXIII, LXXXIV; 6 (1911):103, 266–67; 7 (1912):209–10, 262; 8 (1913):417.

21. John R. Andrews, "Phosphorus Poisoning in the Match Industry in the United States," in United States Department of Commerce and Labor, *Bulletin of the Bureau of Labor,* no. 86 (January 1910): 105.

22. Ibid., 92.

23. *Bulletin of the International Labour Office* 7 (1912):145–48; also 8 (1913):300–01, 310, 346; Treaty of Peace between the Allied and Associated Powers and Germany (28 June 1919), pt. 13, sec. 1, annex (5).

24. Ibid., preamble.

25. Miller, *Drafting of the Covenant,* 2:387, 388.

26. Ibid., 388.

27. Ibid. 1:463.

28. Ibid.

29. Treaty of Peace between the Principal Allied and Associated Powers and Poland (28 June 1919), chap. 1; treaty with Austria (10 September 1919), pt. 3, sec. 5 and sec. 6; with Czechoslovakia (10 September 1919), chap. 1; with the Serb-Croat-Slovene state [Yugoslavia] (10 September 1919), chap. 1; with

Bulgaria (27 November 1919), pt. 3, sec. 4; with Romania (9 December 1919), chap. 1.

30. Bonsal, *Suitors and Suppliants,* 124.

31. H. W. V. Temperley, ed., *A History of the Peace Conference of Paris* (London: Frowde, Hodder and Stoughton, 1920–1924), 5:433.

32. Ibid., 434.

33. Ibid.

34. Miller, *Drafting of the Covenant,* 2:387.

3. New International Approaches

1. League of Nations, *Official Journal,* spec. suppl. 54, Records of the Eighth Ordinary Session of the Assembly, Plenary Meetings, *Text of the Debates* (Geneva, 1927), 59.

2. Robert Cecil, *A Great Experiment* (London: Jonathan Cape, 1941).

3. Arthur Salter, *Memoirs of a Public Servant* (London: Faber and Faber, 1961), 205–6.

4. League of Nations, *Official Journal,* spec. suppl. 54, *Text of the Debates,* 63.

5. Convention for the Pacific Settlement of International Disputes (29 July 1899), preamble, para. 8; Convention for the Pacific Settlement of International Disputes (18 October 1907), Preamble, para. 8.

6. 1899 Convention, preamble, para. 4; 1907 Convention, preamble, para. 4.

7. League of Nations, *Official Journal,* spec. suppl. 54, *Text of Debates,* 39.

8. Jean Monnet, *Memoirs* (Garden City, N.Y.: Doubleday & Co., 1978), 88.

9. Ibid., 90.

10. Ibid., 83.

11. Reply of the Allied and Associated Powers to the German Delegation, 16 June 1919, in U.S. Department of State, *Foreign Relations of the United States The Paris Peace Conference* 6 (Washington, D.C.: Government Printing Office, 1946):930.

12. League of Nations, *The Aaland Islands Question,* Report submitted to the Council of the League of Nations by the Commission of Rapporteurs (Geneva, 16 April 1921), 2, 4.

13. League of Nations, *Official Journal,* spec. suppl. 1 (August, 1920), Correspondence Relating to the Question of the Aaland Islands (London: Harrison & Sons, 1920), 18.

14. Ibid., 29.

15. League, *Aaland Islands Question,* 28, 32.

16. Ibid., 28.

17. League of Nations, *Official Journal,* spec. suppl. 3 (October 1920), Report of the International Committee of Jurists . . . upon the Legal Aspects of the Aaland Island Question (London: Harrison & Sons, 1920), 14.

18. Covenant of the League of Nations (28 June 1919), preamble, para. 1.

19. League of Nations, *Arbitration, Security and Reduction of Armaments,*

General Report Submitted to the Fifth Assembly on Behalf of the First and Third Committees, A.135 (1). 1924. IX (8 October 1924), 20.

20. League of Nations, *Official Journal*, spec. suppl. 54, *Text of Debates*, 62.

21. League of Nations, *Official Journal*, 54th Council sess., 10 (6 March 1929):520.

22. Treaty of Peace between the Principal Allied and Associated Powers and Poland (28 June 1919), art. 7.

23. League of Nations, *Official Journal*, Records of Plenary and Committee Meetings, 7(1926):42.

24. League of Nations, *Official Journal*, spec. suppl 125, Fifteenth Ordinary Assembly Sess., Records of Plenary and Committee Meetings, 15(1934):53.

25. League of Nations, *Official Journal*, Records of Plenary and Committee Meetings, 10(1929):1162.

26. League of Nations, *Official Journal*, Fifty-fourth Council Sess., 10(6 March 1929):520.

27. League of Nations, *Official Journal*, Record of Plenary and Committee Meetings, 7(1926):54.

28. League of Nations, *Official Journal*, Fifty-fourth Council sess., 10(6 March 1929):528–29.

29. Ibid., 528.

30. Convention on Rights and Duties of States (26 December 1933), art. 8, in *The International Conferences of American States, First Supplement, 1933–1940* (Washington, D.C.: Carnegie Endowment for International Peace, 1940), 122.

31. U.S. reservation to the Convention on Rights and Duties of States (1933), ibid., 123–24.

32. *Seventh International Conference of American States* (Montevideo, 1933), First, Second and Eighth Committees . . . Minutes and Antecedents, 104, 105, 117,110.

33. Ibid., 110.

34. Declaration of the Rights of the Child 1925, preamble, in League of Nations, *Official Journal*, spec. suppl. 23, Fifth Ordinary Assembly sess., Plenary Meetings, *Text of the Debates* (Geneva, 1926), 177.

35. Ibid., art. 5.

36. C. A. Macartney, et al., *Survey of International Affairs, 1925* (London: Oxford University Press, 1928), 2:86–91.

37. David Lloyd George, *Memoirs of the Peace Conference* (New Haven: Yale University Press, 1939), 1:445.

4. Search for Authority

1. Georges Kaeckenbeeck, *The International Experiment of Upper Silesia* (London: Oxford University Press, 1942), 514.

2. 1942 Declaration by United Nations, in Charles I. Bevans, comp., *Treaties and Other International Agreements of the United States of America, 1776–1949* (Washington, D.C.: G.P.O., 1968–) 3:697–98.

3. U.S. Department of State, *Foreign Relations of the United States, 1937* (Washington, D.C.: Department of State, 1954) 1:700.

4. Ibid., 701.

5. Ibid., 768.

6. Ibid., 786.

7. Ibid., 787.

8. League of Nations, Conference for the Reduction and Limitation of Armaments, Conf. D. 171 (I), *Preliminary Report on the Work of the Conference* (Geneva: 1936), 149.

9. *Public Papers of the Secretaries-General of the United Nations*, ed. Andrew W. Cordier and Wilder Foote (New York: Columbia University Press, 1969–) 2:411.

10. Ibid., 404.

11. Ibid., 405.

12. Kaeckenbeeck, *International Experiment*, 514.

13. *Resolutions of the Institute of International Law*, comp. James Brown Scott (New York: Oxford University Press for the Carnegie Endowment for International Peace, 1916), xvi.

14. Ibid., xx.

15. *American Journal of International Law* (1907) 1:130.

16. American Institute of International Law, *The Recommendations of Habana Concerning International Organization* (New York: Oxford University Press for the Carnegie Endowment for International Peace, 1917), 80.

17. Quoted in Stévan Tchirkovitch, *L'Institut Américain de Droit International* (Paris: A. Pedone, 1926), 13.

18. *Codification of American International Law* (Washington, D.C.: G.P.O. for the Pan American Union, 1925), 28–32, 35–37.

19. Ibid., 3.

20. James Brierly, "The Draft Code of American International Law," *The British Yearbook of International Law*, 7 (London: Oxford University Press, 1926), 19.

21. Ibid., 20.

22. Nicolas Politis, lectures at Columbia University, published as *Les nouvelles tendances du droit international* (Paris: Hachette, 1927).

23. *Annuaire de l'Institut de Droit International* (1925) 32:241. For the Institut's declaration of the rights and duties of states, see ibid., 238–39.

24. Alejandro Alvarez, *Exposé de motifs et déclaration des grands principes du droit international moderne*, 2d ed. (Paris: Les Editions Internationales, 1938), 49.

25. Ibid.

26. Woodrow Wilson, remarks to the New York Press Club, 30 June 1916, in *The Public Papers of Woodrow Wilson*, ed. Arthur S. Link et al., (Princeton, N.J.: Princeton University Press, 1967) 37:334.

27. Ibid., 41:523.

28. Harold Butler, *The Lost Peace* (London: Faber and Faber, 1941), 219.

29. Cecil, *A Great Experiment*, 336–37.

30. *The International Conferences of American States, First Supplement, 1933–1940* (Washington, D.C.: Carnegie Endowment for International Peace, 1940), 332.

31. "Preliminary Recommendations on Postwar Problems," in Carnegie Endowment for International Peace, *International Conciliation*, no. 387(February 1943):101.

32. Ibid., 103.

33. Ibid.

34. Ellery C. Stowell, *International Law* (New York: Henry Holt, 1931), vii.

35. Ibid., 518–19.

36. Ibid., 525.

37. "Preliminary Recommendations," *International Conciliation*, no. 387(1943):121.

38. Elihu Root, *Addresses on International Subjects* (Cambridge, Mass.: Harvard University Press, 1916), 421.

39. Joint petition from the German National party, the Centre party, and the Social-Democrat party, 4 September 1935, in Permanent Court of International Justice, Thirty-fifth Session, 1935; Ser. C: *Pleadings, Oral Statements and Documents*, no. 77: *Consistency of Certain Danzig Legislative Decrees with the Constitution of the Free City* (Leyden: A. W. Sijthoff, 1935), 18.

40. Ibid., 15.

41. Permanent Court of International Justice, Thirty-fifth Session, 1935; Ser. A/B: *Advisory Opinions*, fasc. 65: *Consistency of Certain Danzig Legislative Decrees with the Constitution of the Free City*. Advisory opinion, 4 December 1935 (Leyden: A. W. Sijthoff, 1935), 57.

42. Ibid.

43. Ibid., 54.

44. Permanent Court of International Justice, Thirty-fifth Sess., 1935. Ser. C, *Pleadings*, no. 77: *Consistency of Certain Danzig Legislative Decrees*, 13.

45. Ibid., 20.

46. Ibid., 64, 65. There are no exact English equivalents for *Gesetz* and *Recht*, the two German terms for *law* used by Gürtner, or for *loi* and *droit*, which are used in the court's French translation of Gürtner's argument. In both languages the words convey the same subtle difference between a statute law and a law that is also right or just. An attempt has been made here to capture some of the difference in English by using the terms *formal law* and *true law*.

47. Ibid., 203.

48. Ibid., 25.

49. Nicolas Politis, *La morale internationale* (Neuchâtel, Switzerland: Editions de la Baconnière, 1943), 100.

50. Ibid., 47.

51. Ibid., 47, 52.

52. Ibid., 7.

53. United Nations, *United Nations Conference on International Organization,*

San Francisco, 1945 (New York: U.N. Information Organization, 1945–1955) 1:705.

54. Ibid., 3:312.

55. L. M. Goodrich, Edvard Hambro, Anne Patricia Simons, *Charter of the United Nations: Commentary and Documents* (New York: Columbia University Press, 1969), 665.

56. *U.N. Conference on International Organization* 3:63.

57. Ibid., 265.

58. The Act of Chapultepec, in *Foreign Policy Reports* 21 (1 May 1945): 49.

59. *U.N. Conference on International Organization* 1:363.

60. U.N. Charter, Art. 2 (7).

5. States and Peoples

1. 1989 Convention on the Rights of the Child, *International Legal Materials (ILM)* 28(November 1989):1468.

2. Conference on Security and Co-operation in Europe (CSCE), concluding document from the Vienna meeting (1986–1989), *ILM* 28(March 1989):532.

3. U.N. General Assembly, Seventy-third Plenary Meeting (18 November 1989), Declaration on the Enhancement of the Effectiveness of the Principles of Refraining from the Threat or Use of Force in International Relations, *ILM* 27(November 1988):1677.

4. CSCE, Final Act (Helsinki, Finland, 1975), 4.

5. 1974 Charter of Economic Rights and Duties of States, in *Basic Documents in International Law,* ed. Ian Brownlie, 3d ed. (Oxford: Clarendon Press, 1983), 242.

6. 1948 Universal Declaration of Human Rights, art. 1, in *Basic Documents on Human Rights,* ed. Ian Brownlie, 2d ed. (Oxford: Clarendon Press, 1981), 22.

7. *Public Papers of the Secretaries-General of the United Nations* 2:476.

8. Quoted in George McTurnan Kahin, *The Asian-African Conference* (Ithaca: N.Y.: Cornell University Press, 1956), 41.

9. Ibid., 74.

10. Ibid.

11. *Selected Documents of the Bandung Conference . . . Bandung, Indonesia, April 18–24, 1955* (New York: Institute of Pacific Relations, 1955), 8.

12. Kahin, *Asian-African Conference,* 41.

13. Ibid., 74.

14. Ibid., 84.

15. *Selected Documents of Bandung,* 27.

16. Kahin, *Asian-African Conference,* 84–85.

17. 1970 Declaration on Principles of International Law Concerning Friendly Relations and Co-operation among States in accordance with the Charter of the United Nations, in *Basic Documents in International Law,* ed. Brownlie, 35–44.

18. UN General Assembly, Sixth Committee, meeting of 26 October 1960 (A/C.6/SR655), p. 27, para. 2; 28 October 1960 (A/C.6/SR657), pp. 38–39, para. 18; 31 October 1960 (A/C.6/SR658), p. 45, para. 18.

19. UN General Assembly, Twenty-fifth Sess. (1970), *Official Records* (A/PV.1860), 5.

20. UN *Conference on International Organization* 3:260.

21. Lusaka Declaration on Peace, Independence, Development, Co-operation and Democritization of International Relations (1970), in *The Third World without Superpowers: The Collected Documents of the Non-Aligned Countries*, ed. Odette Jankowitsch and Karl P. Sauvant (Dobbs Ferry, N.Y.: Oceana Publications, 1978), 1:82.

22. *UN Conference on International Organization* 3:260.

23. Léon Bourgeois, *Solidarité* (Paris: Armand Colin, 1896).

24. 1936 Declaration of Principles of Inter-American Solidarity and Co-operation, in *International Conferences of American States, First Supplement*, 160; 1938 Declaration of the Principles of the Solidarity of America, 309.

25. United Nations Conference on Trade and Development, 3d Sess. (1972), *Proceedings*, 1A:184.

26. *Basic Documents in International Law*, ed. Brownlie, 237.

27. *International Conferences of American States, First Supplement*, 161.

28. League of Nations, *Official Journal*, spec. suppl. 54, *Text of the Debates*, 206.

29. Ibid., 40.

30. *Codification of American International Law*, 25.

31. Ibid., 3.

32. J. M. Yepes, *La codificación del derecho internacional Americano y la Conferencia de Rio de Janeiro* (Bogotá [Colombia]: Imprenta Nacional, 1927), 151.

33. Ibid., 152.

34. *Le Temps* (30 July 1927), quoted in Arnold J. Toynbee, *Survey of International Affairs, 1927* (Oxford: Oxford University Press for the Royal Institute of International Affairs, 1929), 3.

35. 1977 Protocol Additional to the Geneva Conventions of 12 August 1949, relating to the protection of victims of international conflict (Protocol I), in *ILM* 16(1977):1397.

6. Peoples and States

1. 1938 Declaration on Persecution for Racial or Religious Motives, in *International Conferences of American States, First Supplement*, 260.

2. Quoted in Ruth B. Russell, *A History of the United Nations Charter* (Washington, D.C.: The Brookings Institution, 912.

3. *Selections from the Smuts Papers*, ed. W. K. Hancock and Jean van der Poel (Cambridge: University Press, 1966), 4:257.

4. Russell, *History of the Charter*, 912.

5. U.N. Charter, preamble, para. 10.

6. U.N. Charter, art. 1 (2).

7. 1987 Declaration on . . . the Principle of Refraining from the Threat or Use of Force . . . , *ILM* 27:1679.

8. Stephen Bonsal, *Unfinished Business* (Garden City, N.Y.: Doubleday, Doran, 1944), 48.

9. Ibid., 49.

10. Miller, *Making of the Covenant* 2:562.

11. Ibid.

12. Memorandum on the Registration and Publication of Treaties, *League of Nations Treaty Series* 1:9.

13. League of Nations. *Ten Years of World Co-operation* (Geneva: Secretariat of the League of Nations, 1930), 402–3.

14. *International Ethics* (New York: Paulist Press, 1928), 40.

15. Temperley, *History of the Peace Conference* 1:vi.

16. Ibid., vii.

17. *L'Esprit International* 1(January 1927):3.

18. Miller, *Making of the Covenant* 2:280.

19. Ibid., 281.

20. League of Nations, *Ten Years of World Co-operation*, 399.

21. Nicolas Politis, *Le grand problème du XXe siècle: La synthèse de l'ordre et de la liberté* (Lisbon: Faculdade de Direito da Universidade de Lisboa, 1942), 11.

22. *L'Esprit International* (4 April 1930):233.

23. Ibid., 235.

24. 1948 Universal Declaration of Human Rights, proclamatory paragraph preceding the body of the declaration, *Basic Documents on Human Rights*, ed. Brownlie, 22.

25. Kahin, *Asian-African Conference*, 84.

26. "Danger of War and Appeal for Peace," adopted at the Belgrade Conference of Non-Aligned Nations (1961), in *Asian-African States: Texts of International Declarations* (New Delhi: Scindia House for the Indian Society of International Law, 1965), 26.

27. *ILM* 27(1988):1675.

28. Miller, *Making of the Covenant* 1:439.

29. *Seventh International Conference of American States* (Montevideo, 1933), Third Committee, *Minutes and Antecedents*, 43–44.

30. 1972 Declaration of the United Nations Conference on the Human Environment (Stockholm Declaration), principle 1, in *Basic Documents Supplement to International Law, Cases and Materials*, ed. Louis Henkin, Richard Crawford Pugh, et al., 2d. ed. (St. Paul, Minn.: West Publishing, 1987), 635.

31. Treaty of Peace between the United States of America, the British Empire, France, Italy, and Japan, and Poland (1919), art. 3, in U.S. Senate, *Treaties, Conventions, International Acts, Protocols, and Agreements . . . 1910–1923* (Washington, D.C.: G.P.O., 1923) 3:3717.

32. Seventh International Conference of American States, *Plenary Sessions* (Montevideo, 1933), 54.

33. CSCE Final Act, principles 1 and 7.

34. Ibid., 3.

35. Vienna Concluding Document (1989), principle 11, *ILM* 28:533.

36. George Schultz, address at the closing session of CSCE Vienna review conference, 17 January 1989, in U.S. Department of State, *Current Policy Bulletin,* no. 1145 (n.d.):2.

37. Walter Lippmann, *Public Opinion* (New York: Harcourt, Brace, 1922), 411.

38. 1959 Declaration of the Rights of the Child, in *Human Rights: A Compilation of International Instruments* (New York: United Nations, 1988), 366–68.

39. Ibid.; 1960 Convention Against Discrimination in Education, ibid., 88–95.

40. 1948 Universal Declaration of Human Rights, ibid., 1–7; 1966 International Covenant on Economic, Social, and Cultural Rights, ibid., 7–18; 1981 African Charter on Human and Peoples' Rights, in Paul Sieghardt, *The Lawful Rights of Mankind* (Oxford: Oxford University Press, 1985), 231–37.

41. 1950 Convention for the Protection of Human Rights and Fundamental Freedoms (European Convention of Human Rights), *Basic Documents on Human Rights,* ed. Brownlie, 243–57; 1966 International Covenant on Civil and Political Rights, ibid., 128–45; 1948 Freedom of Association and Protection of the Right to Organization Convention, ibid., 190–95; 1962 Social Policy (Basic Aims and Standards) Convention, ibid., 219–27.

42. 1970 Declaration on Principles of International Law concerning Friendly Relations and Co-operation among States in accordance with the Charter of the United Nations, *Basic Documents in International Law,* ed. Brownlie, 35–44; 1974 Charter of Economic Rights and Duties of States, ibid., 235–49; 1948 Convention on the Prevention and Punishment of the Crime of Genocide, *Basic Documents on Human Rights,* ed. Brownlie, 31–34.

Bibliographic Essay

The notes in the text refer the reader to the primary sources from which direct quotations are taken, sources that provide the evidence for the argument of the book. This essay fills out the book's scholarly foundation by discussing some of the works that were influential in the construction of the argument or that provided necessary background information. A work such as *Code of Peace*, which covers a seventy-year period on an international scale, must of necessity rely heavily on the work of other scholars.

Some of the issues raised in the course of the argument have ramifications that extend beyond the limits of this study. For readers who want to pursue these lines of thought, the essay also suggests works for more extended discussion or for a different perspective from that of the text. The purpose of the suggestions is to offer guidance and intellectual stimulation, not to provide an exhaustive survey of the literatures of the various fields that were drawn on for the writing of this particular treatise on international security. The discussion proceeds chapter by chapter, beginning with the Introduction and the general issues addressed there.

Introduction

The formation and character of the modern states system has received extensive treatment, but few studies can match the analytical power and the sensitivity to historical context that F. H. Hinsley brings to the subject in his *Power and the Pursuit of Peace* (Cambridge: Cambridge University Press, 1963). His example is the inspiration for much in this book. Gordon A. Craig and Alexander L. George provide a useful, although less historically informed, treatment of some of the same issues in their *Force and Statecraft* (New York: Oxford University Press, 1983). Its brevity and its clear expository style make it a good introduction to international relations in the period in which this study is set.

In their book's third section, "Ethical Imperatives and Foreign Policy," Craig and George tackle a subject not often dealt with in studies of international relations. Their treatment is more descriptive than analytical, but they raise some of the basic issues that have to be dealt with in any discussion of the subject, beginning with the question, "*Are* there ethical imperatives that apply to foreign policy?" To answer that question, this study goes beyond the brief discussion in Craig and George to draw on the resources of diplomatic history, political science, moral and political philosophy, and the normative aspects of international law.

As a resource for those who are not legal specialists, international law is a special case that requires a special approach: on the one hand, respect; on the other hand, caution. The approach must be made with care since the subject rests in a thicket of unspelled-out assumptions. On this point see William R. Bishin and Christopher D. Stone, *Law, Language, and Ethics* (Mineola, N.Y.: Foundation Press, 1972), in which the authors argue that every legal problem "has its roots and perhaps its analog in traditionally 'philosophical' realms. Strip away the technical legal terms, plumb the debate's assumptions, and a host of implicit philosophical positions will be found" (vii).

Perhaps the most troubling aspect of law, and international law in particular, is its persistent mingling of *is* and *ought*. Those without formal legal training are not the only ones to find this tendency troubling. The legal positivist Hans Kelsen notes in his *General Theory of Law and the State* (Cambridge, Mass.: Harvard University Press, 1945), "Much traditional jurisprudence is characterized by a tendency to confuse the theory of positive law with political ideologies disguised either as metaphysical speculation about justice or as natural-law doctrine. It confounds the question of the essence of law—that is, the question of what the law actually is—with the question of what it should be" (xv).

One of the best introductions to this important but difficult subject still is J. L. Brierly, *The Law of Nations* (Oxford: Clarendon Press, 1928; 6th ed., 1963). Brierly's subtitle, *An Introduction to the International Law of Peace*, points to some of the questions discussed in this book. It points also to the fact that many works on international law, such as Brierly's treatise, are best read as works of speculative philosophy. As Michael Walzer has observed in his *Just and Unjust Wars* (New York: Basic Books, 1977), many of those in international law "are in fact moral and political philosophers, and it would be best if they presented themselves that way" (xiii).

Three other works have informed the treatment of international law in this book: Percy E. Corbett, *The Growth of World Law* (Princeton, N.J.: Princeton University Press, 1971), Charles de Visscher, *Theory and Reality in Public International Law* (Princeton, N.J.: Princeton University Press, 1957), and H. L. A. Hart, *The Concept of Law* (Oxford: Clarendon Press, 1961), especially chapters 9 and 10, "Laws and Morals," and "International Law." With these as background, the reader will be better able to draw intellectual sustenance from the discussion and references in a standard international law text such as that by Louis Henkin, Richard Crawford Pugh, et al., *International Law: Cases and Materials* (2d ed., St. Paul, Minn.: West Publishing, 1987). A witty and erudite plea for greater United States adherence to international law is Daniel Patrick Moynihan, *On the Law of Nations* (Cambridge, Mass.: Harvard University Press, 1990).

Terry Nardin, *Law, Morality, and the Relations of States* (Princeton, N.J.: Princeton University Press, 1983) provides a bridge from discussions of law to discussions of ethics. His conception of international law as an authoritative framework of common rules, within which independent states may coexist, offers original insights into the nature and function of rules in international society—insights that have proved invaluable in this book. Nardin approaches his subject as a moral philosopher, and this approach provides a double freedom. The subject is freed from sterile preconceptions, and this, in turn, frees the reader to seek new relationships among law, ethics, and the society of states.

Debate over the relationship between ethics and international affairs is often cast in the limited (and limiting) terms of realism versus idealism. The debate is thoroughly reviewed by Marshall Cohen in an article that first appeared in *Philosophy and Public Affairs* 13(Fall 1984) and has been reprinted in *International Ethics,* ed. Charles R. Beitz et al. (Princeton, N.J.: Princeton University Press, 1985): "Moral Skepticism and International Relations." Just how limited the realism/idealism vocabulary is for discussion of this complex subject will be made clear with the publication of a jointly written book, *Traditions of International Ethics,* ed. Terry Nardin and David R. Mapel (Cambridge: Cambridge University Press, 1991), in which the resources of many different ethical traditions are explored by the several authors. Specific problems such as intervention and the uses of force are examined in the light of these different traditions of international ethics.

The influx of non-Western states into the international system following World War II has stimulated much discussion of the question, "Is it possible to have universal values in a system where so many cultural traditions are represented?" The answer given in this book is yes. Others do not agree. Adda Bozeman in *The Future of Law in a Multicultural World* (Princeton, N.J.: Princeton University Press, 1971) is one of many who have given a negative answer. To mention only two others: Josef L. Kunz, "Pluralism of Legal and Value Systems and International Law," *American Journal of International Law* 49 (1955):370–76, and A. J. M. Milne, "Human Rights and the Diversity of Morals: A Philosophical Analysis of Rights and Obligations in the Global System," in *Rights and Obligations in North-South Relations,* ed. Moorhead Wright (New York: St. Martin's Press, 1986), 8–33. These authors, like many others, have based their arguments on sources other than the record of what states have actually said and done, and have ignored or discounted the effect of the structure of the international system.

1. The World the Warlords Made

An understanding of the international context within which this chapter is set can be gained from Akira Iriye, *Pacific Estrangement* (Cambridge, Mass.: Harvard University Press, 1972), an analysis of the parallel tendencies of Japanese and American foreign policies in the years 1897 to 1911, and George F. Kennan, *The Decline of Bismarck's European Order* (Princeton, N.J.: Princeton University Press, 1979). Those who want to pursue the subject of military strategy will find rich resources in Edward Mead Earle, ed., *Makers of Modern Strategy* (Princeton, N.J.: Princeton University Press, 1943), and its sequel of the same name, edited by Peter Paret, issued by the same publisher in 1986.

There has been a recent resurgence of scholarly interest in the Russo-Japanese War. Ian Nish in *The Origins of the Russo-Japanese War* (London: Longman, 1985) concludes that concerns about security and fear of armament policies were the primary causes of the war. R. M. Connaughton, *The War of the Rising Sun and Tumbling Bear* (London: Routledge, 1988), offers a detailed military history of the conflict.

At the time the war was being fought, it generated intense interest in several powerful countries. The Austrians published an official account of the war. The historical section of the German general staff issued a six-volume history. The military information division of the U.S. general staff printed five volumes of the reports of U.S. military observers attached to the armies in Manchuria and then published a one-volume summary, *The Epitome of the Russo-Japanese War* (Washington, D.C.: G.P.O., 1907). The historical section of Great Britain's Committee of Imperial Defence published a five-volume account (1908–1910) covering the land operations, followed by a three-volume set with three portfolios of maps (1910–1920) for the naval aspects of the war, the whole entitled *Official History (Naval and Military) of the Russo-Japanese War.*

The account in this book is based chiefly on the British volumes. Other sources drawn on were the U.S. *Epitome* and, for the way the war was presented to a popular audience, a selection from *Collier's* war correspondents: *The Russo-Japanese War: A Photographic and Descriptive Review of the Great Conflict in the Far East* (New York: P. F. Collier & Son, 1905). Frederick Palmer, *With Kuroki in Manchuria* (New York: Charles Scribner's Sons, 1904), is an admiring account of the Japanese war effort.

F. T. Jane, *All the World's Fighting Ships* (Boston: Little Brown, 1898), and Fred T. Jane, *The Imperial Japanese Navy* (London: W. Thacker, 1904), provided some technical details, as did Captain J. S. Cowie, *Mines, Minelayers, and Minelaying* (London: Oxford University Press, 1949). The concerted Japanese campaign to gather intelligence is described by Ian Nish in "Japanese Intelligence and the Approach of the Russo-Japanese War" in *The Missing Dimension*, ed. Christopher Andrews and David Dilks (Urbana, Ill.: University of Illinois Press, 1984), 17–32.

Views by contemporary scholars of the ways that Japanese actions fit or did not fit early twentieth-century standards of international conduct can be found in Amos S. Hershey, *The International Law and Diplomacy of the Russo-Japanese War* (New York: Macmillan, 1906), and Sakuyé Takakashi, *International Law Applied to the Russo-Japanese War* (New York: Banks Law Publishing, 1908).

2. The Ethical Heritage

Understanding of the 1918–1919 peace conference in Paris has been heavily influenced by two works: John Maynard Keynes, *The Economic Consequences of the Peace* (New York: Harcourt, Brace and Howe, 1920), and Arno J. Mayer, *Politics and Diplomacy of Peacemaking* (New York: Alfred A. Knopf, 1967). Keynes's work was written in the heat of anger after he had resigned from the

British delegation to the peace conference. His attack on the economic aspects of the peace settlement is clothed in such brilliant and striking prose that subsequent commentators have seemed compelled to subscribe to his simplistic views on the noneconomic aspects of the conference as well. The account in this study is a non-Keynsian view of some of the moral issues involved.

Mayer covers the conference more thoroughly and in more detail than any other scholar, but the thrust of his coverage is to demonstrate that the peacemakers were chiefly concerned to contain revolutionary movements. Once this has been shown—and disagreements here would center on the word "chiefly"—there remains a lot of conference that does not fit the antirevolutionary conceptual scheme. It is this portion of the conference that has been subjected to close examination here.

The notes in the text make clear the importance of David Hunter Miller's *The Drafting of the Covenant,* 2 vols. (New York: G. P. Putnam's Sons, 1928) as a source. Also important for overall context were H. W. V. Temperley, ed., *A History of the Peace Conference of Paris,* 6 vols. (London: Oxford University Press and Hodder & Stoughton, 1920–1924), and Arnold J. Toynbee, *The World After the Peace Conference* (London: Oxford University Press, 1925), which, despite the title, contains material bearing directly on the conference.

The memoirs of David Lloyd George, *Memoirs of the Peace Conference,* 2 vols. (New Haven, Conn.: Yale University Press, 1929) and Harold Nicolson, *Peacemaking 1919* (Boston: Houghton Mifflin, 1953) were moderately helpful. A scholarly treatment of the Japanese attempt to include a racial equality clause in the League covenant in Paul Gordon Lauren's "Human Rights in History: Diplomacy and Racial Equality at the Paris Peace Conference," in *Diplomatic History* 2 (Summer 1978): 257–78.

Useful as these sources have been in the writing of chapter 2, most of the chapter is based on an ethically oriented reading of the basic data of the conference.

3. New International Approaches

Scholarly studies of the interwar period have concentrated on economic issues, on the rise of totalitarian states, and on the failure of the League of Nations to prevent great power aggression. An exception to this generalization about scholarly studies, and one that does much to show the far-reaching effects of the breakdown of the pre-World War I diplomacy of imperialism, is Akira Iriye's *After Imperialism* (Cambridge, Mass.: Harvard University Press, 1965). Iriye's thesis is not dealt with directly in this book, but his conclusions inform the book's understanding of the world within which the League functioned, particularly in the 1920s.

As with the Russo-Japanese War, there is today renewed scholarly interest in the League of Nations and its accomplishments. The review article by A. Lentin, "What Really Happened at Paris?" *Diplomacy and Statecraft* 1 (July 1990):264–75, summarizes some recent work but much is still in process. The basic source for information about the League remains F. P. Walters, *History of the League of Nations,* 2 vols. (London: Oxford University Press, 1952). An attempt to make some of the later work and interpretations available is Ruth B. Henig, ed., *The League of Nations* (New York: Barnes & Noble, 1973), a selection of excerpts from official records and speeches, with brief introductory remarks that cast the League in a different light from that of the "failure" found in many semipopular treatments. Raymond B. Fosdick, *Letters on the League of Nations* (Princeton, N.J.: Princeton University Press, 1966), gives a clear picture of the hopes held and difficulties faced by early workers in the League, as does the relevant portion of Arthur Salter's *Memoirs of a Public Servant* (London: Faber and Faber, 1961).

The section entitled "Hard Cases" in chapter 3 illustrates one of the basic approaches to the subject of this book. General works of moral or political philosophy provide the understanding and the framework within which a specific analysis is conducted. The general works are not directly cited, but they are essential. In this case, the essential general work is Albert R. Jonsen and Stephen Toulmin, *The Abuse of Casuistry: A History of Moral Reasoning* (Berkeley: University of California Press, 1988). The analysis of the Aaland Islands and Vilna cases is carried out within the framework of understanding provided by these authors' discussion of the application of general principles to specific situations.

James Barros, who has published accounts of several of the specific problems dealt with by the League, has covered the Aaland Islands controversy in detail in *The Aland Islands Question* (New Haven, Conn.: Yale University Press, 1968). Chronology is his organizing concept, but he has done yeoman work in dredging up the relevant documentation. The same could be said of Gerhard P. Pink whose "The Conference of Ambassadors (Paris 1920–1931)," *Geneva Studies* 12 (February 1942) is one of the few accounts of the work of this important group.

A sense of the importance attached to the minority question in the early interwar years can be gained from C. A. Macartney, *National States and National Minorities* (London: Oxford University Press, 1934), and Julius Stone, *International Guarantees of Minority Rights* (London: Oxford University Press, 1932). There is no study in depth of the crucial concept of the rights and duties of states in this or any other period, but Hans Kelsen provides a brief overview, from a positivist stance, in "The Draft Declaration on Rights and Duties of States," *American Journal of International Law* 44 (1950):259–76.

Latin American resentment at U.S. policies during the early interwar years is brought out in the text. Additional evidence can be found in Clarence H. Haring, *South America Looks at the United States* (New York: Macmillan, 1928). An article by Dwight Morrow, "Who Buys Foreign Bonds?" in *Foreign Affairs* 5(1927), is a clear exposition of Latin American–U.S. relations from the investor's point of view. It also helps to explain the stance taken by U.S. Secretary of State Charles Evans Hughes at the 1928 Conference of American States, a stance that caused much Latin American resentment. Hughes makes clear his position in *Our Relations to the Nations of the Western Hemisphere* (Princeton, N.J.: Princeton University Press, 1928).

4. Search for Authority

U.S. secretary of state Cordell Hull's attempt to get universal agreement to his "Fundamental Principles of International Conduct" is described briefly in *The Memoirs of Cordell Hull*, 2 vols. (New York: Macmillan, 1941) 1:535–36. When the subject is treated at all in accounts of U.S. diplomacy of this period, it is put in the context of increasing tension between Japan and the United States following the hostile actions that marked the opening of the Sino-Japanese War. A broader research reach makes it clear that common standards of international behavior was a longstanding concern of Hull's. He had, for example, been instrumental in inserting a similar list of principles into the Democratic party platform for 1932.

Few works of synthesis exist for the study of developments in international law during the interwar period. Almost the only general history is Arthur Nussbaum, *A Concise History of the Law of Nations* (rev. ed., New York: Macmillan, 1954), an episodic, one-thinker-after-another account that is particularly weak on the twentieth century. Richard J. Alfaro, "The Rights and Duties of States," in Academie de droit international, *Recueil des cours, 1959* (Leyden, Netherlands: A. W. Sijthoff, 1960), 91–202, provides in his second appendix a useful guide to the burst of interwar appraisals of the subject: "Chronology of Events Directly or Indirectly Related to the Codification of International Law and to the Formulation of a Declaration of Rights and Duties of States," 181–93.

Those who want to know more about the group characterized in this study as the founders of the search for authority, must be prepared to look in many different locations. Warren F. Kuehl, ed., *Biographical Dictionary of Internationalists* (Westport, Conn.: Greenwood Press, 1983) provides brief biographical sketches of some members of the group. H. B. Jacobini, *A Study of the Philosophy of International Law as Seen in Works of Latin American Writers* (The Hague: Martinus Nijhoff, 1954) emphasizes Latin American opposition to the positivistic tendencies of the interwar period. Latin American members of the group who were also active in the post–World War II period receive some attention in Alan Thomas Leonhard, "The Legal Thought of Latin American Judges on the International Court of Justice" (Ph.D. diss., Duke University, 1966), and the early career of one influential member is treated in more detail by Ralph Dingman Nurnberger in his "James Brown Scott, Peace through Justice" (Ph.D. diss., Georgetown University, 1975). The important European contingent, and the small but active Asian contingent, have been all but ignored.

Further details about the National Socialists in Danzig in the 1930s can be found in Hans L. Leonhardt, *Nazi Conquest of Danzig* (Chicago: University of Chicago Press, 1942). Morality was much appealed to in the period, but with unpredictable consequences, as when a number of Anglican bishops counseled acquiescence to Hitler's demands on the grounds of a higher morality than that embodied in the terms of the treaty that Hitler was unilaterally breaking. See Catherine Ann Cline, "Ecumenism and Appeasement: the Bishops of the Church of England and the Treaty of Versailles," *Journal of Modern History* 61(1989):683–703.

There is no scholarly study of Nicolas Politis or of his thought, which, it would appear, owes something to the ideas of Léon Duguit. In his *Law in the Modern State* (New York: B. W. Huebsch, 1919), Duguit postulates a sociological base for law, a conception that resonates in the thought of many in this period. For a closely related, but separate, argument, that grounds international behavior not on sociological needs but rather on the requirements of a functioning international system, see Adam Watson, *Diplomacy* (New York: McGraw-Hill, 1983). Watson's *raison de système* is akin to Politis's argument, but without the moral context that, for Politis, gave both meaning and justification.

Secondary works on the San Francisco conference tend toward organizational detail, or reminiscence. The notes in the text refer the reader to the sources found most useful for the purposes of this study.

5. States and Peoples

On the Afro-Asian conference at Bandung, a work by C. S. Jha, an Indian diplomat, is useful for providing a non-Western perspective beyond that provided by the speakers at Bandung and by the Final Communiqué: *From Bandung to Tashkent* (Madras: Sangam Books, 1983). Considering the emotional and symbolic importance attached to this conference by non-Western states, it has attracted surprisingly little scholarly attention in the West.

The case for a New International Economic Order is presented with great persuasiveness by José Figueres in "Some Economic Foundations of Human Rights," in *Basic Documents on Human Rights,* ed. Ian Brownlie (2d ed., Oxford: Clarendon Press, 1981), 495–513. The question of distributive justice raised by Figueres has been dealt with at length and with sympathy by a number of scholars including Charles R. Beitz, *Political Theory and International Relations* (Princeton, N.J.: Princeton University Press, 1979); Henry Shue, *Basic Rights* (Princeton, N.J.: Princeton University Press, 1980); and Oscar Schachter, *Sharing the World's Resources* (New York: Columbia University Press, 1977).

For a detailed study of the 1974 Charter of Economic Rights and Duties of States that stresses the role of the oil embargo of 1973–1974 in giving the developing countries enough leverage to get their concerns taken seriously, see Robert F. Meagher, *An International Redistribution of Wealth and Power* (New York: Pergamon Press, 1979). A richly detailed study of the way that rhetoric can sometimes outrun practice in economic matters is Charles Lipson, *Standing Guard* (Berkeley: University of California Press, 1985). Lipson's subtitle gives an indication of the underlying practice: *Protecting Foreign Capital in the Nineteenth and Twentieth Centuries.* Many of his examples deal with Latin America.

Thomas G. Weiss, a former official within the United Nations Conference on Trade and Development, takes a close look at the group negotiating system that has evolved as developing states have tried to gain international leverage for their economic advantage. His *Multilateral Development Diplomacy in UNCTAD* (New York: St. Martin's Press, 1986), recommends changes in the system, and a strengthening of South/South relations and trade.

The adaptation of traditional rules of warfare and justifications for war to modern conditions is not one of the central concerns of this book. The effort has attracted much scholarly attention, however. The issues are carefully explored in the works of James Turner Johnson, whose *Can Modern War Be Just?* (New Haven, Conn.: Yale University Press, 1984) is a thoughtful guide as well as an affirmation of the possibility. The states' repeated assertions that struggle against colonial domination or exploitation is a legitimate form of warfare is analyzed by Gidon Gottlieb in "The New International Law: Toward the Legitimation of War," *Ethics* 78(1968):144–47.

6. Peoples and States

The section of this chapter that deals with expectation that the public would keep watch over the new international order was developed almost entirely from the primary sources quoted in the text. A fuller explanation of what was meant in the 1920s by "the international mind" can be found in an explanation by the man who coined the term: Nicholas Murray Butler, "The Development of the International Mind," speech before the Hague Academy of International Law, 20 July 1923, in *International Conciliation*, no. 192 (1923): 771–85.

The continuing concerns and work of the International Labour Organization can be followed in outline in the ILO's publication *International Labour Conventions and Recommendations, 1919–1981* (Geneva: International Labour Office, 1982), and in greater detail in C. Wilfrid Jenks, *Social Justice in the Law of Nations* (London: Oxford University Press, 1970).

No other aspect of the states' efforts at standard setting has attracted more attention than their efforts in the area of human rights. *Rights* is the accepted, the common, the all-justifying term in most ethical discourse today, a fact that Thomas L. Haskell has noted in his "The Curious Persistence of Rights Talk in the 'Age of Interpretation,'" *Journal of American History* 74(1987):984–1012. The literature of *rights* is vast, and it increases daily. The following is a sampling of those works that readers might find most useful.

For a general philosophical introduction, Ronald Dworkin, *Taking Rights Seriously* (Cambridge, Mass.: Harvard University Press, 1978). More briefly, but with philosophical depth, Richard McKeon, "The Philosophic Bases and Material Circumstances of the Rights of Man," in *Human Rights*, ed. UNESCO (London: Allan Wingate, 1949), 35–46.

Specific to the concerns of this book but treated separately from the general code-making effort that has been analyzed here: R. J. Vincent, *Human Rights and International Relations* (Cambridge: Cambridge University Press, 1986) and Jack Donnelly, *Universal Human Rights in Theory and Practice* (Ithaca, N.Y.: Cornell University Press, 1989). Two of the strengths of Donnelly's book are his clear assertion of the universality of human rights and his facing the difficulties this raises as regards cultural diversity and economic development.

Hewing more closely to the actions of the states than the sources listed above is Paul Sieghart, *The Lawful Rights of Mankind* (Oxford: Oxford University Press, 1985). For an analysis of one of the lesser-known components of the code of international ethics studied here, see Emmanuel G. Bello, "The African Charter on Human and Peoples' Rights, A Legal Analysis," in Hague Academy of International Law, *Collection of Courses, 1985* (Dordrecht, Netherlands: Martinus Nijhoff, 1987) 194:21–268.

Documentary background on the Conference on Security and Cooperation in Europe can be found in Igor I. Kavass, Jacqueline Paquin Granier, and Mary Frances Dominick, eds., *Human Rights, European Politics, and the Helsinki Accord: the Documentary Evolution of the Conference on Security and Co-operation in Europe, 1973–75*, 6 vols. (Buffalo, N.Y.: William S. Hein, 1981). For an account of the negotiations by a senior U.S. official who was involved from start to finish, see John J. Maresca, *To Helsinki* (Durham, N.C.: Duke University Press, 1985). Vojtech Mastny, *Helsinki, Human Rights, and European Security* (Durham, N.C.: Duke University Press, 1986), has selected writings on the CSCE review process from Belgrade through Madrid, while A. Bloed and P. van Dijk, eds., *Essays on Human Rights in the Helsinki Process* (Dordrecht, Netherlands: Martinus Nijhoff, 1985), concentrate on the negotiating process and the legal implications of the Madrid follow-up meeting, 1980–83.

For those who want to pursue the emphasis on environmental protection, the place to start is Lynton Keith Caldwell, *International Environmental Policy* (Durham, N.C.: Duke University Press, 1984). Caldwell emphasizes the importance of the 1972 Stockholm Conference in making the environment a matter for legitimate international concern. For a later, broadly based treatment of the subject, see John E. Carroll, ed., *International Environmental Diplomacy* (Cambridge: Cambridge University Press, 1988).

Index

201

Respect for human rights and fundamental freedoms, basic principle of code of international ethics, xii, 164. *See also* Human rights

Revolution, after World War I, 24, 30–31

Rhetoric of revolution and purity, 114–15, 121–27, 130–32

Rights and duties of states: as context for human rights, 154–55; and writing of UN Charter, 107–12. *See also* Convention on Rights and Duties of States (1933)

Rolin-Jacquemyns, Gustave, on role of Institut de Droit International, 90

Roosevelt, Franklin: and Latin-American relations, 79; loss of, 109–10

Roosevelt, Theodore: on defense and peace, 9–10; opinion of international law, 57

Root, Elihu, on dangers of morality in international affairs, 99

Russia: and Dogger Bank incident, 26–28; in Russo-Japanese War (1904–5), 5–6, 11–14, 16–19; revolution in, 24. *See also* Soviet Union

Russian navy, 5–6, 12–13, 19; in Dogger Bank incident, 26–28

Russo-Japanese War (1904–5), 5–6, 11–14, 16–19

Saar Basin, 55, 59–60

Salter, Sir Arthur, on character of League of Nations, 54–55

San Francisco Conference (1945), 107–12

Schultz, George, on human rights, 161

Scott, James Brown: at Paris Peace Conference, 49; and international law, 89

Seldes, Gilbert, on war's devastation, 24–25

Self-determination: basic principle of code of international ethics, xii, 163; at Paris Peace Conference, 49; in Aaland Islands dispute, 61–66; meaning determined by context, 164

Shotwell, James T., at Paris Peace Conference, 40

Smuts, Jan Christian: contributions to UN Charter, 144–45

Solidarity: in Hague Conventions, 57; transformation of meaning of term, 114, 131–32

Sovereign equality of states: basic principle of code of international ethics, xii, 163; in Convention on Rights and Duties of States, 80

Sovereignty, devolution of, 153–54

Sovereignty, of states: and Aaland Islands dispute, 64–66; Danzig dispute, 100; minority treaty dispute, 76; extreme assertion of (1933), 77–80; in charter of OAS (1948), 77; in Final Act CSCE, 159

Soviet Union: and Vilna dispute, 69; Helsinki Watch group in, 160; relations with League of Nations, 58; revolutionary origins, 24; sponsor of Dumbarton Oaks proposals, 107. *See also* Russia

Sphere of influence, role of, 9, 69

Standards of social justice, 31–41

States: as moral communities, 11; as oppressors, vii; as warlords, xv, 5–21, 29, 50, 67–68, 135, 137–38; rights of, interwar period, 71

Stockholm Declaration (on environment, 1972), 158

Stowell, Ellery C., on practice as basis of international law, 97–98

Stresemann, Gustav, on minority treaties, 71–72; shares Nobel peace prize, 75

Sukarno, Achmed, on meaning of revolution, 121, 123

Sweden, and Aaland Islands dispute, 61–66

Territorial integrity and political independence of states: basic principle of code of international ethics, xii, 163; in Convention on Rights and Duties of States, 80; interwar concern for, 71–72

Third World, effect on code of international ethics, 126–34

Transformation of meanings, 146–47. *See also* Cooperation with other states; Interdependence; People (or peoples); *Public;* Self-determination; Solidarity; Sovereignty

Trans-Siberian Railway, 7, 12